Python® Machine Learning

Python® Machine Learning

Wei-Meng Lee

WILEY

Python® Machine Learning

Published by
John Wiley & Sons, Inc.
10475 Crosspoint Boulevard
Indianapolis, IN 46256
www.wiley.com

Copyright © 2019 by John Wiley & Sons, Inc., Indianapolis, Indiana
Published simultaneously in Canada

ISBN: 978-1-119-54563-7
ISBN: 978-1-119-54569-9 (ebk)
ISBN: 978-1-119-54567-5 (ebk)

Manufactured in the United States of America
SKY10078445_062724

For general information on our other products and services please contact our Customer Care Department within the United States at (877) 762-2974, outside the United States at (317) 572-3993 or fax (317) 572-4002.

Wiley publishes in a variety of print and electronic formats and by print-on-demand. Some material included with standard print versions of this book may not be included in e-books or in print-on-demand. If this book refers to media such as a CD or DVD that is not included in the version you purchased, you may download this material at http://booksupport.wiley.com. For more information about Wiley products, visit www.wiley.com.

Library of Congress Control Number: 2019931301

I dedicate this book with love to my dearest wife (Sze Wa) and girl (Chloe), who have to endure my irregular work schedule and for their companionship when I am trying to meet writing deadlines!

About the Author

Wei-Meng Lee is a technologist and founder of Developer Learning Solutions (http://www.learn2develop.net), a company specializing in hands-on training on the latest technologies.

Wei-Meng has many years of training experience, and his training courses place special emphasis on the learning-by-doing approach. His hands-on approach to learning programming makes understanding the subject much easier than just reading books, tutorials, and documentations.

Wei-Meng's name regularly appears in online and print publications such as DevX.com, MobiForge.com, and CoDe Magazine. You can contact Wei-Meng at: weimenglee@learn2develop.net.

About the Technical Editor

Doug Mahugh is a software developer who began his career in 1978 as a Fortran programmer for Boeing. Doug has worked for Microsoft since 2005 in a variety of roles including developer advocacy, standards engagement, and content development. Since learning Python in 2008, Doug has written samples and tutorials on topics ranging from caching and continuous integration to Azure Active Directory authentication and Microsoft Graph. Doug has spoken at industry events in over 20 countries, and he has been Microsoft's technical representative to standards bodies including ISO/IEC, Ecma International, OASIS, CalConnect, and others.

Doug currently lives in Seattle with his wife Megan and two Samoyeds named Jamie and Alice.

Credits

Acquisitions Editor
Devon Lewis

Associate Publisher
Jim Minatel

Editorial Manager
Pete Gaughan

Production Manager
Katie Wisor

Project Editor
Gary Schwartz

Production Editor
Barath Kumar Rajasekaran

Technical Editor
Doug Mahugh

Copy Editor
Kim Cofer

Proofreader
Nancy Bell

Indexer
Potomac Indexing, LLC

Cover Designer
Wiley

Cover Image
©Lidiia Moor/iStockphoto-
background texture
© Rick_Jo/iStockphoto-digital
robotic brain

Acknowledgments

Writing a book is always exciting, but along with it come long hours of hard work, straining to get things done accurately and correctly. To make a book possible, a lot of unsung heroes work tirelessly behind the scenes. For this, I would like to take this opportunity to thank a number of special people who made this book possible.

First, I want to thank my acquisitions editor Devon Lewis, who was my first point of contact for this book. Thank you, Devon, for giving me this opportunity and for your trust in me!

Next, a huge thanks to Gary Schwartz, my project editor, who was always a pleasure to work with. Gary is always contactable, even when he is at the airport! Gary has been very patient with me, even though I have missed several of my deadlines for the book. I know it threw a spanner into his plan, but he is always accommodating. Working with him, I know my book is in good hands. Thank you very much, Gary!

Equally important is my technical editor—Doug Mahugh. Doug has been very eager-eyed editing and testing my code, and never fails to let me know if things do not work the way I intended. Thanks for catching my errors and making the book a better read, Doug! I would also like to take this opportunity to thank my production editor—Barath Kumar Rajasekaran. Without his hard work, this book would not be even possible. Thanks, Barath!

Last, but not least, I want to thank my parents and my wife, Sze Wa, for all the support they have given me. They have selflessly adjusted their schedules to accommodate my busy schedule when I was working on this book. I love you all!

Contents at a glance

Introduction   xxiii

Chapter 1   Introduction to Machine Learning   1

Chapter 2   Extending Python Using NumPy   19

Chapter 3   Manipulating Tabular Data Using Pandas   39

Chapter 4   Data Visualization Using matplotlib   67

Chapter 5   Getting Started with Scikit-learn for Machine Learning   93

Chapter 6   Supervised Learning—Linear Regression   119

Chapter 7   Supervised Learning—Classification Using
             Logistic Regression   151

Chapter 8   Supervised Learning—Classification Using Support
             Vector Machines   177

Chapter 9   Supervised Learning—Classification Using K-Nearest
             Neighbors (KNN)   205

Chapter 10   Unsupervised Learning—Clustering Using K-Means   221

Chapter 11   Using Azure Machine Learning Studio   243

Chapter 12   Deploying Machine Learning Models   269

Index   285

Contents

Introduction		xxiii
Chapter 1	**Introduction to Machine Learning**	**1**
	What Is Machine Learning?	2
	What Problems Will Machine Learning Be Solving in This Book?	3
	Classification	4
	Regression	4
	Clustering	5
	Types of Machine Learning Algorithms	5
	Supervised Learning	5
	Unsupervised Learning	7
	Getting the Tools	8
	Obtaining Anaconda	8
	Installing Anaconda	9
	Running Jupyter Notebook for Mac	9
	Running Jupyter Notebook for Windows	10
	Creating a New Notebook	11
	Naming the Notebook	12
	Adding and Removing Cells	13
	Running a Cell	14
	Restarting the Kernel	16
	Exporting Your Notebook	16
	Getting Help	17
Chapter 2	**Extending Python Using NumPy**	**19**
	What Is NumPy?	19
	Creating NumPy Arrays	20
	Array Indexing	22

Boolean Indexing		22
Slicing Arrays		23
NumPy Slice Is a Reference		25
Reshaping Arrays		26
Array Math		27
Dot Product		29
Matrix		30
Cumulative Sum		31
NumPy Sorting		32
Array Assignment		34
Copying by Reference		34
Copying by View (Shallow Copy)		36
Copying by Value (Deep Copy)		37
Chapter 3	**Manipulating Tabular Data Using Pandas**	**39**
	What Is Pandas?	39
	Pandas Series	40
	Creating a Series Using a Specified Index	41
	Accessing Elements in a Series	41
	Specifying a Datetime Range as the Index of a Series	42
	Date Ranges	43
	Pandas DataFrame	45
	Creating a DataFrame	45
	Specifying the Index in a DataFrame	46
	Generating Descriptive Statistics on the DataFrame	47
	Extracting from DataFrames	49
	Selecting the First and Last Five Rows	49
	Selecting a Specific Column in a DataFrame	50
	Slicing Based on Row Number	50
	Slicing Based on Row and Column Numbers	51
	Slicing Based on Labels	52
	Selecting a Single Cell in a DataFrame	54
	Selecting Based on Cell Value	54
	Transforming DataFrames	54
	Checking to See If a Result Is a DataFrame or Series	55
	Sorting Data in a DataFrame	55
	Sorting by Index	55
	Sorting by Value	56
	Applying Functions to a DataFrame	57
	Adding and Removing Rows and Columns in a DataFrame	60
	Adding a Column	61
	Removing Rows	61
	Removing Columns	62
	Generating a Crosstab	63
Chapter 4	**Data Visualization Using matplotlib**	**67**
	What Is matplotlib?	67
	Plotting Line Charts	68

Adding Title and Labels   69
Styling   69
Plotting Multiple Lines in the Same Chart   71
Adding a Legend   72
Plotting Bar Charts   73
Adding Another Bar to the Chart   74
Changing the Tick Marks   75
Plotting Pie Charts   77
Exploding the Slices   78
Displaying Custom Colors   79
Rotating the Pie Chart   80
Displaying a Legend   81
Saving the Chart   82
Plotting Scatter Plots   83
Combining Plots   83
Subplots   84
Plotting Using Seaborn   85
Displaying Categorical Plots   86
Displaying Lmplots   88
Displaying Swarmplots   90

Chapter 5   Getting Started with Scikit-learn for Machine Learning   93
Introduction to Scikit-learn   93
Getting Datasets   94
Using the Scikit-learn Dataset   94
Using the Kaggle Dataset   97
Using the UCI (University of California, Irvine)
    Machine Learning Repository   97
Generating Your Own Dataset   98
    Linearly Distributed Dataset   98
    Clustered Dataset   98
    Clustered Dataset Distributed in Circular Fashion   100
Getting Started with Scikit-learn   100
Using the LinearRegression Class for Fitting the Model   101
Making Predictions   102
Plotting the Linear Regression Line   102
Getting the Gradient and Intercept of the Linear
    Regression Line   103
Examining the Performance of the Model by Calculating the
    Residual Sum of Squares   104
Evaluating the Model Using a Test Dataset   105
Persisting the Model   106
Data Cleansing   107
Cleaning Rows with NaNs   108
    Replacing NaN with the Mean of the Column   109
    Removing Rows   109
Removing Duplicate Rows   110
Normalizing Columns   112

	Removing Outliers	113
	Tukey Fences	113
	Z-Score	116
Chapter 6	**Supervised Learning—Linear Regression**	**119**
	Types of Linear Regression	119
	Linear Regression	120
	Using the Boston Dataset	120
	Data Cleansing	125
	Feature Selection	126
	Multiple Regression	128
	Training the Model	131
	Getting the Intercept and Coefficients	133
	Plotting the 3D Hyperplane	133
	Polynomial Regression	135
	Formula for Polynomial Regression	138
	Polynomial Regression in Scikit-learn	138
	Understanding Bias and Variance	141
	Using Polynomial Multiple Regression on the Boston Dataset	144
	Plotting the 3D Hyperplane	146
Chapter 7	**Supervised Learning—Classification Using**	
Logistic Regression		**151**
	What Is Logistic Regression?	151
	Understanding Odds	153
	Logit Function	153
	Sigmoid Curve	154
	Using the Breast Cancer Wisconsin (Diagnostic) Data Set	156
	Examining the Relationship Between Features	156
	Plotting the Features in 2D	157
	Plotting in 3D	158
	Training Using One Feature	161
	Finding the Intercept and Coefficient	162
	Plotting the Sigmoid Curve	162
	Making Predictions	163
	Training the Model Using All Features	164
	Testing the Model	166
	Getting the Confusion Matrix	166
	Computing Accuracy, Recall, Precision, and Other Metrics	168
	Receiver Operating Characteristic (ROC) Curve	171
	Plotting the ROC and Finding the Area Under the	
	Curve (AUC)	174
Chapter 8	**Supervised Learning—Classification Using Support**	
Vector Machines		**177**
	What Is a Support Vector Machine?	177
	Maximum Separability	178
	Support Vectors	179

Formula for the Hyperplane 180
Using Scikit-learn for SVM 181
Plotting the Hyperplane and the Margins 184
Making Predictions 185
Kernel Trick 186
Adding a Third Dimension 187
Plotting the 3D Hyperplane 189
Types of Kernels 191
C 194
Radial Basis Function (RBF) Kernel 196
Gamma 197
Polynomial Kernel 199
Using SVM for Real-Life Problems 200

Chapter 9   Supervised Learning—Classification Using K-Nearest Neighbors (KNN)   205
What Is K-Nearest Neighbors? 205
Implementing KNN in Python 206
Plotting the Points 206
Calculating the Distance Between the Points 207
Implementing KNN 208
Making Predictions 209
Visualizing Different Values of K 209
Using Scikit-Learn's KNeighborsClassifier Class for KNN . 211
Exploring Different Values of K 213
Cross-Validation 216
Parameter-Tuning K 217
Finding the Optimal K 218

Chapter 10   Unsupervised Learning—Clustering Using K-Means   221
What Is Unsupervised Learning? 221
Unsupervised Learning Using K-Means 222
How Clustering in K-Means Works 222
Implementing K-Means in Python 225
Using K-Means in Scikit-learn 230
Evaluating Cluster Size Using the Silhouette Coefficient . 232
Calculating the Silhouette Coefficient 233
Finding the Optimal K 234
Using K-Means to Solve Real-Life Problems 236
Importing the Data 237
Cleaning the Data 237
Plotting the Scatter Plot 238
Clustering Using K-Means 239
Finding the Optimal Size Classes 240

Chapter 11   Using Azure Machine Learning Studio   243
What Is Microsoft Azure Machine Learning Studio? 243
An Example Using the Titanic Experiment 244
Using Microsoft Azure Machine Learning Studio 246

Uploading Your Dataset	247
Creating an Experiment	248
Filtering the Data and Making Fields Categorical	252
Removing the Missing Data	254
Splitting the Data for Training and Testing	254
Training a Model	256
Comparing Against Other Algorithms	258
Evaluating Machine Learning Algorithms	260
Publishing the Learning Model as a Web Service	261
Publishing the Experiment	261
Testing the Web Service	263
Programmatically Accessing the Web Service	263

Chapter 12	**Deploying Machine Learning Models**	**269**
	Deploying ML	269
	Case Study	270
	Loading the Data	271
	Cleaning the Data	271
	Examining the Correlation Between the Features	273
	Plotting the Correlation Between Features	274
	Evaluating the Algorithms	277
	Logistic Regression	277
	K-Nearest Neighbors	277
	Support Vector Machines	278
	Selecting the Best Performing Algorithm	279
	Training and Saving the Model	279
	Deploying the Model	280
	Testing the Model	282
	Creating the Client Application to Use the Model	283

Index	**285**

Introduction

This book covers machine learning, one of the hottest topics in more recent years. With computing power increasing exponentially and prices decreasing simultaneously, there is no better time for machine learning. With machine learning, tasks that usually require huge processing power are now possible on desktop machines. Nevertheless, machine learning is not for the faint of heart—it requires a good foundation in statistics, as well as programming knowledge. Most books on the market either are too superficial or go into too much depth that often leaves beginning readers gasping for air.

This book will take a gentle approach to this topic. First, it will cover some of the fundamental libraries used in Python that make machine learning possible. In particular, you will learn how to manipulate arrays of numbers using the NumPy library, followed by using the Pandas library to deal with tabular data. Once that is done, you will learn how to visualize data using the matplotlib library, which allows you to plot different types of charts and graphs so that you can visualize your data easily.

Once you have a firm foundation in the basics, I will discuss machine learning using Python and the Scikit-Learn libraries. This will give you a solid understanding of how the various machine learning algorithms work behind the scenes.

For this book, I will cover the common machine learning algorithms, such as regression, clustering, and classification.

This book also contains a chapter where you will learn how to perform machine learning using the Microsoft Azure Machine Learning Studio, which allows developers to start building machine learning models using drag-and-drop without needing to code. And most importantly, without requiring a deep knowledge of machine learning.

Finally, I will discuss how you can deploy the models that you have built, so that they can be used by client applications running on mobile and desktop devices.

It is my key intention to make this book accessible to as many developers as possible. To get the most out of this book, you should have some basic knowledge of Python programming, and some foundational understanding of basic statistics. And just like you will never be able to learn how to swim just by reading a book, I strongly suggest that you try out the sample code while you are going through the chapters. Go ahead and modify the code and see how the output varies, and very often you would be surprised by what you can do.

All the sample code in this book are available as Jupyter Notebooks (available for download from Wiley's support page for this book, www.wiley.com/go/ leepythonmachinelearning). So you could just download them and try them out immediately.

Without further delay, welcome to *Python Machine Learning*!

Introduction to Machine Learning

Welcome to *Python Machine Learning*! The fact that you are reading this book is a clear indication of your interest in this very interesting and exciting topic.

This book covers *machine learning,* one of the hottest programming topics in more recent years. *Machine learning (ML)* is a collection of algorithms and techniques used to design systems that learn from data. These systems are then able to perform predictions or deduce patterns from the supplied data.

With computing power increasing exponentially and prices decreasing simultaneously, there is no better time for machine learning. Machine learning tasks that usually require huge processing power are now possible on desktop machines. Nevertheless, machine learning is not for the faint of heart—it requires a good foundation in mathematics, statistics, as well as programming knowledge. The majority of the books in the market on machine learning go into too much detail, which often leaves beginning readers gasping for air. Most of the discussion on machine learning revolves heavily around statistical theories and algorithms, so unless you are a mathematician or a PhD candidate, you will likely find them difficult to digest. For most people, developers in particular, what they want is to have a foundational understanding of how machine learning works, and most importantly, how to apply machine learning in their applications. It is with this motive in mind that I set out to write this book.

This book will take a *gentle* approach to machine learning. I will attempt to do the following:

➤ Cover the libraries in Python that lay the foundation for machine learning, namely NumPy, Pandas, and matplotlib.

➤ Discuss machine learning using Python and the Scikit-learn libraries. Where possible, I will manually implement the relevant machine learning algorithm using Python. This will allow you to understand how the various machine learning algorithms work behind the scenes. Once this is done, I will show how to use the Scikit-learn libraries, which make it really easy to integrate machine learning into your own apps.

➤ Cover the common machine learning algorithms—regressions, clustering, and classifications.

TIP   It is not the intention of this book to go into a deep discussion of machine learning algorithms. Although there are chapters that discuss some of the mathematical concepts behind the algorithms, it is my intention to make the subject easy to understand and hopefully motivate you to learn further.

Machine learning is indeed a very complex topic. But instead of discussing the complex mathematical theories behind it, I will cover it using easy-to-understand examples and walk you through numerous code samples. This code-intensive book encourages readers to try out the numerous examples in the various chapters, which are designed to be independent, compact, and easy to follow and understand.

What Is Machine Learning?

If you have ever written a program, you will be familiar with the diagram shown in Figure 1.1. You write a program, feed some data into it, and get your output. For example, you might write a program to perform some accounting tasks for your business. In this case, the data collected would include your sales records, your inventory lists, and so on. The program would then take in the data and calculate your profits or loss based on your sales records. You may also perhaps churn out some nice and fanciful charts showing your sales performance. In this case, the output is the profit/loss statement, as well as other charts.

Traditional Programming

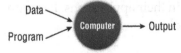

Figure 1.1: In traditional programming, the data and the program produce the output

For many years, traditional desktop and web programming have dominated the landscape, and many algorithms and methodologies have evolved to make programs run more efficiently. In more recent years, however, machine learning has taken over the programming world. Machine learning has transformed the paradigm in Figure 1.1 to a new paradigm, which is shown in Figure 1.2. Instead of feeding the data to the program, you now use the data and the output that you have collected to derive your program (also known as the *model*). Using the same accounting example, with the machine learning paradigm, you would take the detailed sales records (which are collectively both the data and output) and use them to derive a set of rules to make predictions. You may use this model to predict the most popular items that will sell next year, or which items will be less popular going forward.

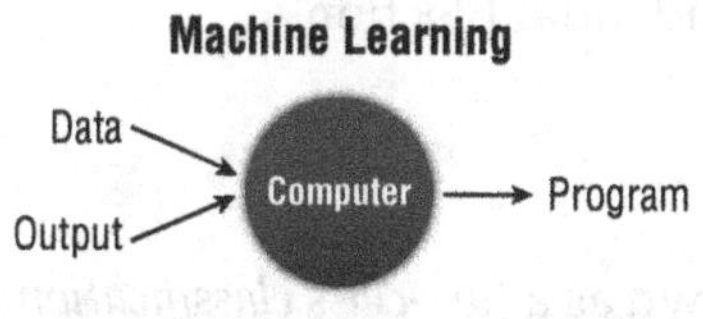

Machine Learning

Figure 1.2: In machine learning, the data and the output produce the program

> **TIP** Machine learning is about finding *patterns* in data.

What Problems Will Machine Learning Be Solving in This Book?

So, what exactly is machine learning? Machine learning (ML) is a collection of algorithms and techniques used to design systems that learn from data. ML algorithms have a strong mathematical and statistical basis, but they do not take into account domain knowledge. ML consists of the following disciplines:

- Scientific computing
- Mathematics
- Statistics

A good application of machine learning is trying to determine if a particular credit card transaction is fraudulent. Given past transaction records, the data scientist's job is to clean up and transform the data based on domain knowledge so that the right ML algorithm can be applied in order to solve the problem (in this case determine if a transaction is fraudulent). A data scientist needs to know about which method of machine learning will best help in completing this task and how to apply it. The data scientist does not necessarily need to know how that method works, although knowing this will always help in building a more accurate learning model.

In this book, there are three main types of problems that we want to solve using machine learning. These problem types are as follows:

Classification: Is this A or B?

Regression: How much or how many?

Clustering: How is this organized?

Classification

In machine learning, *classification* is identifying to which set of categories a new observation belongs based on the set of training data containing in the observed categories. Here are some examples of classification problems:

- Predicting the winner for the U.S. 2020 Presidential Election
- Predicting if a tumor is cancerous
- Classifying the different types of flowers

A classification problem with two classes is known as a *two-class classification* problem. Those with more than two classes are known as *multi-class classification* problems.

The outcome of a classification problem is a discrete value indicating the predicted class in which an observation lies. The outcome of a classification problem can also be a continuous value, indicating the likelihood of an observation belonging to a particular class. For example, candidate A is predicted to win the election with a probability of 0.65 (or 65 percent). Here, 0.65 is the continuous value indicating the confidence of the prediction, and it can be converted to a class value ("win" in this case) by selecting the prediction with the highest probability.

Chapter 7 through Chapter 9 will discuss classifications in more detail.

Regression

Regression helps in forecasting the future by estimating the relationship between variables. Unlike classification (which predicts the class to which an observation belongs), regression returns a continuous output variable. Here are some examples of regression problems:

- Predicting the sales number for a particular item for the next quarter
- Predicting the temperatures for next week
- Predicting the lifespan of a particular model of tire

Chapter 5 and Chapter 6 will discuss regressions in more detail.

Clustering

Clustering helps in grouping similar data points into intuitive groups. Given a set of data, clustering helps you discover how they are organized by grouping them into natural clumps.

Examples of clustering problems are as follows:

- Which viewers like the same genre of movies
- Which models of hard drives fail in the same way

Clustering is very useful when you want to discover a specific pattern in the data. Chapter 10 will discuss clustering in more detail.

Types of Machine Learning Algorithms

Machine learning algorithms fall into two broad categories:

- *Supervised learning algorithms* are trained with labeled data. In other words, data composed of examples of the desired answers. For instance, a model that identifies fraudulent credit card use would be trained from a dataset with labeled data points of known fraudulent and valid charges. Most machine learning is supervised.

- *Unsupervised learning algorithms* are used on data with no labels, and the goal is to find relationships in the data. For instance, you might want to find groupings of customer demographics with similar buying habits.

Supervised Learning

In supervised learning, a labeled dataset is used. A *labeled dataset* means that a group of data has been tagged with a label. This label provides informative meaning to the data. Using the label, unlabeled data can be predicted to obtain a new label. For example, a dataset may contain a series of records containing the following fields, which record the size of the various houses and the prices for which they were sold:

House Size, Price Sold

In this very simple example, *Price Sold* is the label. When plotted on a chart (see Figure 1.3), this dataset can help you predict the price of a house that is yet to be sold. Predicting a price for the house is a *regression* problem.

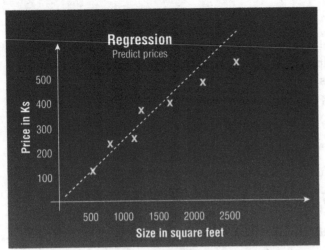

Figure 1.3: Using regression to predict the expected selling price of a house

Using another example, suppose that you have a dataset containing the following:

Tumor Size, Age, Malignant

The *Malignant* field is a label indicating if a tumor is cancerous. When you plot the dataset on a chart (see Figure 1.4), you will be able to classify it into two distinct groups, with one group containing the cancerous tumors and the other containing the benign tumors. Using this grouping, you can now predict if a new tumor is cancerous or not. This type of problem is known as a *classification* problem.

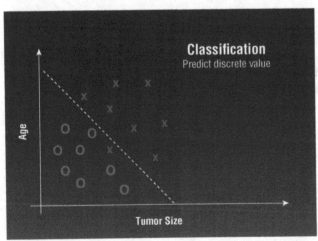

Figure 1.4: Using classification to categorize data into distinct classes

> **TIP**   Chapter 6 through Chapter 9 will discuss supervised learning algorithms in more detail.

Unsupervised Learning

In unsupervised learning, the dataset used is not labeled. An easy way to visualize unlabeled data is to consider the dataset containing the waist size and leg length of a group of people:

Waist Size, Leg Length

Using unsupervised learning, your job is to try to predict a pattern in the dataset. You may plot the dataset in a chart, as shown in Figure 1.5.

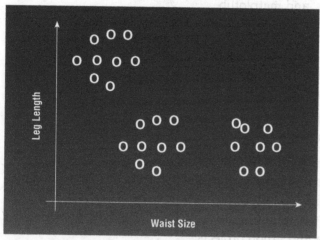

Figure 1.5: Plotting the unlabeled data

You can then use some clustering algorithms to find the patterns in the dataset. The end result might be the discovery of three distinct groups of clusters in the data, as shown in Figure 1.6.

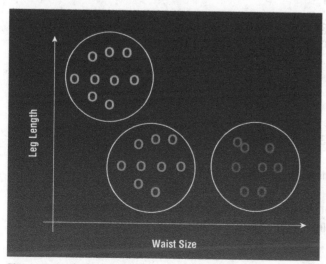

Figure 1.6: Clustering the points into distinct groups

> **TIP**   Chapter 10 will discuss unsupervised learning algorithms in more detail.

Getting the Tools

For this book, all of the examples are tested using Python 3 and the Scikit-learn library, a Python library that implements the various types of machine learning algorithms, such as classification, regression, clustering, decision tree, and more. Besides Scikit-learn, you will also be using some complementary Python libraries—NumPy, Pandas, and matplotlib.

While you can install the Python interpreter and the other libraries individually on your computer, the trouble-free way to install all of these libraries is to install the Anaconda package. *Anaconda* is a free Python distribution that comes with all of the necessary libraries that you need to create data science and machine learning projects.

Anaconda includes the following:

- The core Python language
- The various Python packages (libraries)
- *conda*, Anaconda's own package manager for updating Anaconda and packages
- Jupyter Notebook (formerly known as *iPython Notebook*), a web-based editor for working with Python projects

With Anaconda, you have the flexibility to install different languages (R, JavaScript, Julia, and so on) to work in Jupyter Notebook.

Obtaining Anaconda

To download Anaconda, go to `https://www.anaconda.com/download/`. You will be able to download Anaconda for these operating systems (see Figure 1.7):

- Windows
- macOS
- Linux

Download the Python 3 for the platform you are using.

> **NOTE**   At the time of this writing, Python is in version 3.7.

> **TIP**   For this book, we will be using Python 3. So be sure to download the correct version of Anaconda containing Python 3.

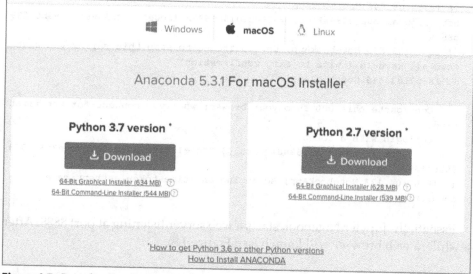

Figure 1.7: Downloading Anaconda for Python 3

Installing Anaconda

Installing Anaconda is mostly a non-event process. Double-click the file that you have downloaded, and follow the instructions displayed on the screen. In particular, Anaconda for Windows has the option to be installed only for the local user. This option does not require administrator rights, and hence it is very useful for users who are installing Anaconda on company-issued computers, which are usually locked down with limited user privileges.

Once Anaconda is installed, you will want to launch Jupyter Notebook. Jupyter Notebook is an open source web application, which allows you to create and share documents that contain documentation, code, and more.

Running Jupyter Notebook for Mac

To launch Jupyter from macOS, launch *Terminal* and type the following command:

```
$ jupyter notebook
```

You will see the following:

```
$ jupyter notebook
[I 18:57:03.642 NotebookApp] JupyterLab extension loaded from
/Users/weimenglee/anaconda3/lib/python3.7/site-packages/jupyterlab
[I 18:57:03.643 NotebookApp] JupyterLab application directory is
/Users/weimenglee/anaconda3/share/jupyter/lab
[I 18:57:03.648 NotebookApp] Serving notebooks from local directory:
/Users/weimenglee/Python Machine Learning
[I 18:57:03.648 NotebookApp] The Jupyter Notebook is running at:
```

```
[I 18:57:03.648 NotebookApp]
http://localhost:8888/?token=3700cfe13b65982612c0e1975ce3a68107399b07f89
b85fa
[I 18:57:03.648 NotebookApp] Use Control-C to stop this server and shut
down all kernels (twice to skip confirmation).
[C 18:57:03.649 NotebookApp]

    Copy/paste this URL into your browser when you connect for the first
time,
    to login with a token:
        http://localhost:8888/?token=3700cfe13b65982612c0e1975ce3a681073
99b07f89b85fa
[I 18:57:04.133 NotebookApp] Accepting one-time-token-authenticated
connection from ::1
```

Essentially, Jupyter Notebook starts a web server listening at port 8888. After a while, a web browser will launch (see Figure 1.8).

Figure 1.8: The Jupyter Notebook Home page

TIP   The Home page of Jupyter Notebook shows the content of the directory from where it is launched. Hence, it is always useful to change to the directory that contains your source code first, prior to launching Jupyter Notebook.

Running Jupyter Notebook for Windows

The best way to launch Jupyter Notebook in Windows is to launch it from the *Anaconda Prompt*. The Anaconda Prompt automatically runs the batch file located at C:\Anaconda3\Scripts\activate.bat with the following argument:

```
C:\Anaconda3\Scripts\activate.bat C:\Anaconda3
```

TIP   Note that the exact location of the Anaconda3 folder can vary. For example, by default Windows 10 will install Anaconda in `C:\Users\<username>\AppData\Local\Continuum\anaconda3` instead of `C:\Anaconda3`.

This sets up the necessary paths for accessing Anaconda and its libraries.

To launch the Anaconda Prompt, type **Anaconda Prompt** in the Windows Run textbox. To launch Jupyter Notebook from the Anaconda Prompt, type the following:

```
(base) C:\Users\Wei-Meng Lee\Python Machine Learning>jupyter notebook
```

You will then see this:

```
[I 21:30:48.048 NotebookApp] JupyterLab beta preview extension loaded from
C:\Anaconda3\lib\site-packages\jupyterlab
[I 21:30:48.048 NotebookApp] JupyterLab application directory is
C:\Anaconda3\share\jupyter\lab
[I 21:30:49.315 NotebookApp] Serving notebooks from local directory:
C:\Users\Wei-Meng Lee\Python Machine Learning
[I 21:30:49.315 NotebookApp] 0 active kernels
[I 21:30:49.322 NotebookApp] The Jupyter Notebook is running at:
[I 21:30:49.323 NotebookApp]
http://localhost:8888/?token=482bfe023bd77731dc132b5340f335b9e450ce5e1c4
d7b2f
[I 21:30:49.324 NotebookApp] Use Control-C to stop this server and shut
down all kernels (twice to skip confirmation).
[C 21:30:49.336 NotebookApp]

    Copy/paste this URL into your browser when you connect for the first
time,
    to login with a token:
        http://localhost:8888/?token=482bfe023bd77731dc132b5340f335b9e45
0ce5e1c4d7b2f
[I 21:30:49.470 NotebookApp] Accepting one-time-token-authenticated
connection from ::1
```

Essentially, Jupyter Notebook starts a web server listening at port 8888. It then launches your web browser showing you the page in Figure 1.9.

Creating a New Notebook

To create a new notebook, locate the New button on the right side of the screen and click it. You should be able to see Python 3 in the dropdown (see Figure 1.10). Click this option.

Your new notebook will now appear (see Figure 1.11).

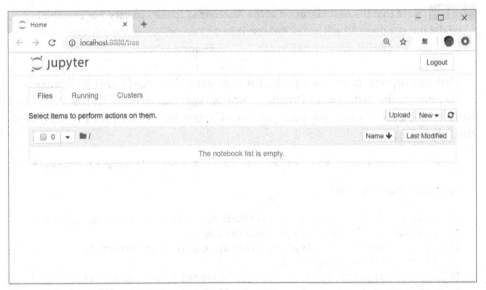

Figure 1.9: Jupyter Notebook showing the Home page

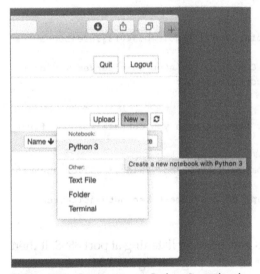

Figure 1.10: Creating a new Python 3 notebook

Naming the Notebook

By default, your notebook will be named "Untitled". To give it a suitable name, click "Untitled" and type in a new name. Your notebook will be saved in the directory from which you have launched Jupyter Notebook. The notebook will be saved with a filename that you have given it, together with the .ipynb extension.

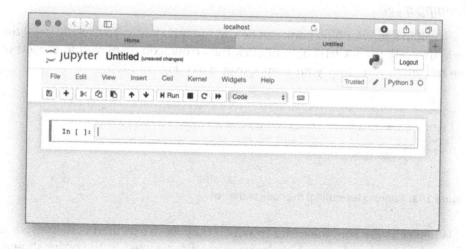

Figure 1.11: The Python 3 notebook created in Jupyter Notebook

TIP   Jupyter Notebook was previously known as *iPython Notebook*; hence the
`.ipynb` **extension.**

Adding and Removing Cells

A notebook contains one or more cells. You can type Python statements in each
cell. Using Jupyter Notebook, you can divide your code into multiple snippets
and put them into cells so that they can be run individually.

To add more cells to your notebook, click the + button. You can also use
the Insert menu item and select the option Insert Cell Above to add a new
cell above the current cell, or select the Insert Cell Below option to add a
new cell below the current cell.

Figure 1.12 shows the notebook containing two cells.

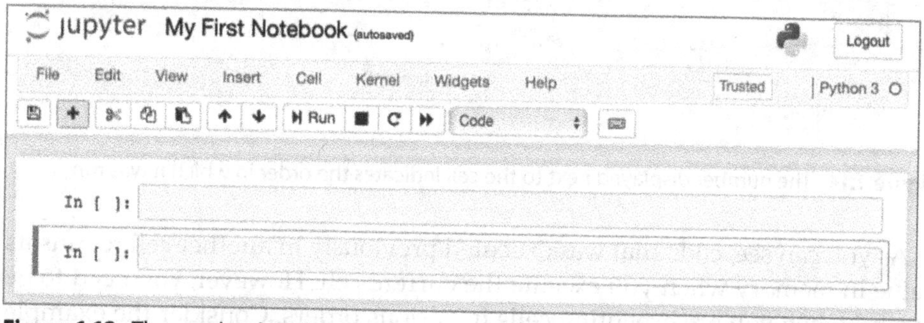

Figure 1.12: The notebook with two cells

Running a Cell

Each cell in a Jupyter Notebook can be run independently. To execute (run) the code in a cell, press Ctrl+Enter, or click the arrow icon displayed to the left of the cell when you hover your mouse over it (see Figure 1.13).

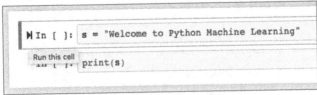

Figure 1.13: Running (executing) the code in the cell

When cells are run, the order in which they were executed is displayed as a running number. Figure 1.14 shows two cells executed in the order shown. The number 1 in the first cell indicates that this cell was executed first, followed by number 2 in the second cell. The output of the cell is displayed immediately after the cell. If you go back to the first cell and run it, the number will then change to 3.

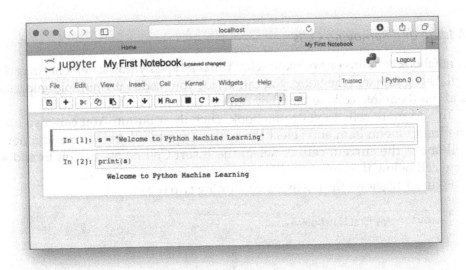

Figure 1.14: The number displayed next to the cell indicates the order in which it was run

As you can see, code that was executed previously in another cell retains its value in memory when you execute the current cell. However, you need to be careful when you are executing cells in various orders. Consider the example in Figure 1.15. Here, we have three cells. In the first cell, we initialize the value of s to a string and print its value in the second cell. In the third cell, we change the value of s to another string.

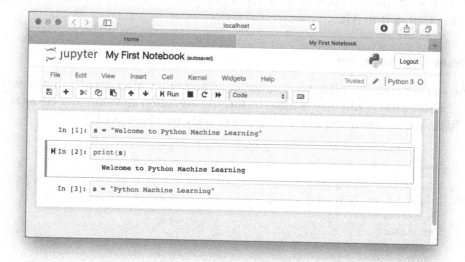

Figure 1.15: The notebook with three cells

Very often, in the midst of testing your code, it is very common that you may make modifications in one cell and go back to an earlier cell to retest the code. In this example, suppose that you go back and rerun the second cell. In this case, you would now print out the new value of s (see Figure 1.16). At first glance, you may be expecting to see the string "Welcome to Python Machine Learning," but since the second cell was rerun after the third cell, the value of s will take on the "Python Machine Learning" string.

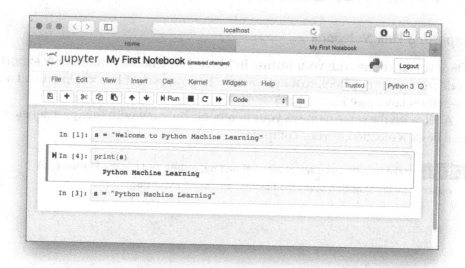

Figure 1.16: Executing the cells in non-linear order

To restart the execution from the first cell, you need to restart the kernel, or select Cell ⇨ Run All.

Restarting the Kernel

As you can run any cell in your notebook in any order, after a while things may get a little messy. You may want to restart the execution and start all over again. This is where restarting the kernel is necessary (see Figure 1.17).

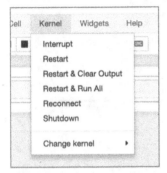

Figure 1.17: Restarting the kernel

> **TIP** When your code goes into an infinite loop, you need to restart the kernel.
> There are two common scenarios for restarting the kernel:
> **Restart & Clear Output** Restart the kernel and clear all of the outputs. You can now run any of the cells in any order you like.
> **Restart & Run All** Restart the kernel and run all of the cells from the first to the last. This is very useful if you are satisfied with your code and want to test it in its entirety.

Exporting Your Notebook

Once you are done with your testing in Jupyter Notebook, you can now export code from your notebook to a Python file. To do so, select File ⇨ Download as ⇨ python (.py). (See Figure 1.18.)

A file with the same name as your notebook, but now with the .py extension, will be downloaded to your computer.

> **TIP** Make sure that you select the python (.py) option and not the Python (.py) option. The latter option saves the file with an .html extension.

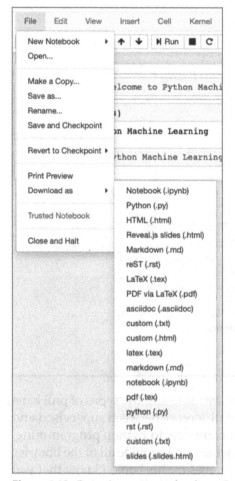

Figure 1.18: Exporting your notebook to a Python file

Getting Help

You can get help in Jupyter Notebook quite easily. To get help on a function in Python, position your cursor on the function name and press Shift+Tab. This will display a pop-up known as the *tooltip* (see Figure 1.19).

To expand the tooltip (see Figure 1.20), click the + button on the upper-right corner of the tooltip. You can also get the expanded version of the tooltip when you press Shift+Tab+Tab.

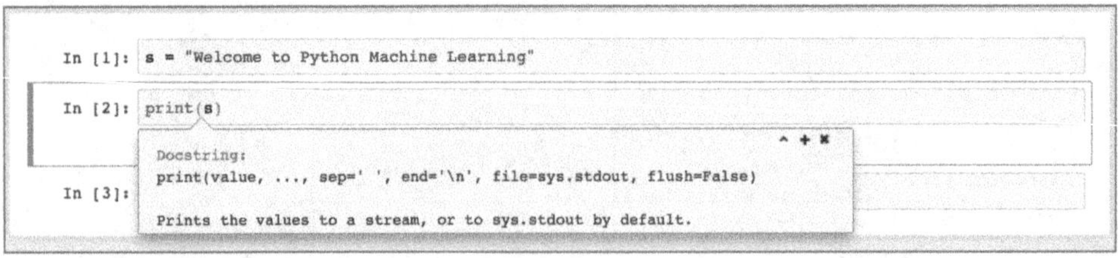

```
In [1]:  s = "Welcome to Python Machine Learning"

In [2]:  print(s)
                                                                    ^ + ✕
              Docstring:
              print(value, ..., sep=' ', end='\n', file=sys.stdout, flush=False)
In [3]:
              Prints the values to a stream, or to sys.stdout by default.
```

Figure 1.19: The tooltip displays help information

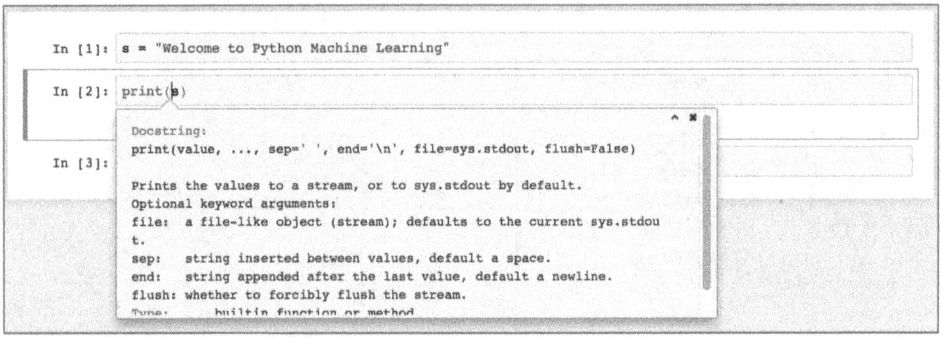

```
In [1]:  s = "Welcome to Python Machine Learning"

In [2]:  print(s)
                                                                    ^ ✕
              Docstring:
              print(value, ..., sep=' ', end='\n', file=sys.stdout, flush=False)
In [3]:
              Prints the values to a stream, or to sys.stdout by default.
              Optional keyword arguments:
              file:  a file-like object (stream); defaults to the current sys.stdou
              t.
              sep:    string inserted between values, default a space.
              end:    string appended after the last value, default a newline.
              flush: whether to forcibly flush the stream.
              Type:      builtin function or method
```

Figure 1.20: Expanding the tooltip to show more detail

Summary

In this chapter, you learned about machine learning and the types of problems that it can solve. You also studied the main difference between supervised and unsupervised learning. For developers who are new to Python programming, I strongly advise you to install Anaconda, which will provide all of the libraries and packages you'll need to follow the examples in this book. I know that you are all eager to start learning, so let's move onward to Chapter 2!

Extending Python Using NumPy

What Is NumPy?

In Python, you usually use the `list` data type to store a collection of items. The Python list is similar to the concept of arrays in languages like Java, C#, and JavaScript. The following code snippet shows a Python list:

```
list1 = [1,2,3,4,5]
```

Unlike arrays, a Python list does not need to contain elements of the same type. The following example is a perfectly legal list in Python:

```
list2 = [1,"Hello",3.14,True,5]
```

While this unique feature in Python provides flexibility when handling multiple types in a list, it has its disadvantages when processing large amounts of data (as is typical in machine learning and data science projects). The key problem with Python's `list` data type is its efficiency. To allow a list to have non-uniform type items, each item in the list is stored in a memory location, with the list containing an "array" of pointers to each of these locations. A Python list requires the following:

- At least 4 bytes per pointer.
- At least 16 bytes for the smallest Python object—4 bytes for a pointer, 4 bytes for the reference count, 4 bytes for the value. All of these together round up to 16 bytes.

Due to the way that a Python list is implemented, accessing items in a large list is computationally expensive. To solve this limitation with Python's list feature, Python programmers turn to *NumPy*, an extension to the Python programming language that adds support for large, multidimensional arrays and matrices, along with a large library of high-level mathematical functions to operate on these arrays.

In NumPy, an array is of type `ndarray` (n-dimensional array), and all elements must be of the same type. An `ndarray` object represents a multidimensional, homogeneous array of fixed-size items, and it is much more efficient than Python's list. The `ndarray` object also provides functions that operate on an entire array at once.

Creating NumPy Arrays

Before using NumPy, you first need to import the NumPy package (you may use its conventional alias *np* if you prefer):

```
import numpy as np
```

The first way to make NumPy arrays is to create them intrinsically, using the functions built right into NumPy. First, you can use the `arange()` function to create an evenly spaced array with a given interval:

```
a1 = np.arange(10)        # creates a range from 0 to 9
print(a1)                 # [0 1 2 3 4 5 6 7 8 9]
print(a1.shape)           # (10,)
```

The preceding statement creates a rank 1 array (one-dimensional) of ten elements. To get the shape of the array, use the `shape` property. Think of `a1` as a 10×1 matrix.

You can also specify a step in the `arange()` function. The following code snippet inserts a step value of 2:

```
a2 = np.arange(0,10,2)    # creates a range from 0 to 9, step 2
print(a2)                 # [0 2 4 6 8]
```

To create an array of a specific size filled with 0s, use the `zeros()` function:

```
a3 = np.zeros(5)          # create an array with all 0s
print(a3)                 # [ 0.  0.  0.  0.  0.]
print(a3.shape)           # (5,)
```

You can also create two-dimensional arrays using the `zeros()` function:

```
a4 = np.zeros((2,3))      # array of rank 2 with all 0s; 2 rows and 3
                          # columns
print(a4.shape)           # (2,3)
```

```
print(a4)
'''

[[ 0.  0.  0.]
 [ 0.  0.  0.]]
'''
```

If you want an array filled with a specific number instead of 0, use the `full()` function:

```
a5 = np.full((2,3), 8)    # array of rank 2 with all 8s
print(a5)
'''

[[8 8 8]
 [8 8 8]]
'''
```

Sometimes, you need to create an array that mirrors an identity matrix. In NumPy, you can do so using the `eye()` function:

```
a6 = np.eye(4)            # 4x4 identity matrix
print(a6)
'''

[[ 1.  0.  0.  0.]
 [ 0.  1.  0.  0.]
 [ 0.  0.  1.  0.]
 [ 0.  0.  0.  1.]]
'''
```

The `eye()` function returns a 2-D array with ones on the diagonal and zeros elsewhere.

To create an array filled with random numbers, you can use the `random()` function from the `numpy.random` module:

```
a7 = np.random.random((2,4)) # rank 2 array (2 rows 4 columns) with
                             # random values
                             # in the half-open interval [0.0, 1.0)
print(a7)
'''

[[ 0.48255806  0.23928884  0.99861279  0.4624779 ]
 [ 0.18721584  0.71287041  0.84619432  0.65990083]]
'''
```

Another way to create a NumPy array is to create it from a Python list as follows:

```
list1 = [1,2,3,4,5]    # list1 is a list in Python
r1 = np.array(list1)   # rank 1 array
print(r1)              # [1 2 3 4 5]
```

The array created in this example is a rank 1 array.

Array Indexing

Accessing elements in the array is similar to accessing elements in a Python list:

```
print(r1[0])           # 1
print(r1[1])           # 2
```

The following code snippet creates another array named *r2*, which is two-dimensional:

```
list2 = [6,7,8,9,0]
r2 = np.array([list1,list2])      # rank 2 array
print(r2)
'''
[[1 2 3 4 5]
 [6 7 8 9 0]]
'''
print(r2.shape)          # (2,5) - 2 rows and 5 columns
print(r2[0,0])           # 1
print(r2[0,1])           # 2
print(r2[1,0])           # 6
```

Here, *r2* is a rank 2 array, with two rows and five columns.

Besides using an index to access elements in an array, you can also use a list as the index as follows:

```
list1 = [1,2,3,4,5]
r1 = np.array(list1)
print(r1[[2,4]])     # [3 5]
```

Boolean Indexing

In addition to using indexing to access elements in an array, there is another very cool way to access elements in a NumPy array. Consider the following:

```
print(r1>2)     # [False False  True  True  True]
```

This statement prints out a list containing Boolean values. What it actually does is to go through each element in *r1* and check if each element is more than two. The result is a Boolean value, and a list of Boolean values is created at the end of the process. You can feed the list results back into the array as the index:

```
print(r1[r1>2])     # [3 4 5]
```

This method of accessing elements in an array is known as *Boolean Indexing*. This method is very useful. Consider the following example:

```
nums = np.arange(20)
print(nums)        # [ 0  1  2  3  4  5  6  7  8  9 10 11 12 13 14 15 16
17 18 19]
```

If you want to retrieve all of the odd numbers from the list, you could simply use Boolean Indexing as follows:

```
odd_num = nums[nums % 2 == 1]
print(odd_num)     # [ 1  3  5  7  9 11 13 15 17 19]
```

Slicing Arrays

Slicing in NumPy arrays is similar to how it works with a Python list. Consider the following example:

```
a = np.array([[1,2,3,4,5],
              [4,5,6,7,8],
              [9,8,7,6,5]])    # rank 2 array
print(a)
'''
[[1 2 3 4 5]
 [4 5 6 7 8]
 [9 8 7 6 5]]
'''
```

To extract the last two rows and first two columns, you can use slicing:

```
b1 = a[1:3, :3]    # row 1 to 3 (not inclusive) and first 3 columns
print(b1)
```

The preceding code snippet will print out the following:

```
[[4 5 6]
 [9 8 7]]
```

Let's dissect this code. Slicing has the following syntax: [start:stop]. For two-dimensional arrays, the slicing syntax becomes [start:stop, start:stop]. The start:stop before the comma (,) refers to the rows, and the start:stop after the comma (,) refers to the columns. Hence for [1:3, :3], this means that you want to extract the rows with index 1 right up to 3 (but not including 3), and columns starting from the first column right up to index 3 (but not including 3). The general confusion regarding slicing is the end index. You need to remember that the end index is not included in the answer. A better way to visualize slicing is to write the index of each row and column between the numbers, instead of at the center of the number, as shown in Figure 2.1.

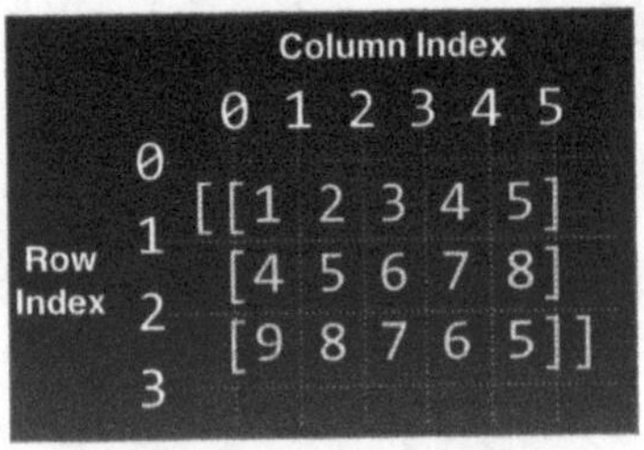

Figure 2.1: Writing the index for row and column in between the numbers

Using this approach, it is now much easier to visualize how slicing works (see Figure 2.2).

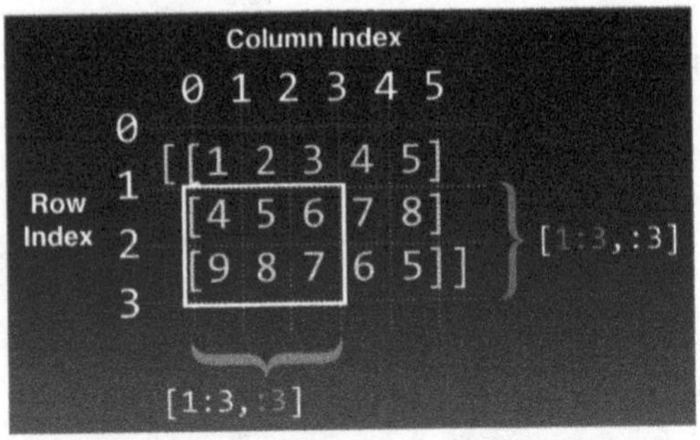

Figure 2.2: Performing slicing using the new approach

What about negative indices? For example, consider the following:

```
b2 = a[-2:,-2:]
print(b2)
```

Using the method just described, you can now write the negative row and column indices, as shown in Figure 2.3.

You should now be able to derive the answer quite easily, which is as follows:

```
[[7 8]
 [6 5]]
```

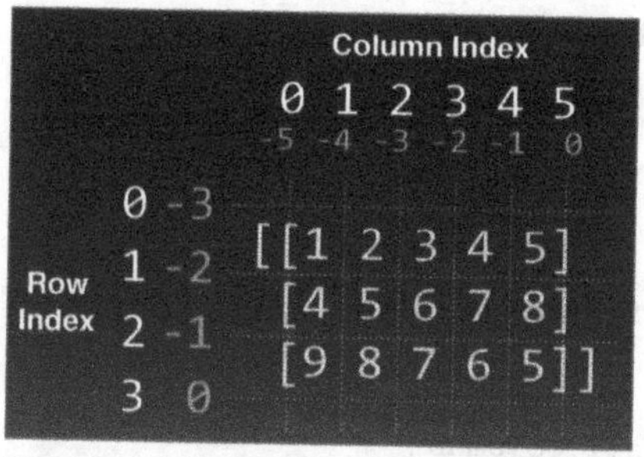

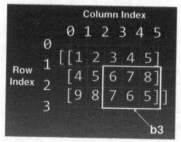

Figure 2.3: Writing the negative indices for rows and columns

NumPy Slice Is a Reference

It is noteworthy that the result of a NumPy slice is a reference and not a copy of the original array. Consider the following:

```
b3 = a[1:, 2:]        # row 1 onwards and column 2 onwards
                      # b3 is now pointing to a subset of a
print(b3)
```

The result is as follows:

```
[[6 7 8]
 [7 6 5]]
```

Here, *b3* is actually a reference to the original array *a* (see Figure 2.4).

Figure 2.4: Slicing returns a reference to the original array and not a copy

Hence, if you were to change one of the elements in *b3* as follows:

```
b3[0,2] = 88          # b3[0,2] is pointing to a[1,4]; modifying it will
                      # modify the original array
print(a)
```

The result will affect the content of a like this:

```
[[ 1  2  3  4  5]
 [ 4  5  6  7 88]
 [ 9  8  7  6  5]]
```

Another salient point to note is that the result of the slicing is dependent on how you slice it. Here is an example:

```
b4 = a[2:, :]        # row 2 onwards and all columns
print(b4)
print(b4.shape)
```

In the preceding statement, you are getting rows with index 2 and above and all of the columns. The result is a rank 2 array, like this:

```
[[9 8 7 6 5]]
(1,5)
```

If you have the following instead . . .

```
b5 = a[2, :]         # row 2 and all columns
print(b5)            # b5 is rank 1
```

. . . then the result would be a rank 1 array:

```
[9 8 7 6 5]
```

Printing the shape of the array confirms this:

```
print(b5.shape)      # (5,)
```

Reshaping Arrays

You can reshape an array to another dimension using the `reshape()` function. Using the b5 (which is a rank 1 array) example, you can reshape it to a rank 2 array as follows:

```
b5 = b5.reshape(1,-1)
print(b5)
'''
[[9 8 7 6 5]]
'''
```

In this example, you call the `reshape()` function with two arguments. The first 1 indicates that you want to convert it into rank 2 array with 1 row, and the

-1 indicates that you will leave it to the `reshape()` function to create the correct number of columns. Of course, in this example, it is clear that after reshaping there will be five columns, so you can call the `reshape()` function as `reshape(1,5)`. In more complex cases, however, it is always convenient to be able to use -1 to let the function decide on the number of rows or columns to create.

Here is another example of how to reshape *b4* (which is a rank 2 array) to rank 1:

```
b4.reshape(-1,)
'''
[9 8 7 6 5]
'''
```

The -1 indicates that you let the function decide how many rows to create as long as the end result is a rank 1 array.

> **TIP** To convert a rank 2 array to a rank 1 array, you can also use the `flatten()` or `ravel()` functions. The `flatten()` function always returns a copy of the array, while the `ravel()` and `reshape()` functions return a view (reference) of the original array.

Array Math

You can perform array math very easily on NumPy arrays. Consider the following two rank 2 arrays:

```
x1 = np.array([[1,2,3],[4,5,6]])
y1 = np.array([[7,8,9],[2,3,4]])
```

To add these two arrays together, you use the + operator as follows:

```
print(x1 + y1)
```

The result is the addition of each individual element in the two arrays:

```
[[ 8 10 12]
 [ 6  8 10]]
```

Array math is important, as it can be used to perform vector calculations. A good example is as follows:

```
x = np.array([2,3])
y = np.array([4,2])
z = x + y
'''
[6 5]
'''
```

Figure 2.5 shows the use of arrays to represent vectors and uses array addition to perform vector addition.

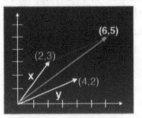

Figure 2.5: Using array addition for vector addition

Besides using the + operator, you can also use the `np.add()` function to add two arrays:

```
np.add(x1,y1)
```

Apart from addition, you can also perform subtraction, multiplication, as well as division with NumPy arrays:

```
print(x1 - y1)      # same as np.subtract(x1,y1)
'''
[[-6 -6 -6]
 [ 2  2  2]]
'''

print(x1 * y1)      # same as np.multiply(x1,y1)
'''
[[ 7 16 27]
 [ 8 15 24]]
'''

print(x1 / y1)      # same as np.divide(x1,y1)
'''
[[ 0.14285714  0.25        0.33333333]
 [ 2.         1.66666667  1.5        ]]
'''
```

What's a practical use of the ability to multiply or divide two arrays? As an example, suppose you have three arrays: one containing the names of a group of people, another the corresponding heights of these individuals, and the last one the corresponding weights of the individuals in the group:

```
names   = np.array(['Ann','Joe','Mark'])
heights = np.array([1.5, 1.78, 1.6])
weights = np.array([65, 46, 59])
```

Now say that you want to calculate the Body Mass Index (BMI) of this group of people. The formula to calculate BMI is as follows:

- Divide the weight in kilograms (kg) by the height in meters (m)
- Divide the answer by the height again

Using the BMI, you can classify a person as healthy, overweight, or underweight using the following categories:

- Underweight if BMI < 18.5
- Overweight if BMI > 25
- Normal weight if 18.5 <= BMI <= 25

Using array division, you could simply calculate BMI using the following statement:

```
bmi = weights/heights **2        # calculate the BMI
print(bmi)                       # [ 28.88888889  14.51836889
23.046875  ]
```

Finding out who is overweight, underweight, or otherwise is now very easy:

```
print("Overweight: " , names[bmi>25])
# Overweight:  ['Ann']
print("Underweight: " , names[bmi<18.5])
# Underweight:  ['Joe']
print("Healthy: " , names[(bmi>=18.5) & (bmi<=25)])
# Healthy:  ['Mark']
```

Dot Product

Note that when you multiply two arrays, you are actually multiplying each of the corresponding elements in the two arrays. Very often, you want to perform a scalar product (also commonly known as *dot product*). The dot product is an algebraic operation that takes two coordinate vectors of equal size and returns a single number. The dot product of two vectors is calculated by multiplying corresponding entries in each vector and adding up all of those products. For example, given two vectors—a = $[a_1, a_2, \ldots, a_n]$ and b = $[b_1, b_2, \ldots, b_n]$—the dot product of these two vectors is $a_1b_1 + a_2b_2 + \ldots + a_nb_n$.

In NumPy, dot product is accomplished using the dot() function:

```
x = np.array([2,3])
y = np.array([4,2])
np.dot(x,y)   # 2x4 + 3x2 = 14
```

Dot products also work on rank 2 arrays. If you perform a dot product of two rank 2 arrays, it is equivalent to the following *matrix multiplication*:

```
x2 = np.array([[1,2,3],[4,5,6]])
y2 = np.array([[7,8],[9,10], [11,12]])
print(np.dot(x2,y2))                          # matrix multiplication
'''
[[ 58  64]
 [139 154]]
'''
```

Figure 2.6 shows how matrix multiplication works. The first result, 58, is derived from the dot product of the first row of the first array and the first column of the second array—1 × 7 + 2 × 9 + 3 × 11 = 58. The second result of 64 is obtained by the dot product of the first row of the first array and the second column of the second array—1 × 8 + 2 × 10 + 3 × 12 = 64. And so on.

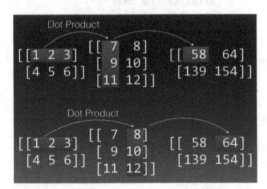

Figure 2.6: Performing matrix multiplication on two arrays

Matrix

NumPy provides another class in addition to arrays (ndarray): matrix. The *matrix* class is a subclass of the ndarray, and it is basically identical to the ndarray with one notable exception—a matrix is strictly two-dimensional, while an ndarray can be multidimensional. Creating a matrix object is similar to creating a NumPy array:

```
x2 = np.matrix([[1,2],[4,5]])
y2 = np.matrix([[7,8],[2,3]])
```

You can also convert a NumPy array to a matrix using the asmatrix() function:

```
x1 = np.array([[1,2],[4,5]])
y1 = np.array([[7,8],[2,3]])
x1 = np.asmatrix(x1)
y1 = np.asmatrix(y1)
```

Another important difference between an `ndarray` and a matrix occurs when you perform multiplications on them. When multiplying two `ndarray` objects, the result is the element-by-element multiplication that we have seen earlier. On the other hand, when multiplying two matrix objects, the result is the dot product (equivalent to the `np.dot()` function):

```
x1 = np.array([[1,2],[4,5]])
y1 = np.array([[7,8],[2,3]])
print(x1 * y1)      # element-by-element multiplication
'''
[[ 7 16]
 [ 8 15]]
'''

x2 = np.matrix([[1,2],[4,5]])
y2 = np.matrix([[7,8],[2,3]])
print(x2 * y2)      # dot product; same as np.dot()
'''
[[11 14]
 [38 47]]
'''
```

Cumulative Sum

Very often, when dealing with numerical data, there is a need to find the cumulative sum of numbers in a NumPy array. Consider the following array:

```
a = np.array([(1,2,3),(4,5,6), (7,8,9)])
print(a)
'''
[[1 2 3]
 [4 5 6]
 [7 8 9]]
'''
```

You can call the `cumsum()` function to get the cumulative sum of the elements:

```
print(a.cumsum())   # prints the cumulative sum of all the
                    # elements in the array
                    # [ 1  3  6 10 15 21 28 36 45]
```

In this case, the `cumsum()` function returns a rank 1 array containing the cumulative sum of all of the elements in the `a` array. The `cumsum()` function also takes in an optional argument—`axis`. Specifying an `axis` of 0 indicates that you want to get the cumulative sum of each column:

```
print(a.cumsum(axis=0))   # sum over rows for each of the 3 columns
'''
```

```
[[ 1  2  3]
 [ 5  7  9]
 [12 15 18]]
'''
```

Specifying an axis of 1 indicates that you want to get the cumulative sum of each row:

```
print(a.cumsum(axis=1))   # sum over columns for each of the 3 rows
'''
[[ 1  3  6]
 [ 4  9 15]
 [ 7 15 24]]
'''
```

Figure 2.7 makes it easy to understand how the `axis` parameter affects the way that cumulative sums are derived.

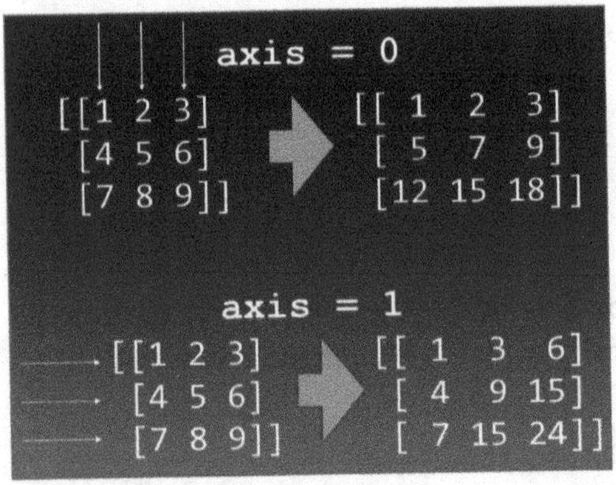

Figure 2.7: Performing cumulative sums on columns and rows

NumPy Sorting

NumPy provides a number of efficient sorting functions that make it very easy to sort an array. The first function for sorting is `sort()`, which takes in an array and returns a sorted array. Consider the following:

```
ages = np.array([34,12,37,5,13])
sorted_ages = np.sort(ages)    # does not modify the original array
print(sorted_ages)             # [ 5 12 13 34 37]
print(ages)                    # [34 12 37  5 13]
```

As you can see from the output, the `sort()` function does not modify the original array. Instead it returns a sorted array. If you want to sort the original array, call the `sort()` function on the array itself as follows:

```
ages.sort()                    # modifies the array
print(ages)                    # [ 5 12 13 34 37]
```

There is another function used for sorting—`argsort()`. To understand how it works, it is useful to examine the following code example:

```
ages = np.array([34,12,37,5,13])
print(ages.argsort())          # [3 1 4 0 2]
```

The `argsort()` function returns the indices that will sort an array. In the preceding example, the first element (3) in the result of the `argsort()` function means that the smallest element after the sort is in index 3 of the original array, which is the number 5. The next number is in index 1, which is the number 12, and so on. Figure 2.8 shows the meaning of the sort indices.

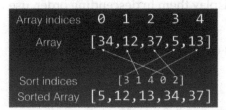

Figure 2.8: Understanding the meaning of the result of the `argsort()` function

To print the sorted *ages* array, use the result of `argsort()` as the index to the *ages* array:

```
print(ages[ages.argsort()])    # [ 5 12 13 34 37]
```

What is the real use of `argsort()`? Imagine that you have three arrays representing a list of people, along with their ages and heights:

```
persons = np.array(['Johnny','Mary','Peter','Will','Joe'])
ages    = np.array([34,12,37,5,13])
heights = np.array([1.76,1.2,1.68,0.5,1.25])
```

Suppose that you want to sort this group of people by age. If you simply sort the *ages* array by itself, the other two arrays would not be sorted correctly based on age. This is where `argsort()` comes in really handy:

```
sort_indices = np.argsort(ages)  # performs a sort based on ages
                                 # and returns an array of indices
                                 # indicating the sort order
```

Once the sort indices are obtained, simply feed them into the three arrays:

```
print(persons[sort_indices])      # ['Will' 'Mary' 'Joe' 'Johnny'
'Peter']
print(ages[sort_indices])         # [ 5 12 13 34 37]
print(heights[sort_indices])      # [ 0.5   1.2   1.25  1.76  1.68]
```

They would now be sorted based on age. As you can see, Will is the youngest, followed by Mary, and so on. The corresponding height for each person would also be in the correct order.

If you wish to sort based on name, then simply use argsort() on the *persons* array and feed the resulting indices into the three arrays:

```
sort_indices = np.argsort(persons)    # sort based on names
print(persons[sort_indices])          # ['Joe' 'Johnny' 'Mary' 'Peter'
'Will']
print(ages[sort_indices])             # [13 34 12 37  5]
print(heights[sort_indices])          # [ 1.25  1.76  1.2   1.68  0.5 ]
```

To reverse the order of the names and display them in descending order, use the Python [::-1] notation:

```
reverse_sort_indices = np.argsort(persons)[::-1] # reverse the order of a list
print(persons[reverse_sort_indices])    # ['Will' 'Peter' 'Mary'
                                         #  'Johnny' 'Joe']
print(ages[reverse_sort_indices])       # [ 5 37 12 34 13]
print(heights[reverse_sort_indices])    # [ 0.5   1.68  1.2   1.76
                                         #  1.25]
```

Array Assignment

When assigning NumPy arrays, you have to take note of how arrays are assigned. Following are a number of examples to illustrate this.

Copying by Reference

Consider an array named *a1*:

```
list1 = [[1,2,3,4], [5,6,7,8]]
a1 = np.array(list1)
print(a1)
'''
[[1 2 3 4]
 [5 6 7 8]]
'''
```

When you try to assign *a1* to another variable, *a2*, a copy of the array is created:

```
a2 = a1    # creates a copy by reference
print(a1)
'''
[[1 2 3 4]
 [5 6 7 8]]
'''

print(a2)
'''
[[1 2 3 4]
 [5 6 7 8]]
'''
```

However, *a2* is actually pointing to the original *a1*. So, any changes made to either array will affect the other as follows:

```
a2[0][0] = 11       # make some changes to a2
print(a1)           # affects a1
'''
[[11  2  3  4]
 [ 5  6  7  8]]
'''

print(a2)
'''
[[11  2  3  4]
 [ 5  6  7  8]]
'''
```

TIP In the "Reshaping Arrays" section earlier in this chapter, you saw how to change the shape of an `ndarray` using the `reshape()` function. In addition to using the `reshape()` function, you can also use the shape property of the `ndarray` to change its dimension.

If *a1* now changes shape, *a2* will also be affected as follows:

```
a1.shape = 1,-1    # reshape a1
print(a1)
'''
[[11  2  3  4  5  6  7  8]]
'''

print(a2)          # a2 also changes shape
'''
[[11  2  3  4  5  6  7  8]]
'''
```

Copying by View (Shallow Copy)

NumPy has a `view()` function that allows you to create a copy of an array by reference, while at the same time ensuring that changing the shape of the original array does not affect the shape of the copy. This is known as a *shallow copy*. Let's take a look at an example to understand how this works:

```
a2 = a1.view()       # creates a copy of a1 by reference; but changes
                     # in dimension in a1 will not affect a2
print(a1)
'''
[[1 2 3 4]
 [5 6 7 8]]
'''

print(a2)
'''
[[1 2 3 4]
 [5 6 7 8]]
'''
```

As usual, modify a value in *a1* and you will see the changes in *a2*:

```
a1[0][0] = 11      # make some changes in a1
print(a1)
'''
[[11  2  3  4]
 [ 5  6  7  8]]
'''

print(a2)          # changes is also seen in a2
'''
[[11  2  3  4]
 [ 5  6  7  8]]
'''
```

Up until now, the shallow copy is identical to the copying performed in the previous section. But with shallow copying, when you change the shape of *a1*, *a2* is unaffected:

```
a1.shape = 1,-1    # change the shape of a1
print(a1)
'''
[[11  2  3  4  5  6  7  8]]
'''
```

```
print(a2)          # a2 does not change shape
'''
[[11  2  3  4]
 [ 5  6  7  8]]  '''
```

Copying by Value (Deep Copy)

If you want to copy an array by value, use the `copy()` function, as in the following example:

```
list1 = [[1,2,3,4], [5,6,7,8]]
a1 = np.array(list1)
a2 = a1.copy()     # create a copy of a1 by value (deep copy)
```

The `copy()` function creates a deep copy of the array—it creates a complete copy of the array and its data. When you assign the copy of the array to another variable, any changes made to the shape of the original array will not affect its copy. Here's the proof:

```
a1[0][0] = 11      # make some changes in a1
print(a1)
'''
[[11  2  3  4]
 [ 5  6  7  8]]
'''


print(a2)          # changes is not seen in a2
'''
[[1 2 3 4]
 [5 6 7 8]]
'''


a1.shape = 1,-1    # change the shape of a1
print(a1)
'''
[[11  2  3  4  5  6  7  8]]
'''


print(a2)          # a2 does not change shape
'''
[[1 2 3 4]
 [5 6 7 8]]
'''
```

Summary

In this chapter, you learned about the use of NumPy as a way to represent data of the same type. You also learned how to create arrays of different dimensions, as well as how to access data stored within the arrays. An important feature of NumPy arrays is their ability to perform array math very easily and efficiently, without requiring you to write lots of code.

In the next chapter, you will learn about another important library that makes dealing with tabular data easy—Pandas.

Manipulating Tabular Data Using Pandas

What Is Pandas?

While NumPy arrays are a much-improved N-dimensional array object version over Python's list, it is insufficient to meet the needs of data science. In the real world, data are often presented in table formats. For example, consider the content of the CSV file shown here:

```
,DateTime,mmol/L
0,2016-06-01 08:00:00,6.1
1,2016-06-01 12:00:00,6.5
2,2016-06-01 18:00:00,6.7
3,2016-06-02 08:00:00,5.0
4,2016-06-02 12:00:00,4.9
5,2016-06-02 18:00:00,5.5
6,2016-06-03 08:00:00,5.6
7,2016-06-03 12:00:00,7.1
8,2016-06-03 18:00:00,5.9
9,2016-06-04 09:00:00,6.6
10,2016-06-04 11:00:00,4.1
11,2016-06-04 17:00:00,5.9
12,2016-06-05 08:00:00,7.6
13,2016-06-05 12:00:00,5.1
14,2016-06-05 18:00:00,6.9
15,2016-06-06 08:00:00,5.0
```

```
16,2016-06-06 12:00:00,6.1
17,2016-06-06 18:00:00,4.9
18,2016-06-07 08:00:00,6.6
19,2016-06-07 12:00:00,4.1
20,2016-06-07 18:00:00,6.9
21,2016-06-08 08:00:00,5.6
22,2016-06-08 12:00:00,8.1
23,2016-06-08 18:00:00,10.9
24,2016-06-09 08:00:00,5.2
25,2016-06-09 12:00:00,7.1
26,2016-06-09 18:00:00,4.9
```

The CSV file contains rows of data that are divided into three columns—index, date and time of recording, and blood glucose readings in mmol/L. To be able to deal with data stored as tables, you need a new data type that is more suited to deal with it—*Pandas*. While Python supports lists and dictionaries for manipulating structured data, it is not well suited for manipulating numerical tables, such as the one stored in the CSV file. *Pandas* is a Python package providing fast, flexible, and expressive data structures designed to make working with "relational" or "labeled" data both easy and intuitive.

NOTE   Pandas stands for *Panel Data Analysis*.

Pandas supports two key data structures: Series and DataFrame. In this chapter, you will learn how to work with Series and DataFrames in Pandas.

Pandas Series

A *Pandas Series* is a one-dimensional NumPy-like array, with each element having an index (0, 1, 2, . . . by default); a Series behaves very much like a dictionary that includes an index. Figure 3.1 shows the structure of a Series in Pandas.

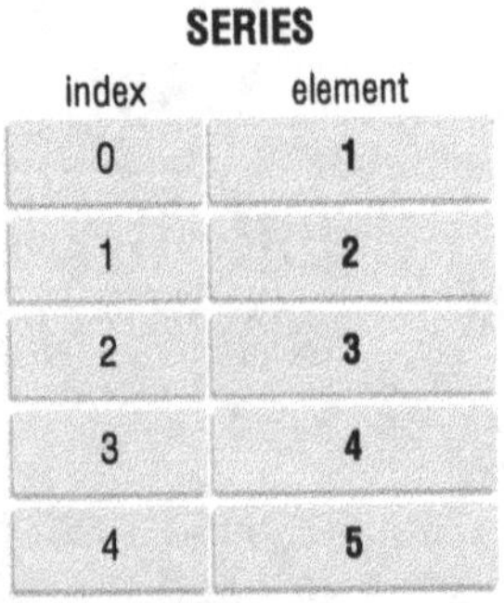

Figure 3.1: A Pandas Series

To create a Series, you first need to import the pandas library (the convention is to use pd as the alias) and then use the Series class:

```
import pandas as pd
series = pd.Series([1,2,3,4,5])
print(series)
```

The preceding code snippet will print the following output:

```
0    1
1    2
2    3
3    4
4    5
dtype: int64
```

By default, the index of a Series starts from 0.

Creating a Series Using a Specified Index

You can specify an optional index for a Series using the index parameter:

```
series = pd.Series([1,2,3,4,5], index=['a','b','c','d','c'])
print(series)
```

The preceding code snippet prints out the following:

```
a    1
b    2
c    3
d    4
c    5
dtype: int64
```

It is worth noting that the index of a Series need not be unique, as the preceding output shows.

Accessing Elements in a Series

Accessing an element in a Series is similar to accessing an element in an array. You can use the position of the element as follows:

```
print(series[2])          # 3
# same as
print(series.iloc[2])     # 3  - based on the position of the index
```

The iloc indexer allows you to specify an element via its position.

Alternatively, you can also specify the value of the index of the element you wish to access like this:

```
print(series['d'])        # 4
# same as
print(series.loc['d'])    # 4 - based on the label in the index
```

The `loc` indexer allows you to specify the *label* (value) of an index.

Note that in the preceding two examples, the result is an integer (which is the type of this Series). What happens if we do the following?

```
print(series['c'])        # more than 1 row has the index 'c'
```

In this case, the result would be another Series:

```
c    3
c    5
dtype: int64
```

You can also perform slicing on a Series:

```
print(series[2:])         # returns a Series
print(series.iloc[2:])    # returns a Series
```

The preceding code snippet generates the following output:

```
c    3
d    4
c    5
dtype: int64
```

Specifying a Datetime Range as the Index of a Series

Often, you want to create a timeseries, such as a running sequence of dates in a month. You could use the `date _ range()` function for this purpose:

```
dates1 = pd.date_range('20190525', periods=12)
print(dates1)
```

The preceding code snippet will display the following:

```
DatetimeIndex(['2019-05-25', '2019-05-26', '2019-05-27', '2019-05-28',
               '2019-05-29', '2019-05-30', '2019-05-31', '2019-06-01',
               '2019-06-02', '2019-06-03', '2019-06-04', '2019-06-05'],
              dtype='datetime64[ns]', freq='D')
```

To assign the range of dates as the index of a Series, use the `index` property of the Series like this:

```
series = pd.Series([1,2,3,4,5,6,7,8,9,10,11,12])
series.index = dates1
print(series)
```

You should see the following output:

```
2019-05-25    1
2019-05-26    2
2019-05-27    3
2019-05-28    4
2019-05-29    5
2019-05-30    6
2019-05-31    7
2019-06-01    8
2019-06-02    9
2019-06-03    10
2019-06-04    11
2019-06-05    12
Freq: D, dtype: int64
```

Date Ranges

In the previous section, you saw how to create date ranges using the `date_range()` function. The `periods` parameter specifies how many dates you want to create, and the default frequency is D (for Daily). If you want to change the frequency to month, use the `freq` parameter and set it to M:

```
dates2 = pd.date_range('2019-05-01', periods=12, freq='M')
print(dates2)
```

This will print out the following dates:

```
DatetimeIndex(['2019-05-31', '2019-06-30', '2019-07-31', '2019-08-31',
               '2019-09-30', '2019-10-31', '2019-11-30', '2019-12-31',
               '2020-01-31', '2020-02-29', '2020-03-31', '2020-04-30'],
              dtype='datetime64[ns]', freq='M')
```

Notice that when the frequency is set to month, the day of each date will be the last day of the month. If you want the date to start with the first day of the month, set the `freq` parameter to MS:

```
dates2 = pd.date_range('2019-05-01', periods=12, freq='MS')
print(dates2)
```

You should now see that each of the dates starts with the first day of every month:

```
DatetimeIndex(['2019-05-01', '2019-06-01', '2019-07-01', '2019-08-01',
               '2019-09-01', '2019-10-01', '2019-11-01', '2019-12-01',
               '2020-01-01', '2020-02-01', '2020-03-01', '2020-04-01'],
              dtype='datetime64[ns]', freq='MS')
```

TIP For other date frequencies, check out the *Offset Aliases* section of the documentation at:
```
http://pandas.pydata.org/pandas-docs/stable/timeseries
.html#offset-aliases
```

Notice that Pandas automatically interprets the date you specified. In this case, *2019-05-01* is interpreted as 1st May, 2019. In some regions, developers will specify the date in the *dd-mm-yyyy* format. Thus to represent 5th January, 2019, you would specify it as follows:

```
dates2 = pd.date_range('05-01-2019', periods=12, freq='MS')
print(dates2)
```

Note however that in this case, Pandas will interpret 05 as the month, 01 as the day, and 2019 as the year, as the following output proves:

```
DatetimeIndex(['2019-05-01', '2019-06-01', '2019-07-01', '2019-08-01',
               '2019-09-01', '2019-10-01', '2019-11-01', '2019-12-01',
               '2020-01-01', '2020-02-01', '2020-03-01', '2020-04-01'],
              dtype='datetime64[ns]', freq='MS')
```

In addition to setting dates, you can also set the time:

```
dates3 = pd.date_range('2019/05/17 09:00:00', periods=8, freq='H')
print(dates3)
```

You should see the following output:

```
DatetimeIndex(['2019-05-17 09:00:00', '2019-05-17 10:00:00',
               '2019-05-17 11:00:00', '2019-05-17 12:00:00',
               '2019-05-17 13:00:00', '2019-05-17 14:00:00',
               '2019-05-17 15:00:00', '2019-05-17 16:00:00'],
              dtype='datetime64[ns]', freq='H')
```

TIP If you review each of the code snippets that you have seen in this section, you will see that Pandas allows you to specify the date in different formats, such as *mm-dd-yyyy*, *yyyy-mm-dd*, and *yyyy/mm/dd*, and it will automatically try to make sense of the dates specified. When in doubt, it is always useful to print out the range of dates to confirm.

Pandas DataFrame

A *Pandas DataFrame* is a two-dimensional NumPy-like array. You can think of it as a table. Figure 3.2 shows the structure of a DataFrame in Pandas. It also shows you that an individual column in a DataFrame (together with the index) is a Series.

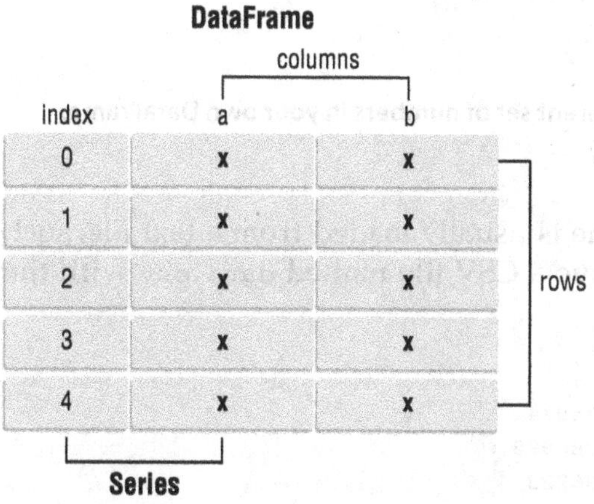

Figure 3.2: A Pandas DataFrame

A DataFrame is very useful in the world of data science and machine learning, as it closely mirrors how data are stored in real-life. Imagine the data stored in a spreadsheet, and you would have a very good visual impression of a DataFrame. A Pandas DataFrame is often used when representing data in machine learning. Hence, for the remaining sections in this chapter, we are going to invest significant time and effort in understanding how it works.

Creating a DataFrame

You can create a Pandas DataFrame using the DataFrame() class:

```
import pandas as pd
import numpy as np

df = pd.DataFrame(np.random.randn(10,4),
                  columns=list('ABCD'))
print(df)
```

In the preceding code snippet, a DataFrame of 10 rows and 4 columns was created, and each cell is filled with a random number using the randn() function. Each column has a label: "A", "B", "C", and "D":

```
          A         B         C         D
0   0.187497  1.122150 -0.988277 -1.985934
```

```
1   0.360803  -0.562243  -0.340693  -0.986988
2  -0.040627   0.067333  -0.452978   0.686223
3  -0.279572  -0.702492   0.252265   0.958977
4   0.537438  -1.737568   0.714727  -0.939288
5   0.070011  -0.516443  -1.655689   0.246721
6   0.001268   0.951517   2.107360  -0.108726
7  -0.185258   0.856520  -0.686285   1.104195
8   0.387023   1.706336  -2.452653   0.260466
9  -1.054974   0.556775  -0.945219  -0.030295
```

NOTE   Obviously, you will see a different set of numbers in your own DataFrame, as the numbers are generated randomly.

More often than not, a DataFrame is usually loaded from a text file, such as a CSV file. Suppose that you have a CSV file named `data.csv` with the following content:

```
A,B,C,D
0.187497,1.122150,-0.988277,-1.985934
0.360803,-0.562243,-0.340693,-0.986988
-0.040627,0.067333,-0.452978,0.686223
-0.279572,-0.702492,0.252265,0.958977
0.537438,-1.737568,0.714727,-0.939288
0.070011,-0.516443,-1.655689,0.246721
0.001268,0.951517,2.107360,-0.108726
-0.185258,0.856520,-0.686285,1.104195
0.387023,1.706336,-2.452653,0.260466
-1.054974,0.556775,-0.945219,-0.030295
```

You can load the content of the CSV file into a DataFrame using the `read_csv()` function:

```
df = pd.read_csv('data.csv')
```

Specifying the Index in a DataFrame

Notice that the DataFrame printed in the previous section has an index starting from 0. This is similar to that of a Series. Like a Series, you can also set the index for the DataFrame using the `index` property, as in the following code snippet:

```
df = pd.read_csv('data.csv')
days = pd.date_range('20190525', periods=10)
df.index = days
print(df)
```

You should see the following output:

```
                   A         B         C         D
2019-05-25  0.187497  1.122150 -0.988277 -1.985934
2019-05-26  0.360803 -0.562243 -0.340693 -0.986988
2019-05-27 -0.040627  0.067333 -0.452978  0.686223
2019-05-28 -0.279572 -0.702492  0.252265  0.958977
2019-05-29  0.537438 -1.737568  0.714727 -0.939288
2019-05-30  0.070011 -0.516443 -1.655689  0.246721
2019-05-31  0.001268  0.951517  2.107360 -0.108726
2019-06-01 -0.185258  0.856520 -0.686285  1.104195
2019-06-02  0.387023  1.706336 -2.452653  0.260466
2019-06-03 -1.054974  0.556775 -0.945219 -0.030295
```

To get the index of the DataFrame, use the `index` property as follows:

```
print(df.index)
```

You will see the following output:

```
DatetimeIndex(['2019-05-25', '2019-05-26', '2019-05-27', '2019-05-28',
               '2019-05-29', '2019-05-30', '2019-05-31', '2019-06-01',
               '2019-06-02', '2019-06-03'],
              dtype='datetime64[ns]', freq='D')
```

If you want to get the values of the entire DataFrame as a two-dimensional ndarray, use the `values` property:

```
print(df.values)
```

You should see the following output:

```
[[ 1.874970e-01  1.122150e+00 -9.882770e-01 -1.985934e+00]
 [ 3.608030e-01 -5.622430e-01 -3.406930e-01 -9.869880e-01]
 [-4.062700e-02  6.733300e-02 -4.529780e-01  6.862230e-01]
 [-2.795720e-01 -7.024920e-01  2.522650e-01  9.589770e-01]
 [ 5.374380e-01 -1.737568e+00  7.147270e-01 -9.392880e-01]
 [ 7.001100e-02 -5.164430e-01 -1.655689e+00  2.467210e-01]
 [ 1.268000e-03  9.515170e-01  2.107360e+00 -1.087260e-01]
 [-1.852580e-01  8.565200e-01 -6.862850e-01  1.104195e+00]
 [ 3.870230e-01  1.706336e+00 -2.452653e+00  2.604660e-01]
 [-1.054974e+00  5.567750e-01 -9.452190e-01 -3.029500e-02]]
```

Generating Descriptive Statistics on the DataFrame

The Pandas DataFrame comes with a few useful functions to provide you with some detailed statistics about the values in the DataFrame. For example, you can use the describe() function to get values such as count, mean, standard deviation, minimum and maximum, as well as the various quartiles:

```
print(df.describe())
```

Using the DataFrame that you have used in the previous section, you should see the following values:

	A	B	C	D
count	10.000000	10.000000	10.000000	10.000000
mean	-0.001639	0.174188	-0.444744	-0.079465
std	0.451656	1.049677	1.267397	0.971164
min	-1.054974	-1.737568	-2.452653	-1.985934
25%	-0.149100	-0.550793	-0.977513	-0.731647
50%	0.035640	0.312054	-0.569632	0.108213
75%	0.317477	0.927768	0.104026	0.579784
max	0.537438	1.706336	2.107360	1.104195

If you simply want to compute the mean in the DataFrame, you can use the mean() function, indicating the axis:

```
print(df.mean(0))    # 0 means compute the mean for each columns
```

You should get the following output:

```
A    -0.001639
B     0.174188
C    -0.444744
D    -0.079465
dtype: float64
```

If you want to get the mean for each row, set the axis to 1:

```
print(df.mean(1))    # 1 means compute the mean for each row
```

You should get the following output:

```
2019-05-25    -0.416141
2019-05-26    -0.382280
2019-05-27     0.064988
2019-05-28     0.057294
2019-05-29    -0.356173
2019-05-30    -0.463850
2019-05-31     0.737855
2019-06-01     0.272293
2019-06-02    -0.024707
2019-06-03    -0.368428
Freq: D, dtype: float64
```

Extracting from DataFrames

In Chapter 2, "Extending Python Using NumPy," you learned about NumPy and how slicing allows you to extract part of a NumPy array. Likewise, in Pandas, slicing applies to both Series and DataFrames.

Because extracting rows and columns in DataFrames is one of the most common tasks that you will perform with DataFrames (and potentially can be confusing), let's walk through the various methods one step at a time so that you have time to digest how they work.

Selecting the First and Last Five Rows

Sometimes, the DataFrame might be too lengthy, and you just want to take a glimpse of the first few rows in the DataFrame. For this purpose, you can use the `head()` function:

```
print(df.head())
```

The `head()` function prints out the first five rows in the DataFrame:

```
                   A          B          C          D
2019-05-25  0.187497   1.122150  -0.988277  -1.985934
2019-05-26  0.360803  -0.562243  -0.340693  -0.986988
2019-05-27 -0.040627   0.067333  -0.452978   0.686223
2019-05-28 -0.279572  -0.702492   0.252265   0.958977
2019-05-29  0.537438  -1.737568   0.714727  -0.939288
```

If you want more than five rows (or less than five), you can indicate the number of rows that you want in the `head()` function as follows:

```
print(df.head(8))      # prints out the first 8 rows
```

There is also a `tail()` function:

```
print(df.tail())
```

The `tail()` function prints the last five rows:

```
                   A          B          C          D
2019-05-30  0.070011  -0.516443  -1.655689   0.246721
2019-05-31  0.001268   0.951517   2.107360  -0.108726
2019-06-01 -0.185258   0.856520  -0.686285   1.104195
2019-06-02  0.387023   1.706336  -2.452653   0.260466
2019-06-03 -1.054974   0.556775  -0.945219  -0.030295
```

Like the `head()` function, the `tail()` function allows you to specify the number of rows to print:

```
print(df.tail(8))      # prints out the last 8 rows
```

Selecting a Specific Column in a DataFrame

To obtain one or more columns in a DataFrame, you can specify the column label as follows:

```
print(df['A'])
# same as
print(df.A)
```

This will print out the "A" column together with its index:

```
2019-05-25     0.187497
2019-05-26     0.360803
2019-05-27    -0.040627
2019-05-28    -0.279572
2019-05-29     0.537438
2019-05-30     0.070011
2019-05-31     0.001268
2019-06-01    -0.185258
2019-06-02     0.387023
2019-06-03    -1.054974
Freq: D, Name: A, dtype: float64
```

Essentially, what you get in return is a Series. If you want to retrieve more than one column, pass in a list containing the column labels:

```
print(df[['A', 'B']])
```

You should see the following output:

```
                   A         B
2019-05-25   0.187497  1.122150
2019-05-26   0.360803 -0.562243
2019-05-27  -0.040627  0.067333
2019-05-28  -0.279572 -0.702492
2019-05-29   0.537438 -1.737568
2019-05-30   0.070011 -0.516443
2019-05-31   0.001268  0.951517
2019-06-01  -0.185258  0.856520
2019-06-02   0.387023  1.706336
2019-06-03  -1.054974  0.556775
```

In this case, instead of a Series, you are now getting a DataFrame.

Slicing Based on Row Number

First, let's extract a range of rows in the DataFrame:

```
print(df[2:4])
```

This extracts row numbers 2 through 4 (not including row 4) from the DataFrame, and you should see the following output:

```
                    A          B          C          D
2019-05-27  -0.040627   0.067333  -0.452978   0.686223
2019-05-28  -0.279572  -0.702492   0.252265   0.958977
```

You can also use the `iloc` indexer for extracting rows based on row number:

```
print(df.iloc[2:4])
```

This will produce the same output as the preceding code snippet.

Note that if you wish to extract specific rows (and not a range of rows) using row numbers, you need to use the `iloc` indexer like this:

```
print(df.iloc[[2,4]])
```

This will print the following output:

```
                    A          B          C          D
2019-05-27  -0.040627   0.067333  -0.452978   0.686223
2019-05-29   0.537438  -1.737568   0.714727  -0.939288
```

Without using the `iloc` indexer, the following will not work:

```
print(df[[2,4]])    # error; need to use the iloc indexer
```

The same applies when extracting a single row using a row number; you need to use `iloc`:

```
print(df.iloc[2])  # prints out row number 2
```

Slicing Based on Row and Column Numbers

If you wish to extract specific rows and columns in a DataFrame, you need to use the `iloc` indexer. The following code snippet extracts row numbers 2 to 3, and column numbers 1 to 3:

```
print(df.iloc[2:4, 1:4])
```

You should get the following output:

```
                    B          C          D
2019-05-27   0.067333  -0.452978   0.686223
2019-05-28  -0.702492   0.252265   0.958977
```

You can also extract specific rows and columns using a list as follows:

```
print(df.iloc[[2,4], [1,3]])
```

The preceding statement prints out row numbers 2 and 4, and column numbers 1 and 3:

```
                  B          D
2019-05-27  0.067333   0.686223
2019-05-29 -1.737568  -0.939288
```

> **TIP** To summarize, if you want to extract a range of rows using slicing, you can simply use the following syntax: `df[start_row:end_row]`. If you want to extract specific rows or columns, use the `iloc` indexer: `df.iloc[[row_1,row_2,...,row_n],[column_1,column_2,...,column_n]]`.

Slicing Based on Labels

Besides extracting rows and columns using their row and column numbers, you can also extract them by label (value). For example, the following code snippet extracts a range of *rows* using their index values (which is of `DatetimeIndex` type):

```
print(df['20190601':'20190603'])
```

This will print out the following output:

```
                  A          B          C          D
2019-06-01 -0.185258   0.856520  -0.686285   1.104195
2019-06-02  0.387023   1.706336  -2.452653   0.260466
2019-06-03 -1.054974   0.556775  -0.945219  -0.030295
```

You can also use the `loc` indexer as follows:

```
print(df.loc['20190601':'20190603'])
```

Using the `loc` indexer is mandatory if you want to extract the *columns* using their values, as the following example shows:

```
print(df.loc['20190601':'20190603', 'A':'C'])
```

The preceding statement prints out the following:

```
                  A          B          C
2019-06-01 -0.185258   0.856520  -0.686285
2019-06-02  0.387023   1.706336  -2.452653
2019-06-03 -1.054974   0.556775  -0.945219
```

> **TIP** Unlike slicing by number, where *start:end* means extracting row *start* through row *end* but not including *end*, slicing by value will include the *end* row.

You can also extract specific columns:

```
print(df.loc['20190601':'20190603', ['A','C']])
```

The preceding statement prints out the following:

```
                   A         C
2019-06-01 -0.185258 -0.686285
2019-06-02  0.387023 -2.452653
2019-06-03 -1.054974 -0.945219
```

If you want to extract a specific row, use the `loc` indexer as follows:

```
print(df.loc['20190601'])
```

It will print out the following:

```
A   -0.185258
B    0.856520
C   -0.686285
D    1.104195
Name: 2019-06-01 00:00:00, dtype: float64
```

Oddly, if you want to extract specific rows with `datetime` as the index, you cannot simply pass the date value to the `loc` indexer as follows:

```
print(df.loc[['20190601','20190603']])    # KeyError
```

First, you need to convert the date into a `datetime` format:

```
from datetime import datetime
date1 = datetime(2019, 6, 1, 0, 0, 0)
date2 = datetime(2019, 6, 3, 0, 0, 0)
print(df.loc[[date1,date2]])
```

You will now see the output like this:

```
                   A         B         C         D
2019-06-01 -0.185258  0.856520 -0.686285  1.104195
2019-06-03 -1.054974  0.556775 -0.945219 -0.030295
```

If you want a specific row and specific columns, you can extract them as follows:

```
print(df.loc[date1, ['A','C']])
```

And the output will look like this:

```
A   -0.185258
C   -0.686285
Name: 2019-06-01 00:00:00, dtype: float64
```

In the preceding example, because there is only a single specified date, the result is a Series.

TIP   To summarize, if you want to extract a range of rows using their labels, you can
simply use the following syntax: df[start _ label:end _ label]. If you want to
extract specific rows or columns, use the loc indexer with the following syntax: df
.loc[[row _ 1 _ label,row _ 2 _ label,...,row _ n _ label],[column _ 1 _
label,column _ 2 _ label,...,column _ n _ label]].

Selecting a Single Cell in a DataFrame

If you simply wish to access a single cell in a DataFrame, there is a function that
does just that: at(). Using the same example as in the previous section, if you
want to get the value of a specific cell, you can use the following code snippet:

```
from datetime import datetime
d = datetime(2019, 6, 3, 0, 0, 0)
print(df.at[d,'B'])
```

You should see the following output:

```
0.556775
```

Selecting Based on Cell Value

If you want to select a subset of the DataFrame based on certain values in the
cells, you can use the Boolean Indexing method, as described in Chapter 2. The
following code snippet prints out all of the rows that have positive values in
the A and B columns:

```
print(df[(df.A > 0) & (df.B>0)])
```

You should see the following output:

```
                   A          B          C          D
2019-05-25  0.187497   1.122150  -0.988277  -1.985934
2019-05-31  0.001268   0.951517   2.107360  -0.108726
2019-06-02  0.387023   1.706336  -2.452653   0.260466
```

Transforming DataFrames

If you need to reflect the DataFrame over its main diagonal (converting columns
to rows and rows to columns), you can use the transpose() function:

```
print(df.transpose())
```

Alternatively, you can just use the T property, which is an accessor to the
transpose() function:

```
print(df.T)
```

In either case, you will see the following output:

```
     2019-05-25  2019-05-26  2019-05-27  2019-05-28  2019-05-29  2019-05-30  \
A      0.187497    0.360803   -0.040627   -0.279572    0.537438    0.070011
B      1.122150   -0.562243    0.067333   -0.702492   -1.737568   -0.516443
C     -0.988277   -0.340693   -0.452978    0.252265    0.714727   -1.655689
D     -1.985934   -0.986988    0.686223    0.958977   -0.939288    0.246721

     2019-05-31  2019-06-01  2019-06-02  2019-06-03
A      0.001268   -0.185258    0.387023   -1.054974
B      0.951517    0.856520    1.706336    0.556775
C      2.107360   -0.686285   -2.452653   -0.945219
D     -0.108726    1.104195    0.260466   -0.030295
```

Checking to See If a Result Is a DataFrame or Series

One of the common problems that you will face with Pandas is knowing if the result that you have obtained is a Series or a DataFrame. To solve this mystery, here is a function that can make your life easier:

```
def checkSeriesOrDataframe(var):
    if isinstance(var, pd.DataFrame):
        return 'Dataframe'
    if isinstance(var, pd.Series):
        return 'Series'
```

Sorting Data in a DataFrame

There are two ways that you can sort the data in a DataFrame:

1. Sort by labels (axis) using the sort_index() function
2. Sort by value using the sort_values() function

Sorting by Index

To sort using the axis, you need to specify if you want to sort by index or column. Setting the axis parameter to 0 indicates that you want to sort by index:

```
print(df.sort_index(axis=0, ascending=False))   # axis = 0 means sort by
                                                 # index
```

Based on the preceding statement, the DataFrame is now sorted according to the index in descending order:

```
                    A         B         C         D
2019-06-03  -1.054974  0.556775 -0.945219 -0.030295
2019-06-02   0.387023  1.706336 -2.452653  0.260466
```

```
2019-06-01 -0.185258  0.856520 -0.686285  1.104195
2019-05-31  0.001268  0.951517  2.107360 -0.108726
2019-05-30  0.070011 -0.516443 -1.655689  0.246721
2019-05-29  0.537438 -1.737568  0.714727 -0.939288
2019-05-28 -0.279572 -0.702492  0.252265  0.958977
2019-05-27 -0.040627  0.067333 -0.452978  0.686223
2019-05-26  0.360803 -0.562243 -0.340693 -0.986988
2019-05-25  0.187497  1.122150 -0.988277 -1.985934
```

TIP Note that the sort _ index() function returns the sorted DataFrame. The original DataFrame is not affected. If you want the original DataFrame to be sorted, use the inplace parameter and set it to True. In general, most operations involving DataFrames do not alter the original DataFrame. So inplace is by default set to False. When inplace is set to True, the function returns None as the result.

Setting the axis parameter to 1 indicates that you want to sort by column labels:

```
print(df.sort_index(axis=1, ascending=False))  # axis = 1 means sort by
                                                # column
```

The DataFrame is now sorted based on the column labels (in descending order):

```
                    D          C          B          A
2019-05-25 -1.985934 -0.988277  1.122150  0.187497
2019-05-26 -0.986988 -0.340693 -0.562243  0.360803
2019-05-27  0.686223 -0.452978  0.067333 -0.040627
2019-05-28  0.958977  0.252265 -0.702492 -0.279572
2019-05-29 -0.939288  0.714727 -1.737568  0.537438
2019-05-30  0.246721 -1.655689 -0.516443  0.070011
2019-05-31 -0.108726  2.107360  0.951517  0.001268
2019-06-01  1.104195 -0.686285  0.856520 -0.185258
2019-06-02  0.260466 -2.452653  1.706336  0.387023
2019-06-03 -0.030295 -0.945219  0.556775 -1.054974
```

Sorting by Value

To sort by value, use the sort _ values() function. The following statement sorts the DataFrame based on the values in column "A":

```
print(df.sort_values('A', axis=0))
```

The output now is now sorted (in ascending order) based on the value of column "A" (the values are highlighted). Notice that the index is now jumbled up:

```
                    A          B          C          D
2019-06-03 -1.054974  0.556775 -0.945219 -0.030295
2019-05-28 -0.279572 -0.702492  0.252265  0.958977
```

```
2019-06-01 -0.185258  0.856520 -0.686285  1.104195
2019-05-27 -0.040627  0.067333 -0.452978  0.686223
2019-05-31  0.001268  0.951517  2.107360 -0.108726
2019-05-30  0.070011 -0.516443 -1.655689  0.246721
2019-05-25  0.187497  1.122150 -0.988277 -1.985934
2019-05-26  0.360803 -0.562243 -0.340693 -0.986988
2019-06-02  0.387023  1.706336 -2.452653  0.260466
2019-05-29  0.537438 -1.737568  0.714727 -0.939288
```

To sort based on a particular index, set the `axis` parameter to 1:

```
print(df.sort_values('20190601', axis=1))
```

You can see that the DataFrame is now sorted (in ascending order) based on the row whose index is 2019-06-01 (the values are highlighted):

```
                    C         A         B         D
2019-05-25 -0.988277  0.187497  1.122150 -1.985934
2019-05-26 -0.340693  0.360803 -0.562243 -0.986988
2019-05-27 -0.452978 -0.040627  0.067333  0.686223
2019-05-28  0.252265 -0.279572 -0.702492  0.958977
2019-05-29  0.714727  0.537438 -1.737568 -0.939288
2019-05-30 -1.655689  0.070011 -0.516443  0.246721
2019-05-31  2.107360  0.001268  0.951517 -0.108726
2019-06-01 -0.686285 -0.185258  0.856520  1.104195
2019-06-02 -2.452653  0.387023  1.706336  0.260466
2019-06-03 -0.945219 -1.054974  0.556775 -0.030295
```

Applying Functions to a DataFrame

You can also apply functions to values in a DataFrame using the `apply()` function. First, let's define two lambda functions as follows:

```
import math
sq_root = lambda x: math.sqrt(x) if x > 0 else x
sq      = lambda x: x**2
```

The first function, `sq_root()`, takes the square root of the value x if it is a positive number. The second function, `sq()`, takes the square of the value x.

It is important to note that objects passed to the `apply()` function are Series objects whose index is either the DataFrame's index (`axis=0`) or the DataFrame's columns (`axis=1`).

We can now apply the functions to the DataFrame. First, apply the `sq_root()` function to column "B":

```
print(df.B.apply(sq_root))
```

Since the result of df.B is a Series, we can apply the sq_root() function to it and it will return the following results:

```
2019-05-25     1.029231
2019-05-26    -0.562243
2019-05-27     0.509398
2019-05-28    -0.702492
2019-05-29    -1.737568
2019-05-30    -0.516443
2019-05-31     0.987652
2019-06-01     0.962021
2019-06-02     1.142921
2019-06-03     0.863813
Freq: D, Name: B, dtype: float64
```

You can also apply the sq() function to df.B:

```
print(df.B.apply(sq))
```

You should see the following results:

```
2019-05-25     1.122150
2019-05-26     0.316117
2019-05-27     0.067333
2019-05-28     0.493495
2019-05-29     3.019143
2019-05-30     0.266713
2019-05-31     0.951517
2019-06-01     0.856520
2019-06-02     1.706336
2019-06-03     0.556775
Freq: D, Name: B, dtype: float64
```

If you apply the sq_root() function to the DataFrame as shown here,

```
df.apply(sq_root)     # ValueError
```

you will get the following error:

```
ValueError: ('The truth value of a Series is ambiguous. Use a.empty,
a.bool(), a.item(), a.any() or a.all().', 'occurred at index A')
```

This is because the object passed into the apply() function in this case is a DataFrame, not a Series. Interestingly, you can apply the sq() function to the DataFrame:

```
df.apply(sq)
```

This will print out the following:

```
                    A          B          C          D
2019-05-25   0.035155   1.259221   0.976691   3.943934
2019-05-26   0.130179   0.316117   0.116072   0.974145
```

```
2019-05-27  0.001651  0.004534  0.205189  0.470902
2019-05-28  0.078161  0.493495  0.063638  0.919637
2019-05-29  0.288840  3.019143  0.510835  0.882262
2019-05-30  0.004902  0.266713  2.741306  0.060871
2019-05-31  0.000002  0.905385  4.440966  0.011821
2019-06-01  0.034321  0.733627  0.470987  1.219247
2019-06-02  0.149787  2.911583  6.015507  0.067843
2019-06-03  1.112970  0.309998  0.893439  0.000918
```

If you want to apply the `sq _ root()` function to the entire DataFrame, you can iterate through the columns and apply the function to each column:

```
for column in df:
    df[column] = df[column].apply(sq_root)
print(df)
```

The result will now look like this:

```
                   A          B          C          D
2019-05-25  0.433009   1.059316  -0.988277  -1.985934
2019-05-26  0.600669  -0.562243  -0.340693  -0.986988
2019-05-27 -0.040627   0.259486  -0.452978   0.828386
2019-05-28 -0.279572  -0.702492   0.502260   0.979274
2019-05-29  0.733102  -1.737568   0.845415  -0.939288
2019-05-30  0.264596  -0.516443  -1.655689   0.496710
2019-05-31  0.035609   0.975457   1.451675  -0.108726
2019-06-01 -0.185258   0.925484  -0.686285   1.050807
2019-06-02  0.622112   1.306268  -2.452653   0.510359
2019-06-03 -1.054974   0.746174  -0.945219  -0.030295
```

The `apply()` function can be applied on either axis: *index* (0; apply function to each column) or *column* (1; apply function to each row). For the two particular lambda functions that we have seen thus far, it does not matter which axis you apply it to, and the result would be the same. However, for some functions, the axis that you apply it to does matter. For example, the following statement uses the `sum()` function from NumPy and applies it to the rows of the DataFrame:

```
print(df.apply(np.sum, axis=0))
```

Essentially, you are summing up all of the values in each column. You should see the following:

```
A    1.128665
B    1.753438
C   -4.722444
D   -0.185696
dtype: float64
```

If you set axis to 1 as follows,

```
print(df.apply(np.sum, axis=1))
```

you will see the summation applied across each row:

```
2019-05-25    -1.481886
2019-05-26    -1.289255
2019-05-27     0.594267
2019-05-28     0.499470
2019-05-29    -1.098339
2019-05-30    -1.410826
2019-05-31     2.354015
2019-06-01     1.104747
2019-06-02    -0.013915
2019-06-03    -1.284314
Freq: D, dtype: float64
```

Adding and Removing Rows and Columns in a DataFrame

So far, all of the previous sections have involved extracting rows and columns from DataFrames, as well as how to sort DataFrames. In this section, we will focus on how to add and remove columns in DataFrames.

Consider the following code snippet, where a DataFrame is created from a dictionary:

```
import pandas as pd

data = {'name': ['Janet', 'Nad', 'Timothy', 'June', 'Amy'],
        'year': [2012, 2012, 2013, 2014, 2014],
        'reports': [6, 13, 14, 1, 7]}

df = pd.DataFrame(data, index =
        ['Singapore', 'China', 'Japan', 'Sweden', 'Norway'])
print(df)
```

The DataFrame looks like this:

```
               name    reports   year
Singapore     Janet          6   2012
China           Nad         13   2012
Japan       Timothy         14   2013
Sweden         June          1   2014
Norway          Amy          7   2014
```

Adding a Column

The following code snippet shows you how to add a new column named "school" to the DataFrame:

```
import numpy as np

schools = np.array(["Cambridge","Oxford","Oxford","Cambridge","Oxford"])
df["school"] = schools
print(df)
```

Printing the DataFrame will look like this:

```
            name   reports  year     school
Singapore   Janet        6  2012  Cambridge
China         Nad       13  2012     Oxford
Japan     Timothy       14  2013     Oxford
Sweden       June        1  2014  Cambridge
Norway        Amy        7  2014     Oxford
```

Removing Rows

To remove one or more rows, use the drop() function. The following code snippet removes the two rows whose index value is "China" and "Japan":

```
print(df.drop(['China', 'Japan'])) # drop rows based on value of index
```

The following output proves that the two rows are removed:

```
            name  reports  year     school
Singapore  Janet        6  2012  Cambridge
Sweden      June        1  2014  Cambridge
Norway       Amy        7  2014     Oxford
```

> **TIP** Like the sort _ index() function, by default the drop() function does not affect the original DataFrame. Use the inplace parameter if you want to modify the original DataFrame.

If you want to drop a row based on a particular column value, specify the column name and the condition like this:

```
print(df[df.name != 'Nad'])           # drop row based on column value
```

The preceding statement drops the row whose name is "Nad":

```
            name  reports  year     school
Singapore  Janet        6  2012  Cambridge
```

```
Japan        Timothy       14  2013      Oxford
Sweden       June           1  2014    Cambridge
Norway       Amy            7  2014      Oxford
```

You can also remove rows based on row number:

```
print(df.drop(df.index[1]))
```

The preceding statement drops row number 1 (the second row):

```
              name  reports  year      school
Singapore    Janet        6  2012    Cambridge
Japan      Timothy       14  2013      Oxford
Sweden        June        1  2014    Cambridge
Norway         Amy        7  2014      Oxford
```

Since `df.index[1]` returns "China", the preceding statement is equivalent to `df.drop['China']`.

If you want to drop multiple rows, specify the row numbers represented as a list:

```
print(df.drop(df.index[[1,2]]))            # remove the second and
                                           third row
```

The preceding statement removes row numbers 1 and 2 (the second and the third row):

```
              name  reports  year      school
Singapore    Janet        6  2012    Cambridge
Sweden        June        1  2014    Cambridge
Norway         Amy        7  2014      Oxford
```

The following removes the second to last row:

```
print(df.drop(df.index[-2]))               # remove second last row
```

You should see the following output:

```
              name  reports  year      school
Singapore    Janet        6  2012    Cambridge
China          Nad       13  2012      Oxford
Japan      Timothy       14  2013      Oxford
Norway         Amy        7  2014      Oxford
```

Removing Columns

The `drop()` function drops rows by default, but if you want to drop columns instead, set the `axis` parameter to `1` like this:

```
print(df.drop('reports', axis=1))    # drop column
```

The preceding code snippet drops the `reports` column:

```
           name   year     school
Singapore  Janet  2012  Cambridge
China        Nad  2012     Oxford
Japan    Timothy  2013     Oxford
Sweden      June  2014  Cambridge
Norway       Amy  2014     Oxford
```

If you want to drop by column number, specify the column number using the `columns` indexer:

```
print(df.drop(df.columns[1], axis=1))    # drop using columns number
```

This will drop the second column ("`reports`"):

```
           name   year     school
Singapore  Janet  2012  Cambridge
China        Nad  2012     Oxford
Japan    Timothy  2013     Oxford
Sweden      June  2014  Cambridge
Norway       Amy  2014     Oxford
```

You can also drop multiple columns:

```
print(df.drop(df.columns[[1,3]], axis=1))    # drop multiple columns
```

This will drop the second and fourth columns ("`reports`" and "`school`"):

```
           name   year
Singapore  Janet  2012
China        Nad  2012
Japan    Timothy  2013
Sweden      June  2014
Norway       Amy  2014
```

Generating a Crosstab

In statistics, a *crosstab* is used to aggregate and jointly display the distribution of two or more variables. It shows the relationships between these variables. Consider the following example:

```
df = pd.DataFrame(
    {
        "Gender": ['Male','Male','Female','Female','Female'],
        "Team"  : [1,2,3,3,1]
    })
print(df)
```

Here you are creating a DataFrame using a dictionary. When the DataFrame is printed out, you will see the following:

```
   Gender  Team
0    Male     1
1    Male     2
2  Female     3
3  Female     3
4  Female     1
```

This DataFrame shows the gender of each person and the team to which the person belongs. Using a crosstab, you would be able to summarize the data and generate a table to show the distribution of each gender for each team. To do that, you use the crosstab() function:

```
print("Displaying the distribution of genders in each team")
print(pd.crosstab(df.Gender, df.Team))
```

You will see the following output:
```
Displaying the distribution of genders in each team

Team     1  2  3
Gender
Female   1  0  2
Male     1  1  0
```

If you want to see the distribution of each team for each gender, you simply reverse the argument:

```
print(pd.crosstab(df.Team, df.Gender))
```

You will see the following output:

```
Gender  Female  Male
Team
1            1     1
2            0     1
3            2     0
```

Summary

In this chapter, you witnessed the use of Pandas to represent tabular data. You learned about the two main Pandas data structures: Series and DataFrame. I attempted to keep things simple and to show you some of the most common operations that you would perform on these data structures. As extracting rows and columns from DataFrames is so common, I have summarized some of these operations in Table 3.1.

Table 3.1: Common DataFrame Operations

DESCRIPTION	CODE EXAMPLES

Extract a range of rows using row numbers	`df[2:4]`
	
	 `df.iloc[2:4]`

Extract a single row using row number	`df.iloc[2]`
Extract a range of rows and range of columns	`df.iloc[2:4, 1:4]`
Extract a range of rows and specific columns using positional values	`df.iloc[2:4, [1,3]]`
Extract specific row(s) and column(s)	`df.iloc[[2,4], [1,3]]`
Extract a range of rows using labels	`df['20190601':'20190603']`
Extract a single row based on its label	`df.loc['20190601']`
Extract specific row(s) using their labels	`df.loc[[date1,date2]]`

Extract specific row(s) and column(s) using their labels	`df.loc[[date1,date2], ['A','C']]`
	
	 `df.loc[[date1,date2], 'A':'C']`

Extract a range of rows and columns using their labels	`df.loc[date1:date2, 'A':'C']`

Data Visualization Using matplotlib

What Is matplotlib?

As the adage goes, "A picture is worth a thousand words." This is probably most true in the world of machine learning. No matter how large or how small your dataset, it is often very useful (and many times, essential) that you are able to visualize the data and see the relationships between the various features within it. For example, given a dataset containing a group of students with their family details (such as examination results, family income, educational background of parents, and so forth), you might want to establish a relationship between the students' results with their family income. The best way to do this would be to plot a chart displaying the related data. Once the chart is plotted, you can then use it to draw your own conclusions and determine whether the results have a positive relationship to family income.

In Python, one of the most commonly used tools for plotting is matplotlib. *Matplotlib* is a Python 2D plotting library that you can use to produce publication-quality charts and figures. Using matplotlib, complex charts and figures can be generated with ease, and its integration with Jupyter Notebook makes it an ideal tool for machine learning.

In this chapter, you will learn the basics of matplotlib. In addition, you will also learn about Seaborn, a complementary data visualization library that is based on matplotlib.

Plotting Line Charts

To see how easy it is to use matplotlib, let's plot a line chart using Jupyter Notebook. Here is a code snippet that plots a line chart:

```
%matplotlib inline
import matplotlib.pyplot as plt

plt.plot(
    [1,2,3,4,5,6,7,8,9,10],
    [2,4.5,1,2,3.5,2,1,2,3,2]
)
```

Figure 4.1 shows the line chart plotted.

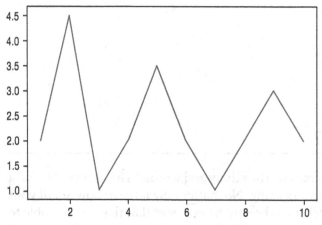

Figure 4.1: A line graph plotted using matplotlib

The first statement tells matplotlib to display the output of the plotting commands in line within front-ends likes Jupyter Notebook. In short, it means display the chart within the same page as your Jupyter Notebook:

```
%matplotlib inline
```

To use matplotlib, you import the `pyplot` module and name it `plt` (its commonly used alias):

```
import matplotlib.pyplot as plt
```

To plot a line chart, you use the `plot()` function from the `pyplot` module, supplying it with two arguments as follows:

1. A list of values representing the x-axis
2. A list of values representing the y-axis

```
    [1,2,3,4,5,6,7,8,9,10],
        [2,4.5,1,2,3.5,2,1,2,3,2]
```

That's it. The chart will be shown in your Jupyter Notebook when you run it.

Adding Title and Labels

A chart without title and labels does not convey meaningful information. Matplotlib allows you to add a title and labels to the axes using the `title()`, `xlabel()`, and `ylabel()` functions as follows:

```
%matplotlib inline
import matplotlib.pyplot as plt

plt.plot(
    [1,2,3,4,5,6,7,8,9,10],
        [2,4.5,1,2,3.5,2,1,2,3,2]
)
plt.title("Results")         # sets the title for the chart
plt.xlabel("Semester")       # sets the label to use for the x-axis
plt.ylabel("Grade")          # sets the label to use for the y-axis
```

Figure 4.2 shows the chart with the title, as well as the labels for the x- and y-axes.

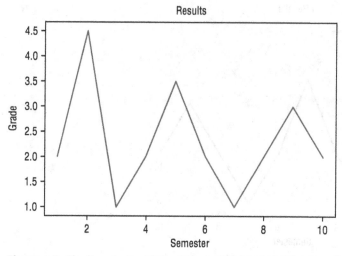

Figure 4.2: The line chart with the title and the labels for the x- and y-axes added

Styling

Matplotlib lets you adjust every aspect of your plot and create beautiful charts. However, it is very time consuming to create really beautiful charts and plots. To help with this, matplotlib ships with a number of predefined styles. Styles allow you to create professional-looking charts using a predefined look-and-feel without requiring you to customize each element of the chart individually.

The following example uses the `ggplot` style, based on a popular data visualization package for the statistical programming language R:

> **TIP**   The "gg" in ggplot comes from Leland Wilkinson's landmark 1999 book, *The Grammar of Graphics: Statistics and Computing,* (Springer, 2005).

```
%matplotlib inline
import matplotlib.pyplot as plt

from matplotlib import style
style.use("ggplot")

plt.plot(
    [1,2,3,4,5,6,7,8,9,10],
    [2,4.5,1,2,3.5,2,1,2,3,2]
)
plt.title("Results")       # sets the title for the chart
plt.xlabel("Semester")     # sets the label to use for the x-axis
plt.ylabel("Grade")        # sets the label to use for the y-axis
```

The chart styled using `ggplot` is shown in Figure 4.3.

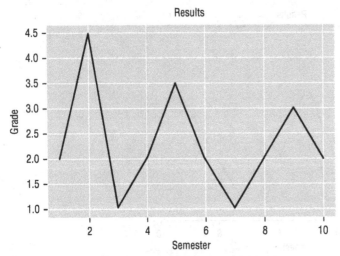

Figure 4.3: The chart with the ggplot style applied to it

Figure 4.4 shows the same chart with the `grayscale` styled applied.

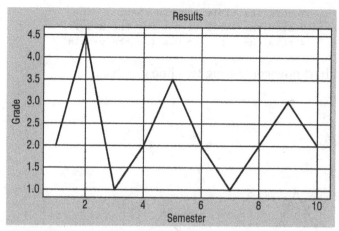

Figure 4.4: The chart with the grayscale style applied to it

You can use the `style.available` property to see the list of styles supported:

```
print(style.available)
```

Here is a sample output:

```
['seaborn-dark', 'seaborn-darkgrid', 'seaborn-ticks', 'fivethirtyeight',
'seaborn-whitegrid', 'classic', '_classic_test', 'fast', 'seaborn-talk',
'seaborn-dark-palette', 'seaborn-bright', 'seaborn-pastel', 'grayscale',
'seaborn-notebook', 'ggplot', 'seaborn-colorblind', 'seaborn-muted',
'seaborn', 'Solarize_Light2', 'seaborn-paper', 'bmh', 'seaborn-white',
'dark_background', 'seaborn-poster', 'seaborn-deep']
```

Plotting Multiple Lines in the Same Chart

You can plot multiple lines in the same chart by calling the `plot()` function one more time, as the following example shows:

```
%matplotlib inline
import matplotlib.pyplot as plt

from matplotlib import style
style.use("ggplot")

plt.plot(
    [1,2,3,4,5,6,7,8,9,10],
    [2,4.5,1,2,3.5,2,1,2,3,2]
)

plt.plot(
    [1,2,3,4,5,6,7,8,9,10],
    [3,4,2,5,2,4,2.5,4,3.5,3]
)
```

```
plt.title("Results")      # sets the title for the chart
plt.xlabel("Semester")    # sets the label to use for the x-axis
plt.ylabel("Grade")       # sets the label to use for the y-axis
```

Figure 4.5 shows the chart now containing two line graphs.

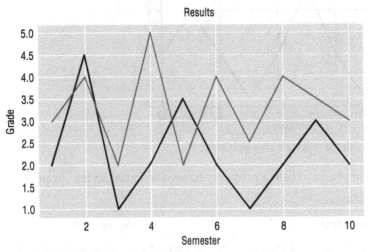

Figure 4.5: The chart with two line graphs

Adding a Legend

As you add more lines to a chart, it becomes more important to have a way to distinguish between the lines. Here is where a legend is useful. Using the previous example, you can add a label to each line plot and then show a legend using the `legend()` function as follows:

```
%matplotlib inline
import matplotlib.pyplot as plt

from matplotlib import style
style.use("ggplot")

plt.plot(
    [1,2,3,4,5,6,7,8,9,10],
    [2,4.5,1,2,3.5,2,1,2,3,2],
    label="Jim"
)

plt.plot(
    [1,2,3,4,5,6,7,8,9,10],
    [3,4,2,5,2,4,2.5,4,3.5,3],
    label="Tom"
)
```

```
plt.title("Results")      # sets the title for the chart
plt.xlabel("Semester")    # sets the label to use for the x-axis
plt.ylabel("Grade")       # sets the label to use for the y-axis
plt.legend()
```

Figure 4.6 shows the chart with a legend displayed.

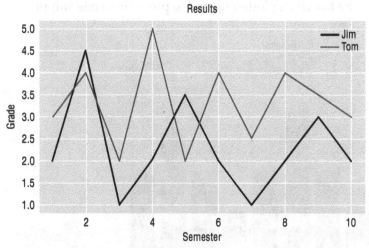

Figure 4.6: The chart with a legend displayed

Plotting Bar Charts

Besides plotting line charts, you can also plot bar charts using matplotlib. *Bar charts* are useful for comparing data. For example, you want to be able to compare the grades of a student over a number of semesters.

Using the same dataset that you used in the previous section, you can plot a bar chart using the bar() function as follows:

```
%matplotlib inline
import matplotlib.pyplot as plt
from matplotlib import style

style.use("ggplot")

plt.bar(
    [1,2,3,4,5,6,7,8,9,10],
    [2,4.5,1,2,3.5,2,1,2,3,2],
    label = "Jim",
    color = "m",                  # m for magenta
    align = "center"
)
```

```
plt.title("Results")
plt.xlabel("Semester")
plt.ylabel("Grade")

plt.legend()
plt.grid(True, color="y")
```

Figure 4.7 shows the bar chart plotted using the preceding code snippet.

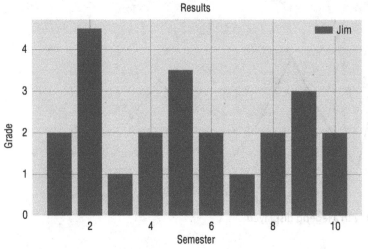

Figure 4.7: Plotting a bar chart

Adding Another Bar to the Chart

Just like adding an additional line chart to the chart, you can add another bar graph to an existing chart. The following statements in bold do just that:

```
%matplotlib inline
import matplotlib.pyplot as plt
from matplotlib import style

style.use("ggplot")

plt.bar(
    [1,2,3,4,5,6,7,8,9,10],
    [2,4.5,1,2,3.5,2,1,2,3,2],
    label = "Jim",
    color = "m",                    # for magenta
    align = "center",
    alpha = 0.5
)
```

```
plt.bar(
    [1,2,3,4,5,6,7,8,9,10],
    [1.2,4.1,0.3,4,5.5,4.7,4.8,5.2,1,1.1],
    label = "Tim",
    color = "g",                    # for green
    align = "center",
    alpha = 0.5
)


plt.title("Results")
plt.xlabel("Semester")
plt.ylabel("Grade")

plt.legend()
plt.grid(True, color="y")
```

Because the bars might overlap each with other, it is important to be able to distinguish them by setting their alpha to 0.5 (making them translucent). Figure 4.8 shows the two bar graphs in the same chart.

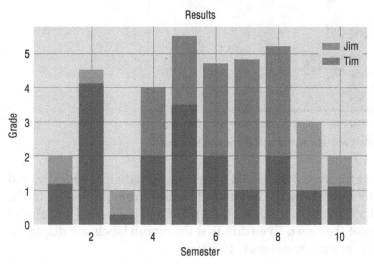

Figure 4.8: Plotting two overlapping bar charts on the same figure

Changing the Tick Marks

So far in our charts, the tick marks on the x-axis always displays the value that was supplied (such as 2, 4, 6, and so on). But what if your x-axis label is in the form of strings like this?

```
rainfall = [17,9,16,3,21,7,8,4,6,21,4,1]
months = ['Jan','Feb','Mar','Apr','May','Jun',
          'Jul','Aug','Sep','Oct','Nov','Dec']
```

In this case, you might be tempted to plot the chart directly as follows:

```
%matplotlib inline
import matplotlib.pyplot as plt

rainfall = [17,9,16,3,21,7,8,4,6,21,4,1]
months = ['Jan','Feb','Mar','Apr','May','Jun',
          'Jul','Aug','Sep','Oct','Nov','Dec']

plt.bar(months, rainfall, align='center', color='orange' )
plt.show()
```

The preceding code snippet will create the chart shown in Figure 4.9.

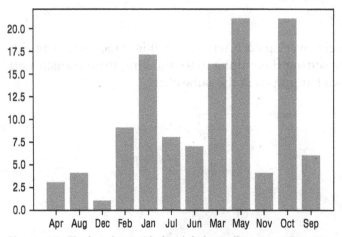

Figure 4.9: The bar chart with the alphabetically arranged x-axis

Look carefully at the x-axis: the labels have been sorted alphabetically, and hence the chart does not show the amount of rainfall from Jan to Dec in the correct order. To fix this, create a `range` object matching the size of the rainfall list, and use it to plot the chart. To ensure that the month labels are displayed correctly on the x-axis, use the `xticks()` function:

```
%matplotlib inline
import matplotlib.pyplot as plt

rainfall = [17,9,16,3,21,7,8,4,6,21,4,1]
months = ['Jan','Feb','Mar','Apr','May','Jun',
          'Jul','Aug','Sep','Oct','Nov','Dec']

plt.bar(range(len(rainfall)), rainfall, align='center', color='orange' )
plt.xticks(range(len(rainfall)), months, rotation='vertical')
plt.show()
```

The `xticks()` function sets the tick labels on the x-axis, as well the positioning of the ticks. In this case, the labels are displayed vertically, as shown in Figure 4.10.

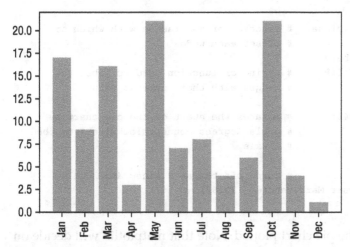

Figure 4.10: The bar chart with the correct x-axis

Plotting Pie Charts

Another chart that is popular is the pie chart. A *pie chart* is a circular statistical graphic divided into slices to illustrate numerical proportions. A pie chart is useful when showing percentage or proportions of data. Consider the following sets of data representing the various browser market shares:

```
labels      = ["Chrome", "Internet Explorer", "Firefox",
               "Edge","Safari","Sogou Explorer","Opera","Others"]
marketshare = [61.64, 11.98, 11.02, 4.23, 3.79, 1.63, 1.52, 4.19]
```

In this case, it would be really beneficial to be able to represent the total market shares as a complete circle, with each slice representing the percentage held by each browser.

The following code snippet shows how you can plot a pie chart using the data that we have:

```
%matplotlib inline
import matplotlib.pyplot as plt

labels      = ["Chrome", "Internet Explorer",
               "Firefox", "Edge","Safari",
               "Sogou Explorer","Opera","Others"]
```

```
marketshare = [61.64, 11.98, 11.02, 4.23, 3.79, 1.63, 1.52, 4.19]
explode     = (0,0,0,0,0,0,0,0)

plt.pie(marketshare,
        explode = explode,     # fraction of the radius with which to
                               # offset each wedge
        labels = labels,
        autopct="%.1f%%",      # string or function used to label the
                               # wedges with their numeric value
        shadow=True,
        startangle=45)         # rotates the start of the pie chart by
                               # angle degrees counterclockwise from the
                               # x-axis

plt.axis("equal")              # turns off the axis lines and labels
plt.title("Web Browser Marketshare - 2018")
plt.show()
```

Figure 4.11 shows the pie chart plotted. Note that matplotlib will decide on the colors to use for each of the slices in the pie chart.

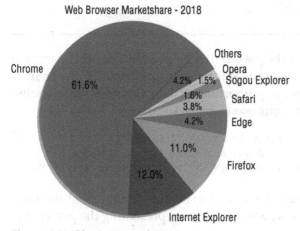

Figure 4.11: Plotting a pie chart

Exploding the Slices

The *explode parameter* specifies the fraction of the radius with which to offset each wedge. In the preceding example, we have set the `explode` parameter to all zeros:

```
explode     = (0,0,0,0,0,0,0,0)
```

Say that we need to highlight the market share of the Firefox and Safari browsers. In that case, we could modify the `explode` list as follows:

```
explode     = (0,0,0.5,0,0.8,0,0,0)
```

Refreshing the chart, you will see the two slices exploding (separating) from the main pie (see Figure 4.12).

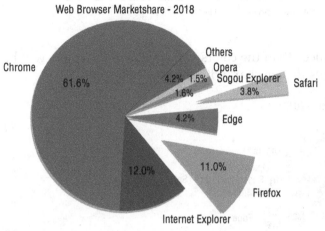

Figure 4.12: The pie chart with two exploded slices

Displaying Custom Colors

By default, matplotlib will decide on the colors to use for each of the slices in the pie chart. Sometimes the colors that are selected may not appeal to you. But you can certainly customize the chart to display using your desired colors.

You can create a list of colors and then pass it to the `colors` parameter:

```
%matplotlib inline
import matplotlib.pyplot as plt

labels      = ["Chrome", "Internet Explorer",
              "Firefox", "Edge","Safari",
              "Sogou Explorer","Opera","Others"]

marketshare = [61.64, 11.98, 11.02, 4.23, 3.79, 1.63, 1.52, 4.19]
explode     = (0,0,0.5,0,0.8,0,0,0)
colors      = ['yellowgreen', 'gold', 'lightskyblue', 'lightcoral']

plt.pie(marketshare,
        explode = explode,   # fraction of the radius with which to
                             # offset each wedge
        labels = labels,
        colors = colors,
        autopct="%.1f%%",    # string or function used to label the
                             # wedges with their numeric value
        shadow=True,
```

```
            startangle=45)        # rotates the start of the pie chart by
                                  # angle degrees counterclockwise from the
                                  # x-axis
plt.axis("equal")                 # turns off the axis lines and labels
plt.title("Web Browser Marketshare - 2018")
plt.show()
```

Since there are more slices than the colors you specified, the colors will be recycled. Figure 4.13 shows the pie chart with the new colors.

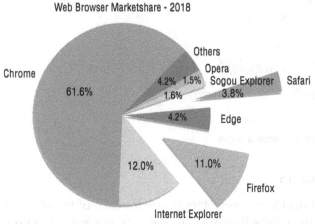

Figure 4.13: Displaying the pie chart with custom colors

Rotating the Pie Chart

Observe that we have set the startangle parameter to 45. This parameter specifies the degrees by which to rotate the start of the pie chart, counterclockwise from the x-axis. Figure 4.14 shows the effect of setting the startangle to 0 versus 45.

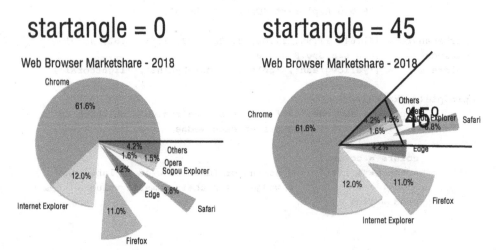

Figure 4.14: Setting the start angle for the pie chart

Displaying a Legend

Like the line and bar charts, you can also display a legend in your pie charts. But before you can do that, you need to handle the return values from the `pie()` function:

```
pie = plt.pie(marketshare,
        explode = explode,    # fraction of the radius with which to
                              # offset each wedge
        labels = labels,
        colors = colors,
        autopct="%.1f%%",     # string or function used to label the
                              # wedges with their numeric value
        shadow=True,
        startangle=45)        # rotates the start of the pie chart by
                              # angle degrees counterclockwise from the
                              # x-axis
```

The `pie()` function returns a tuple containing the following values:

`patches`: A list of `matplotlib.patches.Wedge` instances.

`texts`: A list of the label `matplotlib.text.Text` instances.

`autotexts`: A list of `Text` instances for the numeric labels. This will only be returned if the parameter `autopct` is not `None`.

To display the legend, use the `legend()` function as follows:

```
plt.axis("equal")               # turns off the axis lines and labels
plt.title("Web Browser Marketshare - 2018")
plt.legend(pie[0], labels, loc="best")
plt.show()
```

Figure 4.15 shows the legend displaying on the pie chart.

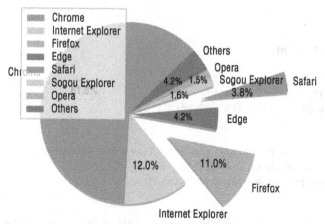

Figure 4.15: Displaying the legend on the pie chart

> **TIP**   If the autopct **parameter is not set to** None, **the** pie() **function returns the tuple** (patches, texts, autotexts).

The positioning of the legend can be modified through the loc parameter. It can take in either a string value or an integer value. Table 4.1 shows the various values that you can use for the loc parameter.

Table 4.1: Location Strings and Corresponding Location Codes

LOCATION STRING	LOCATION CODE
'best'	0
'upper right'	1
'upper left'	2
'lower left'	3
'lower right'	4
'right'	5
'center left'	6
'center right'	7
'lower center'	8
'upper center'	9
'center'	10

Saving the Chart

So far, you have been displaying the charts in a browser. At times, it is useful to be able to save the image to disk. You can do so using the savefig() function as follows:

```
%matplotlib inline
import matplotlib.pyplot as plt

labels      = ["Chrome", "Internet Explorer",
              "Firefox", "Edge","Safari",
              "Sogou Explorer","Opera","Others"]

...
plt.axis("equal")            # turns off the axis lines and labels
plt.title("Web Browser Marketshare - 2018")
plt.savefig("Webbrowsers.png", bbox_inches="tight")
plt.show()
```

Setting the bbox_inches parameter to tight removes all of the extra white space around your figure.

Plotting Scatter Plots

A *scatter plot* is a two-dimensional chart that uses dots (or other shapes) to represent the values for two different variables. Scatter plots are often used to show how much the value of one variable is affected by another.

The following code snippet shows a scatter plot with the x-axis containing a list of numbers from 1 to 4, and the y-axis showing the cube of the x-axis values:

```
%matplotlib inline
import matplotlib.pyplot as plt

plt.plot([1,2,3,4],          # x-axis
         [1,8,27,64],        # y-axis
         'bo')               # blue circle marker
plt.axis([0, 4.5, 0, 70])   # xmin, xmax, ymin, ymax
plt.show()
```

Figure 4.16 shows the scatter plot.

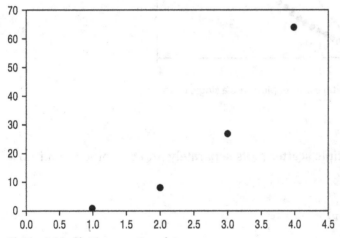

Figure 4.16: Plotting a scatter plot

Combining Plots

You can combine multiple scatter plots into one chart as follows:

```
%matplotlib inline
import matplotlib.pyplot as plt

import numpy as np

a = np.arange(1,4.5,0.1)    # 1.0, 1.1, 1.2, 1.3...4.4
plt.plot(a, a**2, 'y^',     # yellow triangle_up marker
```

```
     a, a**3, 'bo',      # blue circle
     a, a**4, 'r--',)    # red dashed line

plt.axis([0, 4.5, 0, 70])   # xmin, xmax, ymin, ymax
plt.show()
```

Figure 4.17 shows the chart displaying three scatter plots. You can customize the shape of the points to draw on the scatter plot. For example, y^ indicates a yellow triangle-up marker, bo indicates a blue circle, and so on.

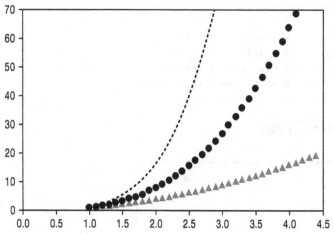

Figure 4.17: Combining multiple scatter plots into a single chart

Subplots

You can also plot multiple scatter plots separately and combine them into a single figure:

```
%matplotlib inline
import matplotlib.pyplot as plt
import numpy as np

a = np.arange(1,5,0.1)

plt.subplot(121)              # 1 row, 2 cols, chart 1
plt.plot([1,2,3,4,5],
         [1,8,27,64,125],
         'y^')

plt.subplot(122)              # 1 row, 2 cols, chart 2
plt.plot(a, a**2, 'y^',
         a, a**3, 'bo',
         a, a**4, 'r--',)
```

```
plt.axis([0, 4.5, 0, 70])    # xmin, xmax, ymin, ymax
plt.show()
```

Figure 4.18 shows two charts displayed in a single figure.

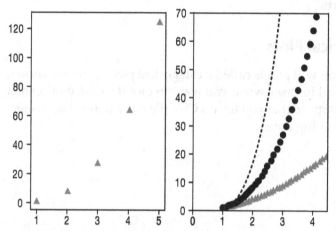

Figure 4.18: Combining two charts into a single figure

The subplot() function adds a subplot to the current figure. One of the arguments it takes in has the following format: *nrow,ncols,index*. In the preceding example, the 121 means "1 row, 2 columns, and chart 1." Using this format, you can have up to a maximum of nine figures. The subplot() function can also be called with the following syntax:

```
plt.subplot(1,2,1)              # 1 row, 2 cols, chart 1
```

Using this syntax, you can now have more than 10 charts in a single figure.

> **TIP**   The scatter() function draws points without lines connecting them, whereas the plot() function may or may not plot the lines, depending on the arguments.

Plotting Using Seaborn

While matplotlib allows you to plot a lot of interesting charts, it takes a bit of effort to get the chart that you want. This is especially true if you are dealing with a large amount of data and would like to examine the relationships between multiple variables.

Introducing *Seaborn*, a complementary plotting library that is based on the matplotlib data visualization library. Seaborn's strength lies in its ability to make statistical graphics in Python, and it is closely integrated with the Pandas data structure (covered in Chapter 3). Seaborn provides high-level abstractions to allow you to build complex visualizations for your data easily. In short, you write less code with Seaborn than with matplotlib, while at the same time you get more sophisticated charts.

Displaying Categorical Plots

The first example that you will plot is called a categorical plot (formerly known as a factorplot). It is useful in cases when you want to plot the distribution of a certain group of data. Suppose that you have a CSV file named `drivinglicense` `.csv` containing the following data:

```
gender,group,license
men,A,1
men,A,0
men,A,1
women,A,1
women,A,0
women,A,0
men,B,0
men,B,0
men,B,0
men,B,1
women,B,1
women,B,1
women,B,1
women,B,1
```

This CSV file shows the distribution of men and women in two groups, A and B, with 1 indicating that the person has a driver's license and a 0 indicating no driver's license. If you are tasked with plotting a chart to show the proportion of men and women in each group that has a driver's license, you can use Seaborn's categorical plot.

First, import the relevant modules:

```
import matplotlib.pyplot as plt
import seaborn as sns
import pandas as pd
```

Load the data into a Pandas dataframe:

```
#---load data---
data = pd.read_csv('drivinglicense.csv')
```

Call the catplot() function with the following arguments:

```
#---plot a factorplot---
g = sns.catplot(x="gender", y="license", col="group",
        data=data, kind="bar", ci=None, aspect=1.0)
```

You pass in the dataframe through the data parameter, and you specify the *gender* as the x-axis. The y-axis will tabulate the proportion of men and women who have a driver's license, and hence you set y to *license*. You want to separate the chart into two groups based on group, hence you set col to *group*.

Next, you set the labels on the chart:

```
#---set the labels---
g.set_axis_labels("", "Proportion with Driving license")
g.set_xticklabels(["Men", "Women"])
g.set_titles("{col_var} {col_name}")

#---show plot---
plt.show()
```

Figure 4.19 shows the categorical plot drawn by Seaborn. As you can see, 2/3 of the men and 1/3 of the women have driver's licenses in Group A, while in Group B, 1/4 of the men and all the women have driver's licenses. Neat, isn't it?

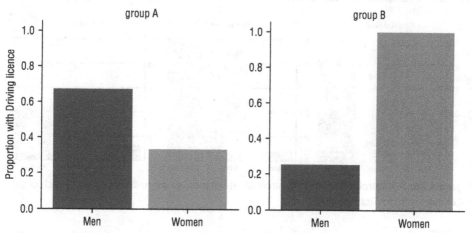

Figure 4.19: Displaying a factorplot showing the distribution of men and women who have driver's licenses in each group

Let's take a look at another example of catplot. Using the Titanic dataset, let's plot a chart and see what the survival rate of men, women, and children looks like in each of the three classes.

> **TIP**   Seaborn has a built-in dataset that you can load directly using the `load_dataset()` function. To see the names of the dataset that you can load, use the `sns.get_dataset_names()` function. Alternatively, if you want to download the dataset for offline use, check out `https://github.com/mwaskom/seaborn-data`. Note that you would need to have an Internet connection, as the `load_dataset()` function loads the specified dataset from the online repository.

```
import matplotlib.pyplot as plt
import seaborn as sns

titanic = sns.load_dataset("titanic")
g = sns.catplot(x="who", y="survived", col="class",
        data=titanic, kind="bar", ci=None, aspect=1)

g.set_axis_labels("", "Survival Rate")
g.set_xticklabels(["Men", "Women", "Children"])
g.set_titles("{col_name} {col_var}")

#---show plot---
plt.show()
```

Figure 4.20 shows the distribution of the data based on classes. As you can see, both women and children have a higher chance of survival if they are in the first- and second-class cabins.

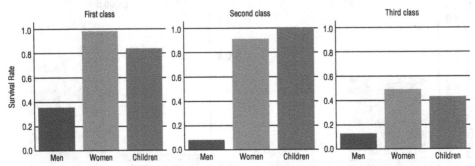

Figure 4.20: A factorplot showing the survival rate of men, women, and children in each of the cabin classes in the Titanic dataset

Displaying Lmplots

Another plot that is popular in Seaborn is the lmplot. An *lmplot* is a scatter plot. Using another built-in dataset from Seaborn, you can plot the relationships between the petal width and petal length of an iris plant and use it to determine the type of iris plants: setosa, versicolor, or virginica.

```
import seaborn as sns
import matplotlib.pyplot as plt

#---load the iris dataset---
iris = sns.load_dataset("iris")

#---plot the lmplot---
sns.lmplot('petal_width', 'petal_length', data=iris,
           hue='species', palette='Set1',
           fit_reg=False, scatter_kws={"s": 70})

#---get the current polar axes on the current figure---
ax = plt.gca()
ax.set_title("Plotting using the Iris dataset")

#---show the plot---
plt.show()
```

Figure 4.21 shows the scatter plot created using the lmplot() function.

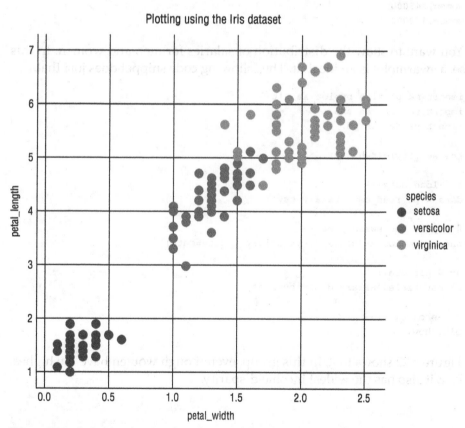

Figure 4.21: An lmplot showing the relationship between the petal length and width of the iris dataset

Displaying Swarmplots

A *swarmplot* is a categorical scatterplot with nonoverlapping points. It is useful for discovering the distribution of data points in a dataset. Consider the following CSV file named `salary.csv`, which contains the following content:

```
gender,salary
men,100000
men,120000
men,119000
men,77000
men,83000
men,120000
men,125000
women,30000
women,140000
women,38000
women,45000
women,23000
women,145000
women,170000
```

You want to show the distribution of salaries for men and women. In this case, a swarmplot is an ideal fit. The following code snippet does just that:

```
import matplotlib.pyplot as plt
import seaborn as sns
import pandas as pd

sns.set_style("whitegrid")

#---load data---
data = pd.read_csv('salary.csv')

#---plot the swarm plot---
sns.swarmplot(x="gender", y="salary", data=data)

ax = plt.gca()
ax.set_title("Salary distribution")

#---show plot---
plt.show()
```

Figure 4.22 shows that, in this group, even though women have the highest salary, it also has the widest income disparity.

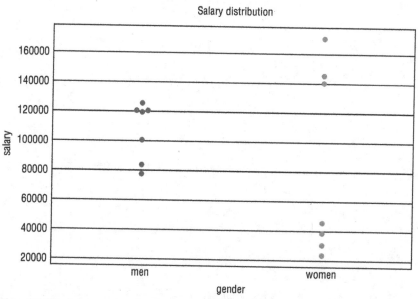

Figure 4.22: A swarmplot showing the distribution of salaries for men and women

Summary

In this chapter, you learned how to use matplotlib to plot the different types of charts that are useful for discovering patterns and relationships in a dataset. A complementary plotting library, Seaborn, simplifies plotting more sophisticated charts. While this chapter does not contain an exhaustive list of charts that you can plot with matplotlib and Seaborn, subsequent chapters will provide more samples and uses for them.

Getting Started with Scikit-learn for Machine Learning

Introduction to Scikit-learn

In Chapters 2–4, you learned how to use Python together with libraries such as NumPy and Pandas to perform number crunching, data visualization, and analysis. For machine learning, you can also use these libraries to build your own learning models. However, doing so would require you to have a strong appreciation of the mathematical foundation for the various machine learning algorithms—not a trivial matter.

Instead of implementing the various machine learning algorithms manually by hand, fortunately, someone else has already done the hard work for you. Introducing *Scikit-learn*, a Python library that implements the various types of machine learning algorithms, such as classification, regression, clustering, decision tree, and more. Using Scikit-learn, implementing machine learning is now simply a matter of calling a function with the appropriate data so that you can fit and train the model.

In this chapter, first you will learn the various venues where you can get the sample datasets to learn how to perform machine learning. You will then learn how to use Scikit-learn to perform simple linear regression on a simple dataset. Finally, you will learn how to perform data cleansing.

Getting Datasets

Often, one of the challenges in machine learning is obtaining sample datasets for experimentation. In machine learning, when you are just getting started with an algorithm, it is often useful to get started with a simple dataset that you can create yourself to test that the algorithm is working correctly according to your understanding. Once you clear this stage, it is time to work with a large dataset, and for this you would need to find the relevant source so that your machine learning model can be as realistic as possible.

Here are some places where you can get the sample dataset to practice your machine learning:

- Scikit-learn's built-in dataset
- Kaggle dataset
- UCI (University of California, Irvine) Machine Learning Repository

Let's take a look at each of these in the following sections.

Using the Scikit-learn Dataset

Scikit-learn comes with a few standard sample datasets, which makes learning machine learning easy. To load the sample datasets, import the datasets module and load the desired dataset. For example, the following code snippets load the *Iris dataset*:

```
from sklearn import datasets
iris = datasets.load_iris()   # raw data of type Bunch
```

TIP   The Iris flower dataset or Fisher's Iris dataset is a multivariate dataset introduced by the British statistician and biologist Ronald Fisher. The dataset consists of 50 samples from each of three species of Iris (Iris setosa, Iris virginica, and Iris versicolor). Four features were measured from each sample: the length and the width of the sepals and petals in centimeters. Based on the combination of these four features, Fisher developed a linear discriminant model to distinguish the species from each other.

The dataset loaded is represented as a `Bunch` object, a Python dictionary that provides attribute-style access. You can use the `DESCR` property to obtain a description of the dataset:

```
print(iris.DESCR)
```

More importantly, however, you can obtain the features of the dataset using the `data` property:

```
print(iris.data)                          # Features
```

The preceding statement prints the following:

```
[[ 5.1  3.5  1.4  0.2]
 [ 4.9  3.   1.4  0.2]
   ...
 [ 6.2  3.4  5.4  2.3]
 [ 5.9  3.   5.1  1.8]]
```

You can also use the `feature_names` property to print the names of the features:

```
print(iris.feature_names)        # Feature Names
```

The preceding statement prints the following:

```
['sepal length (cm)', 'sepal width (cm)',
 'petal length (cm)', 'petal width (cm)']
```

This means that the dataset contains four columns—sepal length, sepal width, petal length, and petal width. If you are wondering what a petal and sepal are, Figure 5.1 shows the Tetramerous flower of Ludwigia octovalvis showing petals and sepals (source: https://en.wikipedia.org/wiki/Sepal).

Figure 5.1: The petal and sepal of a flower

To print the label of the dataset, use the `target` property. For the label names, use the `target_names` property:

```
print(iris.target)              # Labels
print(iris.target_names)        # Label names
```

This prints out the following:

```
[0 0 0 0 0 0 0 0 0 0 0 0 0 0 0 0 0 0 0 ... 2 2 2 2 2
 2 2]
['setosa' 'versicolor' 'virginica']
```

In this case, 0 represents *setosa*, 1 represents *versicolor*, and 2 represents *virginica*.

TIP   Note that not all sample datasets in Scikit-learn support the `feature_names` and `target_names` **properties.**

Figure 5.2 summarizes what the dataset looks like.

sepal length	sepal width	petal length	petal width	target
5.1	3.5	1.4	0.2	0
4.9	3.0	1.4	0.2	0
...	...	...	...	...
5.9	3.0	5.1	1.8	2

0 represents setosa, 1 represents versicolor, 2 represents virginica

Figure 5.2: The fields in the Iris dataset and its target

Often, it is useful to convert the data to a Pandas dataframe, so that you can manipulate it easily:

```
import pandas as pd
df = pd.DataFrame(iris.data)    # convert features
                                # to dataframe in Pandas
print(df.head())
```

These statements print out the following:

```
     0    1    2    3
0  5.1  3.5  1.4  0.2
1  4.9  3.0  1.4  0.2
2  4.7  3.2  1.3  0.2
3  4.6  3.1  1.5  0.2
4  5.0  3.6  1.4  0.2
```

Besides the Iris dataset, you can also load some interesting datasets in Scikit-learn, such as the following:

```
# data on breast cancer
breast_cancer = datasets.load_breast_cancer()

# data on diabetes
diabetes = datasets.load_diabetes()

# dataset of 1797 8x8 images of hand-written digits
digits = datasets.load_digits()
```

For more information on the Scikit-learn dataset, check out the documentation at `http://scikit-learn.org/stable/datasets/index.html`.

Using the Kaggle Dataset

Kaggle is the world's largest community of data scientists and machine learners. What started off as a platform for offering machine learning competitions, Kaggle now also offers a public data platform, as well as a cloud-based workbench for data scientists. Google acquired Kaggle in March 2017.

For learners of machine learning, you can make use of the sample datasets provided by Kaggle at `https://www.kaggle.com/datasets/`. Some of the interesting datasets include:

- **Women's Shoe Prices:** A list of 10,000 women's shoes and the prices at which they are sold (`https://www.kaggle.com/datafiniti/womens-shoes-prices`)
- **Fall Detection Data from China:** Activity of elderly patients along with their medical information (`https://www.kaggle.com/pitasr/falldata`)
- **NYC Property Sales:** A year's worth of properties sold on the NYC real estate market (`https://www.kaggle.com/new-york-city/nyc-property-sales#nyc-rolling-sales.csv`)
- **US Flight Delay:** Flight Delays for year 2016 (`https://www.kaggle.com/niranjan0272/us-flight-delay`)

Using the UCI (University of California, Irvine) Machine Learning Repository

The UCI Machine Learning Repository (`https://archive.ics.uci.edu/ml/datasets.html`) is a collection of databases, domain theories, and data generators that are used by the machine learning community for the empirical analysis of machine learning algorithms. Here are some interesting ones from the huge dataset it contains:

- **Auto MPG Data Set:** A collection of data about the fuel efficiency of different types of cars (`https://archive.ics.uci.edu/ml/datasets/Auto+MPG`)
- **Student Performance Data Set:** Predict student performance in secondary education (high school) (`https://archive.ics.uci.edu/ml/datasets/Student+Performance`)
- **Census Income Data Set:** Predict whether income exceeds $50K/yr. based on census data (`https://archive.ics.uci.edu/ml/datasets/census+income`)

Generating Your Own Dataset

If you cannot find a suitable dataset for experimentation, why not generate one yourself? The `sklearn.datasets.samples_generator` module from the Scikit-learn library contains a number of functions to let you generate different types of datasets for different types of problems. You can use it to generate datasets of different distributions, such as the following:

- Linearly distributed datasets
- Clustered datasets
- Clustered datasets distributed in circular fashion

Linearly Distributed Dataset

The `make_regression()` function generates data that is linearly distributed. You can specify the number of features that you want, as well as the standard deviation of the Gaussian noise applied to the output:

```
%matplotlib inline
from matplotlib import pyplot as plt
from sklearn.datasets.samples_generator import make_regression

X, y = make_regression(n_samples=100, n_features=1, noise=5.4)
plt.scatter(X,y)
```

Figure 5.3 shows the scatter plot of the dataset generated.

Clustered Dataset

The `make_blobs()` function generates *n* number of clusters of random data. This is very useful when performing clustering in unsupervised learning (Chapter 9, "Supervised Learning—Classification using K Nearest Neighbors (KNN)"):

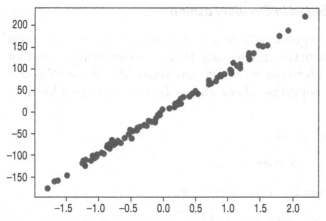

Figure 5.3: Scatter plot showing the linearly distributed data points

```
%matplotlib inline
import matplotlib.pyplot as plt
import numpy as np
from sklearn.datasets import make_blobs

X, y = make_blobs(500, centers=3)   # Generate isotropic Gaussian
                                    # blobs for clustering

rgb = np.array(['r', 'g', 'b'])

# plot the blobs using a scatter plot and use color coding
plt.scatter(X[:, 0], X[:, 1], color=rgb[y])
```

Figure 5.4 shows the scatter plot of the random dataset generated.

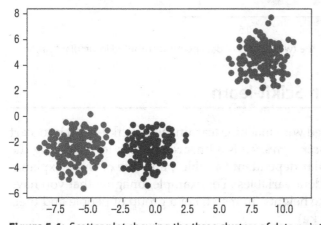

Figure 5.4: Scatter plot showing the three clusters of data points generated

Clustered Dataset Distributed in Circular Fashion

The `make_circles()` function generates a random dataset containing a large circle embedding a smaller circle in two dimensions. This is useful when performing classifications, using algorithms like SVM (Support Vector Machines). SVM will be covered in Chapter 8, "Supervised Learning—Classification using SVM."

```
%matplotlib inline
import matplotlib.pyplot as plt
import numpy as np
from sklearn.datasets import make_circles

X, y = make_circles(n_samples=100, noise=0.09)

rgb = np.array(['r', 'g', 'b'])
plt.scatter(X[:, 0], X[:, 1], color=rgb[y])
```

Figure 5.5 shows the scatter plot of the random dataset generated.

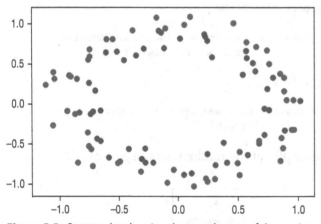

Figure 5.5: Scatter plot showing the two clusters of data points distributed in circular fashion

Getting Started with Scikit-learn

The easiest way to get started with machine learning with Scikit-learn is to start with linear regression. *Linear regression* is a linear approach for modeling the relationship between a scalar dependent variable y and one or more explanatory variables (or independent variables). For example, imagine that you have a set of data comprising the heights (in meters) of a group of people and their corresponding weights (in kg):

```
%matplotlib inline
import matplotlib.pyplot as plt
```

```
# represents the heights of a group of people in meters
heights = [[1.6], [1.65], [1.7], [1.73], [1.8]]

# represents the weights of a group of people in kgs
weights = [[60], [65], [72.3], [75], [80]]

plt.title('Weights plotted against heights')
plt.xlabel('Heights in meters')
plt.ylabel('Weights in kilograms')

plt.plot(heights, weights, 'k.')

# axis range for x and y
plt.axis([1.5, 1.85, 50, 90])
plt.grid(True)
```

When you plot a chart of weights against heights, you will see the chart as shown in Figure 5.6.

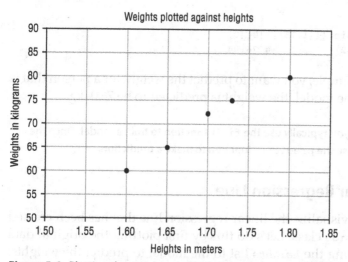

Figure 5.6: Plotting the weights against heights for a group of people

From the chart, you can see that there is a positive correlation between the weights and heights for this group of people. You could draw a straight line through the points and use that to predict the weight of another person based on their height.

Using the LinearRegression Class for Fitting the Model

So how do we draw the straight line that cuts though all of the points? It turns out that the Scikit-learn library has the LinearRegression class that helps you to do just that. All you need to do is to create an instance of this class and use

the *heights* and *weights* lists to create a linear regression model using the fit()
function, like this:

```
from sklearn.linear_model import LinearRegression

# Create and fit the model
model = LinearRegression()
model.fit(X=heights, y=weights)
```

> **TIP**   Observe that the *heights* and *weights* are both represented as
> two-dimensional lists. This is because the fit() function requires both the *X* and *y*
> arguments to be two-dimensional (of type list or ndarray).

Making Predictions

Once you have fitted (trained) the model, you can start to make predictions
using the predict() function, like this:

```
# make prediction
weight = model.predict([[1.75]])[0][0]
print(round(weight,2))          # 76.04
```

In the preceding example, you want to predict the weight for a person that is
1.75m tall. Based on the model, the weight is predicted to be 76.04kg.

> **TIP**   In Scikit-learn, you typically use the fit() function to train a model. Once the
> model is trained, you use the predict() function to make a prediction.

Plotting the Linear Regression Line

It would be useful to visualize the linear regression line that has been created
by the LinearRegression class. Let's do this by first plotting the original data
points and then sending the *heights* list to the model to predict the weights.
We then plot the series of forecasted weights to obtain the line. The following
code snippet shows how this is done:

```
import matplotlib.pyplot as plt

heights = [[1.6], [1.65], [1.7], [1.73], [1.8]]
weights = [[60], [65], [72.3], [75], [80]]

plt.title('Weights plotted against heights')
plt.xlabel('Heights in meters')
plt.ylabel('Weights in kilograms')
```

```
plt.plot(heights, weights, 'k.')

plt.axis([1.5, 1.85, 50, 90])
plt.grid(True)

# plot the regression line
plt.plot(heights, model.predict(heights), color='r')
```

Figure 5.7 shows the linear regression line.

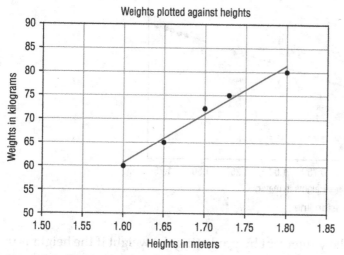

Figure 5.7: Plotting the linear regression line

Getting the Gradient and Intercept of the Linear Regression Line

From Figure 5.7, it is not clear at what value the linear regression line intercepts the y-axis. This is because we have adjusted the x-axis to start plotting at 1.5. A better way to visualize this would be to set the x-axis to start from 0 and enlarge the range of the y-axis. You then plot the line by feeding in two extreme values of the height: 0 and 1.8. The following code snippet re-plots the points and the linear regression line:

```
plt.title('Weights plotted against heights')
plt.xlabel('Heights in meters')
plt.ylabel('Weights in kilograms')

plt.plot(heights, weights, 'k.')

plt.axis([0, 1.85, -200, 200])
plt.grid(True)
```

```
# plot the regression line
extreme_heights = [[0], [1.8]]
plt.plot(extreme_heights, model.predict(extreme_heights), color='b')
```

Figure 5.8 now shows the point where the line cuts the y-axis.

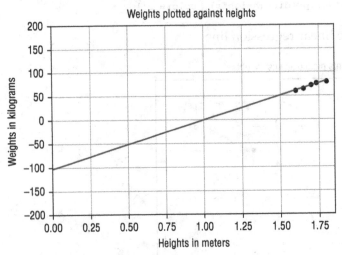

Figure 5.8: The linear regression line

While you can get the y-intercept by predicting the weight if the height is 0:

```
round(model.predict([[0]])[0][0],2)   # -104.75
```

the `model` object provides the answer directly through the `intercept_` property:

```
print(round(model.intercept_[0],2))   # -104.75
```

Using the `model` object, you can also get the gradient of the linear regression line through the `coef_` property:

```
print(round(model.coef_[0][0],2))     # 103.31
```

Examining the Performance of the Model by Calculating the Residual Sum of Squares

To know if your linear regression line is well fitted to all of the data points, we use the *Residual Sum of Squares (RSS)* method. Figure 5.9 shows how the RSS is calculated.

The following code snippet shows how the RSS is calculated in Python:

```
import numpy as np

print('Residual sum of squares: %.2f' %
      np.sum((weights - model.predict(heights)) ** 2))
# Residual sum of squares: 5.34
```

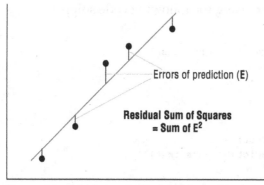

Figure 5.9: Calculating the Residual Sum of Squares for linear regression

The RSS should be as small as possible, with 0 indicating that the regression line fits the points exactly (rarely achievable in the real world).

Evaluating the Model Using a Test Dataset

Now that our model is trained with our training data, we can put it to the test. Assuming that we have the following test dataset:

```
# test data
heights_test = [[1.58], [1.62], [1.69], [1.76], [1.82]]
weights_test = [[58], [63], [72], [73], [85]]
```

we can measure how closely the test data fits the regression line using the *R-Squared method*. The R-Squared method is also known as the *coefficient of determination,* or the *coefficient of multiple determinations for multiple regressions.*

The formula for calculating R-Squared is shown in Figure 5.10.

$$R^2 = 1 - \frac{RSS}{TSS}$$

$$TSS = \sum_{i=1}^{n} (y_i - \bar{y})^2$$

$$RSS = \sum_{i=1}^{n} (y_i - f(x_i))^2$$

Figure 5.10: The formula for calculating R-Squared

Using the formula shown for R-Squared, note the following:

- R^2 is R-squared
- TSS is Total Sum of Squares
- RSS is Residual Sum of Squares

You can now calculate it in Python using the following code snippet:

```
# Total Sum of Squares (TSS)
weights_test_mean = np.mean(np.ravel(weights_test))
TSS = np.sum((np.ravel(weights_test) -
              weights_test_mean) ** 2)
print("TSS: %.2f" % TSS)


# Residual Sum of Squares (RSS)
RSS = np.sum((np.ravel(weights_test) -
              np.ravel(model.predict(heights_test)))
                ** 2)
print("RSS: %.2f" % RSS)


# R_squared
R_squared = 1 - (RSS / TSS)
print("R-squared: %.2f" % R_squared)
```

TIP The `ravel()` function converts the two-dimensional list into a contiguous flattened (one-dimensional) array.

The preceding code snippet yields the following result:

```
TSS: 430.80
RSS: 24.62
R-squared: 0.94
```

Fortunately, you don't have to calculate the R-Squared manually yourself— Scikit-learn has the `score()` function to calculate the R-Squared automatically for you:

```
# using scikit-learn to calculate r-squared
print('R-squared: %.4f' % model.score(heights_test,
                                        weights_test))


# R-squared: 0.9429
```

An R-Squared value of 0.9429 (94.29%) indicates a pretty good fit for your test data.

Persisting the Model

Once you have trained a model, it is often useful to be able to save it for later use. Rather than retraining the model every time you have new data to test, a saved model allows you to load the trained model and make predictions immediately without the need to train the model again.

There are two ways to save your trained model in Python:

- Using the standard `pickle` module in Python to serialize and deserialize objects
- Using the `joblib` module in Scikit-learn that is optimized to save and load Python objects that deal with NumPy data

The first example you will see is saving the model using the `pickle` module:

```
import pickle

# save the model to disk
filename = 'HeightsAndWeights_model.sav'
# write to the file using write and binary mode
pickle.dump(model, open(filename, 'wb'))
```

In the preceding code snippet, you first opened a file in "wb" mode ("w" for write and "b" for binary). You then use the `dump()` function from the `pickle` module to save the model into the file.

To load the model from file, use the `load()` function:

```
# load the model from disk
loaded_model = pickle.load(open(filename, 'rb'))
```

You can now use the model as usual:

```
result = loaded_model.score(heights_test,
                            weights_test)
```

Using the `joblib` module is very similar to using the `pickle` module:

```
from sklearn.externals import joblib

# save the model to disk
filename = 'HeightsAndWeights_model2.sav'
joblib.dump(model, filename)

# load the model from disk
loaded_model = joblib.load(filename)
result = loaded_model.score(heights_test,
                            weights_test)
print(result)
```

Data Cleansing

In machine learning, one of the first tasks that you need to perform is *data cleansing*. Very seldom would you have a dataset that you can use straightaway to train your model. Instead, you have to examine the data carefully for any missing values and either remove them or replace them with some valid values, or you have to normalize them if there are columns with wildly different values. The following sections show some of the common tasks you need to perform when cleaning your data.

Cleaning Rows with NaNs

Consider a CSV file named `NaNDataset.csv` with the following content:

```
A,B,C
1,2,3
4,,6
7,,9
10,11,12
13,14,15
16,17,18
```

Visually, you can spot that there are a few rows with empty fields. Specifically, the second and third rows have missing values for the second columns. For small sets of data, this is easy to spot. But if you have a large dataset, it becomes almost impossible to detect. An effective way to detect for empty rows is to load the dataset into a Pandas dataframe and then use the `isnull()` function to check for null values in the dataframe:

```
import pandas as pd
df = pd.read_csv('NaNDataset.csv')
df.isnull().sum()
```

This code snippet will produce the following output:

```
A    0
B    2
C    0
dtype: int64
```

You can see that column B has two null values. When Pandas loads a dataset containing empty values, it will use NaN to represent those empty fields. The following is the output of the dataframe when you print it out:

```
    A     B   C
0   1   2.0   3
1   4   NaN   6
2   7   NaN   9
3  10  11.0  12
4  13  14.0  15
5  16  17.0  18
```

Replacing NaN with the Mean of the Column

One of the ways to deal with NaNs in your dataset is to replace them with the mean of the columns in which they are located. The following code snippet replaces all of the NaNs in column B with the average value of column B:

```
# replace all the NaNs in column B with the average of column B
df.B = df.B.fillna(df.B.mean())
print(df)
```

The dataframe now looks like this:

```
    A     B    C
0   1   2.0    3
1   4  11.0    6
2   7  11.0    9
3  10  11.0   12
4  13  14.0   15
5  16  17.0   18
```

Removing Rows

Another way to deal with NaNs in your dataset is simply to remove the rows containing them. You can do so using the dropna() function, like this:

```
df = pd.read_csv('NaNDataset.csv')
df = df.dropna()                          # drop all rows with NaN
print(df)
```

This code snippet will produce the following output:

```
    A     B    C
0   1   2.0    3
3  10  11.0   12
4  13  14.0   15
5  16  17.0   18
```

Observe that after removing the rows containing NaN, the index is no longer in sequential order. If you need to reset the index, use the reset_index() function:

```
df = df.reset_index(drop=True)            # reset the index
print(df)
```

The dataframe with the reset index will now look like this:

```
    A     B    C
0   1   2.0    3
1  10  11.0   12
2  13  14.0   15
3  16  17.0   18
```

Removing Duplicate Rows

Consider a CSV file named `DuplicateRows.csv` with the following content:

```
A,B,C
1,2,3
4,5,6
4,5,6
7,8,9
7,18,9
10,11,12
10,11,12
13,14,15
16,17,18
```

To find all of the duplicated rows, first load the dataset into a dataframe and then use the `duplicated()` function, like this:

```
import pandas as pd
df = pd.read_csv('DuplicateRows.csv')
print(df.duplicated(keep=False))
```

This will produce the following output:

```
0    False
1     True
2     True
3    False
4    False
5     True
6     True
7    False
8    False
dtype: bool
```

It shows which rows are duplicated. In this example, rows with index 1, 2, 5, and 6 are duplicates. The `keep` argument allows you to specify how to indicate duplicates:

- The default is `'first'`: All duplicates are marked as `True` except for the first occurrence

- `'last'`: All duplicates are marked as `True` except for the last occurrence

- `False`: All duplicates are marked as `True`

So, if you set `keep` to `'first'`, you will see the following output:

```
0    False
1    False
2     True
```

```
3    False
4    False
5    False
6     True
7    False
8    False
dtype: bool
```

Hence, if you want to see all duplicate rows, you can set `keep` to `False` and use the result of the `duplicated()` function as the index into the dataframe:

```
print(df[df.duplicated(keep=False)])
```

The preceding statement will print all of the duplicate rows:

```
    A    B    C
1   4    5    6
2   4    5    6
5  10   11   12
6  10   11   12
```

To drop duplicate rows, you can use the `drop_duplicates()` function, like this:

```
df.drop_duplicates(keep='first', inplace=True)  # remove
duplicates and keep the first
print(df)
```

> **TIP**   By default, the `drop_duplicates()` function will not modify the original dataframe and will return the dataframe containing the dropped rows. If you want to modify the original dataframe, set the `inplace` parameter to `True`, as shown in the preceding code snippet.

The preceding statements will print the following:

```
    A    B    C
0   1    2    3
1   4    5    6
3   7    8    9
4   7   18    9
5  10   11   12
7  13   14   15
8  16   17   18
```

> **TIP**   To remove all duplicates, set the `keep` parameter to `False`. To keep the last occurrence of duplicate rows, set the `keep` parameter to `'last'`.

Sometimes, you only want to remove duplicates that are found in certain columns in the dataset. For example, if you look at the dataset that we have been using, observe that for row 3 and row 4, the values of column A and C are identical:

```
    A   B   C
3   7   8   9
4   7  18   9
```

You can remove duplicates in certain columns by specifying the `subset` parameter:

```
df.drop_duplicates(subset=['A', 'C'], keep='last',
                        inplace=True)      # remove all duplicates in
                                           # columns A and C and keep
                                           # the last
print(df)
```

This statement will yield the following:

```
    A   B   C
0   1   2   3
1   4   5   6
4   7  18   9
5  10  11  12
7  13  14  15
8  16  17  18
```

Normalizing Columns

Normalization is a technique often applied during the data cleansing process. The aim of *normalization* is to change the values of numeric columns in the dataset to use a common scale, without modifying the differences in the ranges of values.

Normalization is crucial for some algorithms to model the data correctly. For example, one of the columns in your dataset may contain values from 0 to 1, while another column has values ranging from 400,000 to 500,000. The huge disparity in the scale of the numbers could introduce problems when you use the two columns to train your model. Using normalization, you could maintain the ratio of the values in the two columns while keeping them to a limited range. In Pandas, you can use the `MinMaxScaler` class to scale each column to a particular range of values.

Consider a CSV file named `NormalizeColumns.csv` with the following content:

```
A,B,C
1000,2,3
400,5,6
700,6,9
100,11,12
1300,14,15
1600,17,18
```

The following code snippet will scale all the columns' values to the (0,1) range:

```
import pandas as pd
from sklearn import preprocessing

df = pd.read_csv('NormalizeColumns.csv')
x = df.values.astype(float)

min_max_scaler = preprocessing.MinMaxScaler()
x_scaled = min_max_scaler.fit_transform(x)
df = pd.DataFrame(x_scaled, columns=df.columns)
print(df)
```

You should see the following output:

```
     A        B       C
0   0.6  0.000000  0.0
1   0.2  0.200000  0.2
2   0.4  0.266667  0.4
3   0.0  0.600000  0.6
4   0.8  0.800000  0.8
5   1.0  1.000000  1.0
```

Removing Outliers

In statistics, an *outlier* is a point that is distant from other observed points. For example, given a set of values—234, 267, 1, 200, 245, 300, 199, 250, 8999, and 245—it is quite obvious that 1 and 8999 are outliers. They distinctly stand out from the rest of the values, and they "lie outside" most of the other values in the dataset; hence the word *outlier*. Outliers occur mainly due to errors in recording or experimental error, and in machine learning it is important to remove them prior to training your model as it may potentially distort your model if you don't.

There are a number of techniques to remove outliers, and in this chapter we discuss two of them:

- Tukey Fences
- Z-Score

Tukey Fences

Tukey Fences is based on *Interquartile Range (IQR)*. IQR is the difference between the first and third quartiles of a set of values. The first quartile, denoted Q1, is the value in the dataset that holds 25% of the values below it. The third quartile, denoted Q3, is the value in the dataset that holds 25% of the values above it. Hence, by definition, IQR = Q3 – Q1.

Figure 5.11 shows an example of how IQR is obtained for datasets with even and odd numbers of values.

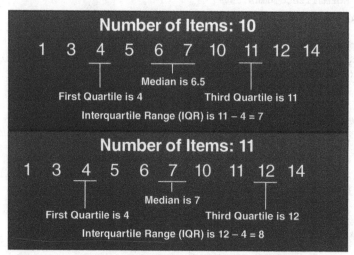

Figure 5.11: Examples of finding the Interquartile Range (IQR)

In Tukey Fences, outliers are values that are as follows:

- Less than Q1 – (1.5 × IQR), or
- More than Q3 + (1.5 × IQR)

The following code snippet shows the implementation of Tukey Fences using Python:

```python
import numpy as np

def outliers_iqr(data):
    q1, q3 = np.percentile(data, [25, 75])
    iqr = q3 - q1
    lower_bound = q1 - (iqr * 1.5)
    upper_bound = q3 + (iqr * 1.5)
    return np.where((data > upper_bound) | (data < lower_bound))
```

TIP The np.where() function returns the location of items satisfying the conditions.

The outliers_iqr() function returns a tuple of which the first element is an array of indices of those rows that have outlier values.

To test the Tukey Fences, let's use the famous Galton dataset on the heights of parents and their children. The dataset contains data based on the famous 1885 study of Francis Galton exploring the relationship between the heights of adult children and the heights of their parents. Each case is an adult child, and the variables are as follows:

Family: The family that the child belongs to, labeled by the numbers from
        1 to 204 and 136A
Father: The father's height, in inches
Mother: The mother's height, in inches
Gender: The gender of the child, male (M) or female (F)
Height: The height of the child, in inches
Kids: The number of kids in the family of the child

The dataset has 898 cases.
First, import the data:

```
import pandas as pd
df = pd.read_csv("http://www.mosaic-web.org/go/datasets/galton.csv")
print(df.head())
```

You should see the following:

```
   family  father  mother sex  height  nkids
0       1    78.5    67.0   M    73.2      4
1       1    78.5    67.0   F    69.2      4
2       1    78.5    67.0   F    69.0      4
3       1    78.5    67.0   F    69.0      4
4       2    75.5    66.5   M    73.5      4
```

If you want to find the outliers in the `height` column, you can call the `outliers_iqr()` function as follows:

```
print("Outliers using outliers_iqr()")
print("==============================")
for i in outliers_iqr(df.height)[0]:
    print(df[i:i+1])
```

You should see the following output:

```
Outliers using outliers_iqr()
==============================
     family  father  mother sex  height  nkids
288      72    70.0    65.0   M    79.0      7
```

Using the Tukey Fences method, you can see that the `height` column has a single outlier.

Z-Score

The second method for determining outliers is to use the *Z-score* method. A Z-score indicates how many standard deviations a data point is from the mean. The Z-score has the following formula:

$$Z = \left(x_i - \mu\right) / \sigma$$

where x_i is the data point, μ is the mean of the dataset, and σ is the standard deviation.

This is how you interpret the Z-score:

- A negative Z-score indicates that the data point is less than the mean, and a positive Z-score indicates the data point in question is larger than the mean

- A Z-score of 0 tells you that the data point is right in the middle (mean), and a Z-score of 1 tells you that your data point is 1 standard deviation above the mean, and so on

- Any Z-score greater than 3 or less than –3 is considered to be an outlier

The following code snippet shows the implementation of the Z-score using Python:

```
def outliers_z_score(data):
    threshold = 3
    mean = np.mean(data)
    std = np.std(data)
    z_scores = [(y - mean) / std for y in data]
    return np.where(np.abs(z_scores) > threshold)
```

Using the same Galton dataset that you used earlier, you can now find the outliers for the height column using the outliers_z_score() function:

```
print("Outliers using outliers_z_score()")
print("==================================")
for i in outliers_z_score(df.height)[0]:
    print(df[i:i+1])
print()
```

You should see the following output:

```
Outliers using outliers_z_score()
==================================
```

	family	father	mother	sex	height	nkids
125	35	71.0	69.0	M	78.0	5

	family	father	mother	sex	height	nkids
288	72	70.0	65.0	M	79.0	7

	family	father	mother	sex	height	nkids
672	155	68.0	60.0	F	56.0	7

Using the Z-score method, you can see that the `height` column has three outliers.

Summary

In this chapter, you have seen how to get started with the Scikit-learn library to solve a linear regression problem. In addition, you have also learned how to get sample datasets, generate your own, perform data cleansing, as well as the two techniques that you can use to remove outliers from your datasets.

In subsequent chapters, you will learn more about the various machine learning algorithms and how to use them to solve real-life problems.

## CHAPTER 6

Supervised Learning—Linear Regression

Types of Linear Regression

In the previous chapter, you learned how to get started with machine learning using simple linear regression, first using Python, and then followed by using the Scikit-learn library. In this chapter, we will look into linear regression in more detail and discuss another variant of linear regression known as *polynomial regression*.

To recap, Figure 6.1 shows the Iris dataset used in Chapter 5, "Getting Started with Scikit-learn for Machine Learning." The first four columns are known as the *features*, or also commonly referred to as the *independent variables*. The last column is known as the *label*, or commonly called the *dependent variable* (or *dependent variables* if there is more than one label).

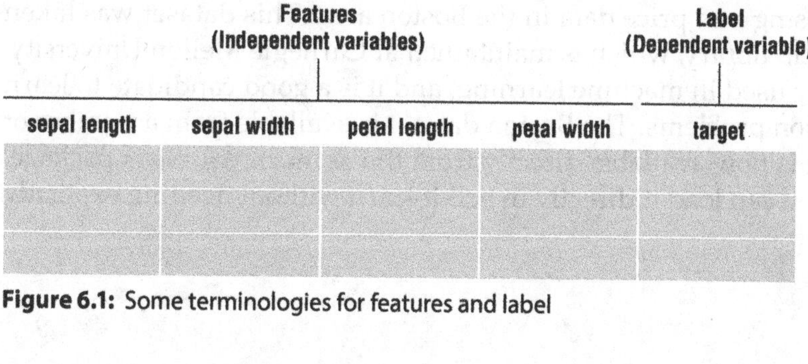

Figure 6.1: Some terminologies for features and label

> **TIP**   Features are also sometimes called *explanatory variables*, while labels are also sometimes called *targets*.

In simple linear regression, we talked about the linear relationship between one independent variable and one dependent variable. In this chapter, besides simple linear regression, we will also discuss the following:

Multiple Regression   Linear relationships between two or more independent variables and one dependent variable.

Polynomial Regression   Modeling the relationship between one independent variable and one dependent variable using an nth degree polynomial function.

Polynomial Multiple Regression   Modeling the relationship between two or more independent variables and one dependent variable using an nth degree polynomial function.

> **TIP**   There is another form of linear regression, called *multivariate linear regression*, where there is more than one correlated dependent variable in the relationship. Multivariate linear regression is beyond the scope of this book.

Linear Regression

In machine learning, *linear regression* is one of the simplest algorithms that you can apply to a dataset to model the relationships between features and labels. In Chapter 5, we started by exploring simple linear regression, where we could explain the relationship between a feature and a label by using a straight line. In the following section, you will learn about a variant of simple linear regression, called *multiple linear regression*, by predicting house prices based on multiple features.

Using the Boston Dataset

For this example, we will use the Boston dataset, which contains data about the housing and price data in the Boston area. This dataset was taken from the StatLib library, which is maintained at Carnegie Mellon University. It is commonly used in machine learning, and it is a good candidate to learn about regression problems. The Boston dataset is available from a number of sources, but it is now available directly from the `sklearn.datasets` package. This means you can load it directly in Scikit-learn without needing explicitly to download it.

First, let's import the necessary libraries and then load the dataset using the `load_boston()` function:

```
import matplotlib.pyplot as plt
import pandas as pd
import numpy as np

from sklearn.datasets import load_boston
dataset = load_boston()
```

It is always good to examine the data before you work with it. The `data` property contains the data for the various columns of the dataset:

```
print(dataset.data)
```

You should see the following:

```
[[  6.32000000e-03   1.80000000e+01   2.31000000e+00 ...,   1.53000000e+01
    3.96900000e+02   4.98000000e+00]
 [  2.73100000e-02   0.00000000e+00   7.07000000e+00 ...,   1.78000000e+01
    3.96900000e+02   9.14000000e+00]
 [  2.72900000e-02   0.00000000e+00   7.07000000e+00 ...,   1.78000000e+01
    3.92830000e+02   4.03000000e+00]
 ...,
 [  6.07600000e-02   0.00000000e+00   1.19300000e+01 ...,   2.10000000e+01
    3.96900000e+02   5.64000000e+00]
 [  1.09590000e-01   0.00000000e+00   1.19300000e+01 ...,   2.10000000e+01
    3.93450000e+02   6.48000000e+00]
 [  4.74100000e-02   0.00000000e+00   1.19300000e+01 ...,   2.10000000e+01
    3.96900000e+02   7.88000000e+00]]
```

The data is a two-dimensional array. To know the name of each column (feature), use the `feature_names` property:

```
print(dataset.feature_names)
```

You should see the following:

```
['CRIM' 'ZN' 'INDUS' 'CHAS' 'NOX' 'RM' 'AGE' 'DIS' 'RAD' 'TAX' 'PTRATIO'
 'B' 'LSTAT']
```

For the description of each feature, you can use the `DESCR` property:

```
print(dataset.DESCR)
```

The preceding statement will print out the following:

```
Boston House Prices dataset
===========================

Notes
------
```

Data Set Characteristics:

    :Number of Instances: 506

    :Number of Attributes: 13 numeric/categorical predictive

    :Median Value (attribute 14) is usually the target

    :Attribute Information (in order):
        - CRIM   per capita crime rate by town
        - ZN   proportion of residential land zoned for lots over
25,000 sq.ft.
        - INDUS   proportion of non-retail business acres per town
        - CHAS   Charles River dummy variable (= 1 if tract bounds
river; 0 otherwise)
        - NOX   nitric oxides concentration (parts per 10 million)
        - RM   average number of rooms per dwelling
        - AGE   proportion of owner-occupied units built prior to 1940
        - DIS   weighted distances to five Boston employment centres
        - RAD   index of accessibility to radial highways
        - TAX   full-value property-tax rate per $10,000
        - PTRATIO pupil-teacher ratio by town
        - B   1000(Bk - 0.63)^2 where Bk is the proportion of
blacks by town
        - LSTAT   % lower status of the population
        - MEDV   Median value of owner-occupied homes in $1000's

    :Missing Attribute Values: None

    :Creator: Harrison, D. and Rubinfeld, D.L.

This is a copy of UCI ML housing dataset: http://archive.ics.uci.edu/
ml/datasets/Housing

This dataset was taken from the StatLib library which is maintained at
Carnegie Mellon University.

The Boston house-price data of Harrison, D. and Rubinfeld, D.L. 'Hedonic
prices and the demand for clean air', J. Environ. Economics & Management,
vol.5, 81-102, 1978.   Used in Belsley, Kuh & Welsch, 'Regression
diagnostics
...', Wiley, 1980.   N.B. Various transformations are used in the table on
pages 244-261 of the latter.

The Boston house-price data has been used in many machine learning
papers that address regression
problems.

References

- Belsley, Kuh & Welsch, 'Regression diagnostics: Identifying Influential Data and Sources of Collinearity', Wiley, 1980. 244-261.
- Quinlan,R. (1993). Combining Instance-Based and Model-Based Learning. In Proceedings on the Tenth International Conference of Machine Learning, 236-243, University of Massachusetts, Amherst. Morgan Kaufmann.
- many more! (see http://archive.ics.uci.edu/ml/datasets/ Housing)

The prices of houses is the information we are seeking, and it can be accessed via the `target` property:

```
print(dataset.target)
```

You will see the following:

```
[ 24.   21.6  34.7  33.4  36.2  28.7  22.9  27.1  16.5  18.9  15.   18.9
  21.7  20.4  18.2  19.9  23.1  17.5  20.2  18.2  13.6  19.6  15.2  14.5
  15.6  13.9  16.6  14.8  18.4  21.   12.7  14.5  13.2  13.1  13.5  18.9
  20.   21.   24.7  30.8  34.9  26.6  25.3  24.7  21.2  19.3  20.   16.6
  14.4  19.4  19.7  20.5  25.   23.4  18.9  35.4  24.7  31.6  23.3  19.6
  18.7  16.   22.2  25.   33.   23.5  19.4  22.   17.4  20.9  24.2  21.7
  22.8  23.4  24.1  21.4  20.   20.8  21.2  20.3  28.   23.9  24.8  22.9
  23.9  26.6  22.5  22.2  23.6  28.7  22.6  22.   22.9  25.   20.6  28.4
  21.4  38.7  43.8  33.2  27.5  26.5  18.6  19.3  20.1  19.5  19.5  20.4
  19.8  19.4  21.7  22.8  18.8  18.7  18.5  18.3  21.2  19.2  20.4  19.3
  22.   20.3  20.5  17.3  18.8  21.4  15.7  16.2  18.   14.3  19.2  19.6
  23.   18.4  15.6  18.1  17.4  17.1  13.3  17.8  14.   14.4  13.4  15.6
  11.8  13.8  15.6  14.6  17.8  15.4  21.5  19.6  15.3  19.4  17.   15.6
  13.1  41.3  24.3  23.3  27.   50.   50.   50.   22.7  25.   50.   23.8
  23.8  22.3  17.4  19.1  23.1  23.6  22.6  29.4  23.2  24.6  29.9  37.2
  39.8  36.2  37.9  32.5  26.4  29.6  50.   32.   29.8  34.9  37.   30.5
  36.4  31.1  29.1  50.   33.3  30.3  34.6  34.9  32.9  24.1  42.3  48.5
  50.   22.6  24.4  22.5  24.4  20.   21.7  19.3  22.4  28.1  23.7  25.
  23.3  28.7  21.5  23.   26.7  21.7  27.5  30.1  44.8  50.   37.6  31.6
  46.7  31.5  24.3  31.7  41.7  48.3  29.   24.   25.1  31.5  23.7  23.3
  22.   20.1  22.2  23.7  17.6  18.5  24.3  20.5  24.5  26.2  24.4  24.8
  29.6  42.8  21.9  20.9  44.   50.   36.   30.1  33.8  43.1  48.8  31.
  36.5  22.8  30.7  50.   43.5  20.7  21.1  25.2  24.4  35.2  32.4  32.
  33.2  33.1  29.1  35.1  45.4  35.4  46.   50.   32.2  22.   20.1  23.2
  22.3  24.8  28.5  37.3  27.9  23.9  21.7  28.6  27.1  20.3  22.5  29.
  24.8  22.   26.4  33.1  36.1  28.4  33.4  28.2  22.8  20.3  16.1  22.1
  19.4  21.6  23.8  16.2  17.8  19.8  23.1  21.   23.8  23.1  20.4  18.5
  25.   24.6  23.   22.2  19.3  22.6  19.8  17.1  19.4  22.2  20.7  21.1
  19.5  18.5  20.6  19.   18.7  32.7  16.5  23.9  31.2  17.5  17.2  23.1
  24.5  26.6  22.9  24.1  18.6  30.1  18.2  20.6  17.8  21.7  22.7  22.6
  25.   19.9  20.8  16.8  21.9  27.5  21.9  23.1  50.   50.   50.   50.
  50.   13.8  13.8  15.   13.9  13.3  13.1  10.2  10.4  10.9  11.3  12.3
   8.8   7.2  10.5   7.4  10.2  11.5  15.1  23.2   9.7  13.8  12.7  13.1
  12.5   8.5   5.    6.3   5.6   7.2  12.1   8.3   8.5   5.   11.9  27.9
  17.2  27.5  15.   17.2  17.9  16.3   7.    7.2   7.5  10.4   8.8   8.4
```

```
16.7  14.2  20.8  13.4  11.7   8.3  10.2  10.9  11.    9.5  14.5  14.1
16.1  14.3  11.7  13.4   9.6   8.7   8.4  12.8  10.5  17.1  18.4  15.4
10.8  11.8  14.9  12.6  14.1  13.   13.4  15.2  16.1  17.8  14.9  14.1
12.7  13.5  14.9  20.   16.4  17.7  19.5  20.2  21.4  19.9  19.   19.1
19.1  20.1  19.9  19.6  23.2  29.8  13.8  13.3  16.7  12.   14.6  21.4
23.   23.7  25.   21.8  20.6  21.2  19.1  20.6  15.2   7.    8.1  13.6
20.1  21.8  24.5  23.1  19.7  18.3  21.2  17.5  16.8  22.4  20.6  23.9
22.   11.9]
```

Now let's load the data into a Pandas DataFrame:

```
df = pd.DataFrame(dataset.data, columns=dataset.feature_names)
df.head()
```

The DataFrame would look like the one shown in Figure 6.2.

	CRIM	ZN	INDUS	CHAS	NOX	RM	AGE	DIS	RAD	TAX	PTRATIO	B	LSTAT
0	0.00632	18.0	2.31	0.0	0.538	6.575	65.2	4.0900	1.0	296.0	15.3	396.90	4.98
1	0.02731	0.0	7.07	0.0	0.469	6.421	78.9	4.9671	2.0	242.0	17.8	396.90	9.14
2	0.02729	0.0	7.07	0.0	0.469	7.185	61.1	4.9671	2.0	242.0	17.8	392.83	4.03
3	0.03237	0.0	2.18	0.0	0.458	6.998	45.8	6.0622	3.0	222.0	18.7	394.63	2.94
4	0.06905	0.0	2.18	0.0	0.458	7.147	54.2	6.0622	3.0	222.0	18.7	396.90	5.33

Figure 6.2: The DataFrame containing all of the features

You would also want to add the prices of the houses to the DataFrame, so let's add a new column to the DataFrame and call it MEDV:

```
df['MEDV'] = dataset.target
df.head()
```

Figure 6.3 shows the complete DataFrame with the features and label.

	CRIM	ZN	INDUS	CHAS	NOX	RM	AGE	DIS	RAD	TAX	PTRATIO	B	LSTAT	MEDV
0	0.00632	18.0	2.31	0.0	0.538	6.575	65.2	4.0900	1.0	296.0	15.3	396.90	4.98	24.0
1	0.02731	0.0	7.07	0.0	0.469	6.421	78.9	4.9671	2.0	242.0	17.8	396.90	9.14	21.6
2	0.02729	0.0	7.07	0.0	0.469	7.185	61.1	4.9671	2.0	242.0	17.8	392.83	4.03	34.7
3	0.03237	0.0	2.18	0.0	0.458	6.998	45.8	6.0622	3.0	222.0	18.7	394.63	2.94	33.4
4	0.06905	0.0	2.18	0.0	0.458	7.147	54.2	6.0622	3.0	222.0	18.7	396.90	5.33	36.2

Figure 6.3: The DataFrame containing all of the features and the label

Data Cleansing

The next step would be to clean the data and perform any conversion if necessary. First, use the `info()` function to check the data type of each field:

```
df.info()
```

You should see the following:

```
<class 'pandas.core.frame.DataFrame'>
RangeIndex: 506 entries, 0 to 505
Data columns (total 14 columns):
CRIM       506 non-null float64
ZN         506 non-null float64
INDUS      506 non-null float64
CHAS       506 non-null float64
NOX        506 non-null float64
RM         506 non-null float64
AGE        506 non-null float64
DIS        506 non-null float64
RAD        506 non-null float64
TAX        506 non-null float64
PTRATIO    506 non-null float64
B          506 non-null float64
LSTAT      506 non-null float64
MEDV       506 non-null float64
dtypes: float64(14)
memory usage: 55.4 KB
```

As Scikit-learn only works with fields that are numeric, you need to encode string values into numeric values. Fortunately, the dataset contains all numerical values, and so no encoding is necessary.

Next, we need to check to see if there are any missing values. To do so, use the `isnull()` function:

```
print(df.isnull().sum())
```

Again, the dataset is good, as it does not have any missing values:

```
CRIM       0
ZN         0
INDUS      0
CHAS       0
NOX        0
RM         0
AGE        0
DIS        0
RAD        0
TAX        0
PTRATIO    0
B          0
```

```
LSTAT      0
MEDV       0
dtype: int64
```

Feature Selection

Now that the data is good to go, we are ready to move on to the next step of the process. As there are 13 features in the dataset, we do not want to use all of these features for training our model, because not all of them are relevant. Instead, we want to choose those features that directly influence the result (that is, prices of houses) to train the model. For this, we can use the corr() function. The corr() function computes the pairwise correlation of columns:

```
corr = df.corr()
print(corr)
```

You will see the following:

```
         CRIM        ZN     INDUS      CHAS       NOX        RM       AGE  \
CRIM     1.000000 -0.199458  0.404471 -0.055295  0.417521 -0.219940
0.350784
ZN      -0.199458  1.000000 -0.533828 -0.042697 -0.516604  0.311991
-0.569537
INDUS    0.404471 -0.533828  1.000000  0.062938  0.763651 -0.391676
0.644779
CHAS    -0.055295 -0.042697  0.062938  1.000000  0.091203  0.091251
0.086518
NOX      0.417521 -0.516604  0.763651  0.091203  1.000000 -0.302188
0.731470
RM      -0.219940  0.311991 -0.391676  0.091251 -0.302188  1.000000
-0.240265
AGE      0.350784 -0.569537  0.644779  0.086518  0.731470 -0.240265
1.000000
DIS     -0.377904  0.664408 -0.708027 -0.099176 -0.769230  0.205246
-0.747881
RAD      0.622029 -0.311948  0.595129 -0.007368  0.611441 -0.209847
0.456022
TAX      0.579564 -0.314563  0.720760 -0.035587  0.668023 -0.292048
0.506456
PTRATIO  0.288250 -0.391679  0.383248 -0.121515  0.188933 -0.355501
0.261515
B       -0.377365  0.175520 -0.356977  0.048788 -0.380051  0.128069
-0.273534
LSTAT    0.452220 -0.412995  0.603800 -0.053929  0.590879 -0.613808
0.602339
MEDV    -0.385832  0.360445 -0.483725  0.175260 -0.427321  0.695360
-0.376955
```

	DIS	RAD	TAX	PTRATIO	B	LSTAT	MEDV
CRIM	-0.377904	0.622029	0.579564	0.288250	-0.377365	0.452220	-0.385832
ZN	0.664408	-0.311948	-0.314563	-0.391679	0.175520	-0.412995	0.360445
INDUS	-0.708027	0.595129	0.720760	0.383248	-0.356977	0.603800	-0.483725
CHAS	-0.099176	-0.007368	-0.035587	-0.121515	0.048788	-0.053929	0.175260
NOX	-0.769230	0.611441	0.668023	0.188933	-0.380051	0.590879	-0.427321
RM	0.205246	-0.209847	-0.292048	-0.355501	0.128069	-0.613808	0.695360
AGE	-0.747881	0.456022	0.506456	0.261515	-0.273534	0.602339	-0.376955
DIS	1.000000	-0.494588	-0.534432	-0.232471	0.291512	-0.496996	0.249929
RAD	-0.494588	1.000000	0.910228	0.464741	-0.444413	0.488676	-0.381626
TAX	-0.534432	0.910228	1.000000	0.460853	-0.441808	0.543993	-0.468536
PTRATIO	-0.232471	0.464741	0.460853	1.000000	-0.177383	0.374044	-0.507787
B	0.291512	-0.444413	-0.441808	-0.177383	1.000000	-0.366087	0.333461
LSTAT	-0.496996	0.488676	0.543993	0.374044	-0.366087	1.000000	-0.737663
MEDV	0.249929	-0.381626	-0.468536	-0.507787	0.333461	-0.737663	1.000000

A *positive correlation* is a relationship between two variables in which both variables move in tandem. A positive correlation exists when one variable decreases as the other variable decreases, or one variable increases while the other variable increases. Similarly, a *negative correlation* is a relationship between two variables in which one variable increases as the other decreases. A perfect negative correlation is represented by the value –1.00: a 0.00 indicates no correlation and a +1.00 indicates a perfect positive correlation.

From the MEDV column in the output, you can see that the RM and LSTAT features have high correlation factors (positive and negative correlations) with the MEDV:

```
MEDV
CRIM    -0.385832
ZN       0.360445
INDUS   -0.483725
CHAS     0.175260
NOX     -0.427321
RM       0.695360
AGE     -0.376955
```

```
DIS       0.249929
RAD      -0.381626
TAX      -0.468536
PTRATIO  -0.507787
B         0.333461
LSTAT    -0.737663
MEDV      1.000000
```

This means that as LSTAT ("% of lower status of the population") increases, the prices of houses go down. When LSTAT decreases, the prices go up. Similarly, as RM ("average number of rooms per dwelling") increases, so will the price. And when RM goes down, the prices go down as well.

Instead of visually finding the top two features with the highest correlation factors, we can do it programmatically as follows:

```
#---get the top 3 features that has the highest correlation---
print(df.corr().abs().nlargest(3, 'MEDV').index)

#---print the top 3 correlation values---
print(df.corr().abs().nlargest(3, 'MEDV').values[:,13])
```

The result confirms our findings:

```
Index(['MEDV', 'LSTAT', 'RM'], dtype='object')
[ 1.          0.73766273  0.69535995]
```

> **TIP**   We will ignore the first result, as MEDV definitely has a perfect correlation with itself!

Since RM and LSTAT have high correlation values, we will use these two features to train our model.

Multiple Regression

In the previous chapter, you saw how to perform a simple linear regression using a single feature and a label. Often, you might want to train your model using more than one independent variable and a label. This is known as *multiple regression*. In multiple regression, two or more independent variables are used to predict the value of a dependent variable (label).

Now let's plot a scatter plot showing the relationship between the LSTAT feature and the MEDV label:

```
plt.scatter(df['LSTAT'], df['MEDV'], marker='o')
plt.xlabel('LSTAT')
plt.ylabel('MEDV')
```

Figure 6.4 shows the scatter plot. It appears that there is a linear correlation between the two.

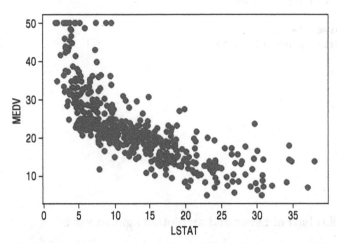

Figure 6.4: Scatter plot showing the relationship between LSTAT and MEDV

Let's also plot a scatter plot showing the relationship between the RM feature and the MEDV label:

```
plt.scatter(df['RM'], df['MEDV'], marker='o')
plt.xlabel('RM')
plt.ylabel('MEDV')
```

Figure 6.5 shows the scatter plot. Again, it appears that there is a linear correlation between the two, albeit with some outliers.

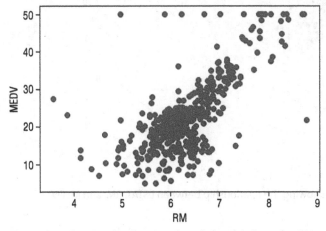

Figure 6.5: Scatter plot showing the relationship between RM and MEDV

Better still, let's plot the two features and the label on a 3D chart:

```
from mpl_toolkits.mplot3d import Axes3D

fig = plt.figure(figsize=(18,15))
ax = fig.add_subplot(111, projection='3d')

ax.scatter(df['LSTAT'],
           df['RM'],
           df['MEDV'],
           c='b')

ax.set_xlabel("LSTAT")
ax.set_ylabel("RM")
ax.set_zlabel("MEDV")
plt.show()
```

Figure 6.6 shows the 3D chart of LSTAT and RM plotted against MEDV.

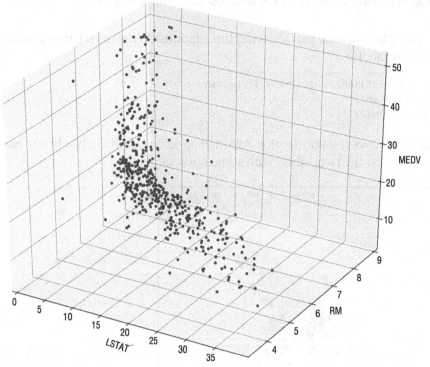

Figure 6.6: The 3D scatter plot showing the relationship between LSTAT, RM, and MEDV

Training the Model

We can now train the model. First, create two DataFrames: x and y. The x DataFrame will contain the combination of the LSTAT and RM features, while the y DataFrame will contain the MEDV label:

```
x = pd.DataFrame(np.c_[df['LSTAT'], df['RM']], columns = ['LSTAT','RM'])
Y = df['MEDV']
```

We will split the dataset into 70 percent for training and 30 percent for testing:

```
from sklearn.model_selection import train_test_split
x_train, x_test, Y_train, Y_test = train_test_split(x, Y, test_size = 0.3,
                                                    random_state=5)
```

> **TIP** Chapter 7, "Supervised Learning—Classification Using Logistic Regression," will discuss more about the train_test_split() function.

After the split, let's print out the shape of the training sets:

```
print(x_train.shape)
print(Y_train.shape)
```

You will see the following:

```
(354, 2)
(354,)
```

This means that the x training set now has 354 rows and 2 columns, while the y training set (which contains the label) has 354 rows and 1 column.
Let's also print out the testing set:

```
print(x_test.shape)
print(Y_test.shape)
```

This time, the testing set has 152 rows:

```
(152, 2)
(152,)
```

We are now ready to begin the training. As you learned from the previous chapter, you can use the LinearRegression class to perform linear regression. In this case, we will use it to train our model:

```
from sklearn.linear_model import LinearRegression

model = LinearRegression()
model.fit(x_train, Y_train)
```

Once the model is trained, we will use the testing set to perform some predictions:

```
price_pred = model.predict(x_test)
```

To learn how well our model performed, we use the R-Squared method that you learned in the previous chapter. The R-Squared method lets you know how close the test data fits the regression line. A value of 1.0 means a perfect fit. So, you aim for a value of R-Squared that is close to 1:

```
print('R-Squared: %.4f' % model.score(x_test,
                                       Y_test))
```

For our model, it returns an R-Squared value as follows:

```
R-Squared: 0.6162
```

We will also plot a scatter plot showing the actual price vs. the predicted price:

```
from sklearn.metrics import mean_squared_error

mse = mean_squared_error(Y_test, price_pred)
print(mse)

plt.scatter(Y_test, price_pred)
plt.xlabel("Actual Prices")
plt.ylabel("Predicted prices")
plt.title("Actual prices vs Predicted prices")
```

Figure 6.7 shows the plot. Ideally, it should be a straight line, but for now it is good enough.

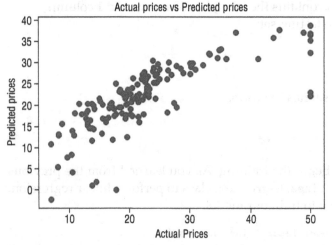

Figure 6.7: A scatter plot showing the predicted prices vs. the actual prices

Getting the Intercept and Coefficients

The formula for multiple regression is as follows:

$$Y = \beta_0 + \beta_1 x_1 + \beta_2 x_2$$

where Y is the dependent variable, β_0 is the intercept, and β_1 and β_2 are the coefficient of the two features x_1 and x_2, respectively.

With the model trained, we can obtain the intercept as well as the coefficients of the features:

```
print(model.intercept_)
print(model.coef_)
```

You should see the following:

```
0.3843793678034899
[-0.65957972  4.83197581]
```

We can use the model to make a prediction for the house price when LSTAT is 30 and RM is 5:

```
print(model.predict([[30,5]]))
```

You should see the following:

```
[4.75686695]
```

You can verify the predicted value by using the formula that was given earlier:

$$Y = \beta_0 + \beta_1 x_1 + \beta_2 x_2$$

$$Y = 0.3843793678034899 + 30(-0.65957972) + 5(4.83197581)$$

$$Y = 4.7568$$

Plotting the 3D Hyperplane

Let's plot a 3D regression hyperplane showing the predictions:

```
import matplotlib.pyplot as plt
import pandas as pd
import numpy as np
from mpl_toolkits.mplot3d import Axes3D

from sklearn.datasets import load_boston
dataset = load_boston()

df = pd.DataFrame(dataset.data, columns=dataset.feature_names)
df['MEDV'] = dataset.target
```

```
x = pd.DataFrame(np.c_[df['LSTAT'], df['RM']], columns = ['LSTAT','RM'])
Y = df['MEDV']

fig = plt.figure(figsize=(18,15))
ax = fig.add_subplot(111, projection='3d')

ax.scatter(x['LSTAT'],
           x['RM'],
           Y,
           c='b')

ax.set_xlabel("LSTAT")
ax.set_ylabel("RM")
ax.set_zlabel("MEDV")

#---create a meshgrid of all the values for LSTAT and RM---
x_surf = np.arange(0, 40, 1)    #---for LSTAT---
y_surf = np.arange(0, 10, 1)    #---for RM---
x_surf, y_surf = np.meshgrid(x_surf, y_surf)

from sklearn.linear_model import LinearRegression
model = LinearRegression()
model.fit(x, Y)

#---calculate z(MEDC) based on the model---
z = lambda x,y: (model.intercept_ + model.coef_[0] * x + model.coef_[1] * y)

ax.plot_surface(x_surf, y_surf, z(x_surf,y_surf),
                rstride=1,
                cstride=1,
                color='None',
                alpha = 0.4)

plt.show()
```

Here, we are training the model using the entire dataset. We then make predictions by passing a combination of values for LSTAT (x _ surf) and RM (y_surf) and calculating the predicted values using the model's intercept and coefficients. The hyperplane is then plotted using the plot_surface() function. The end result is shown in Figure 6.8.

As the chart shown in Jupyter Notebook is static, save the preceding code snippet in a file named boston.py and run it in Terminal, like this:

```
$ python boston.py
```

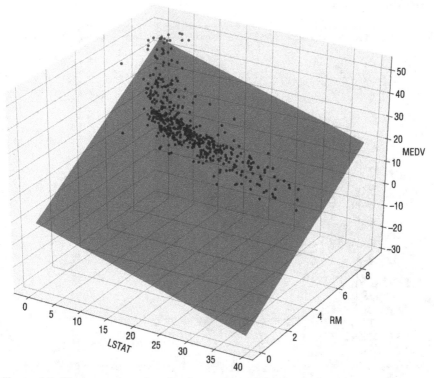

Figure 6.8: The hyperplane showing the predictions for the two features—LSTAT and RM

You will now be able to rotate the chart and move it around to have a better perspective, as shown in Figure 6.9.

Polynomial Regression

In the previous section, you saw how to apply linear regression to predict the prices of houses in the Boston area. While the result is somewhat acceptable, it is not very accurate. This is because sometimes a linear regression line might not be the best solution to capture the relationships between the features and label accurately. In some cases, a curved line might do better.

Consider the series of points shown in Figure 6.10.

The series of points are stored in a file named `polynomial.csv`:

```
x,y
1.5,1.5
2,2.5
3,4
4,4
5,4.5
6,5
```

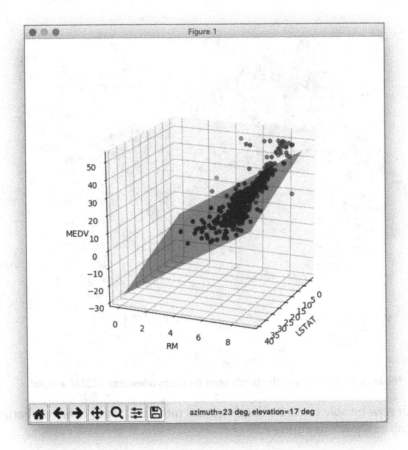

Figure 6.9: Rotating the chart to have a better view of the hyperplane

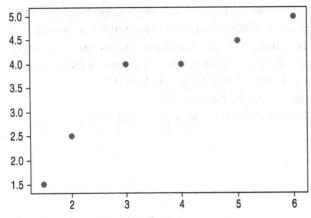

Figure 6.10: A scatter plot of points

And plotted using a scatter plot:

```
df = pd.read_csv('polynomial.csv')
plt.scatter(df.x,df.y)
```

Using linear regression, you can try to plot a straight line cutting through most of the points:

```
model = LinearRegression()

x = df.x[0:6, np.newaxis] #---convert to 2D array---
y = df.y[0:6, np.newaxis] #---convert to 2D array---

model.fit(x,y)

#---perform prediction---
y_pred = model.predict(x)

#---plot the training points---
plt.scatter(x, y, s=10, color='b')

#---plot the straight line---
plt.plot(x, y_pred, color='r')
plt.show()

#---calculate R-Squared---
print('R-Squared for training set: %.4f' % model.score(x,y))
```

You will see the straight regression line, as shown in Figure 6.11.

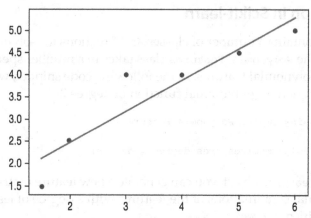

Figure 6.11: The regression line fitting the points

The R-Squared value for the training set is:

```
R-Squared for training set: 0.8658
```

We want to see if there is a more accurate way to fit the points. For instance, instead of a straight line, we want to investigate the possibility of a curved line. This is where *polynomial regression* comes in.

Formula for Polynomial Regression

Polynomial regression is an attempt to create a polynomial function that fits a set of data points.

A polynomial function of degree 1 has the following form:

$$Y = \beta_0 + \beta_1 x$$

This is the simple linear regression that we have seen in the previous chapter. *Quadratic regression* is a degree 2 polynomial:

$$Y = \beta_0 + \beta_1 x + \beta_2 x^2$$

For a polynomial of degree 3, the formula is as follows:

$$Y = \beta_0 + \beta_1 x + \beta_2 x^2 + \beta_3 x^3$$

In general, a polynomial of degree *n* has the formula of:

$$Y = \beta_0 + \beta_1 x + \beta_2 x^2 + \beta_3 x^3 + \ldots + \beta_n x^n$$

The idea behind polynomial regression is simple—find the coefficients of the polynomial function that best fits the data.

Polynomial Regression in Scikit-learn

The Scikit-learn library contains a number of classes and functions for solving polynomial regression. The `PolynomialFeatures` class takes in a number specifying the degree of the polynomial features. In the following code snippet, we are creating a quadratic equation (polynomial function of degree 2):

```
from sklearn.preprocessing import PolynomialFeatures
degree = 2
polynomial_features = PolynomialFeatures(degree = degree)
```

Using this `PolynomialFeatures` object, you can generate a new feature matrix consisting of all polynomial combinations of the features with a degree of less than or equal to the specified degree:

```
x_poly = polynomial_features.fit_transform(x)
print(x_poly)
```

You should see the following:

```
[[ 1.    1.5    2.25]
 [ 1.    2.     4.  ]
 [ 1.    3.     9.  ]
 [ 1.    4.    16.  ]
 [ 1.    5.    25.  ]
 [ 1.    6.    36.  ]]
```

The matrix that you see is generated as follows:

- The first column is always 1.
- The second column is the value of x.
- The third column is the value of x^2.

This can be verified using the `get_feature_names()` function:

```
print(polynomial_features.get_feature_names('x'))
```

It prints out the following:

```
['1', 'x', 'x^2']
```

> **TIP** The math behind finding the coefficients of a polynomial function is beyond the scope of this book. For those who are interested, however, check out the following link on the math behind polynomial regression: http://polynomialregression. drque.net/math.html.

You will now use this generated matrix with the `LinearRegression` class to train your model:

```
model = LinearRegression()
model.fit(x_poly, y)
y_poly_pred = model.predict(x_poly)

#---plot the points---
plt.scatter(x, y, s=10)

#---plot the regression line---
plt.plot(x, y_poly_pred)
plt.show()
```

Figure 6.12 now shows the regression line, a nice curve trying to fit the points. You can print out the intercept and coefficients of the polynomial function:

```
print(model.intercept_)
print(model.coef_)
```

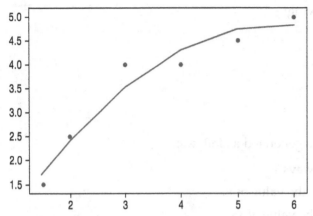

Figure 6.12: A curved line trying to fit the points

You should see the following:

```
[-0.87153912]
[[ 0.          1.98293207 -0.17239897]]
```

By plugging these numbers $Y = -0.87153912 + 1.98293207\,x + (-0.17239897)\,x^2$ into the formula $Y = \beta_0 + \beta_1 x + \beta_2 x^2$, you can make predictions using the preceding formula.

If you evaluate the regression by printing its R-Squared value,

```
print('R-Squared for training set: %.4f' % model.score(x_poly,y))
```

you should get a value of 0.9474:

```
R-Squared for training set: 0.9474
```

Can the R-Squared value be improved? Let's try a degree 3 polynomial. Using the same code and changing `degree` to 3, you should get the curve shown in Figure 6.13 and a value of 0.9889 for R-Squared.

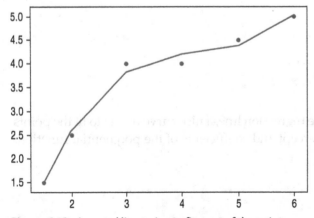

Figure 6.13: A curved line trying to fit most of the points

You now see a curve that more closely fits the points and a much-improved R-Squared value. Moreover, since raising the polynomial degree by 1 improves the R-Squared value, you might be tempted to increase it further. In fact, Figure 6.14 shows the curve when the `degree` is set to 4. It fits all the points perfectly.

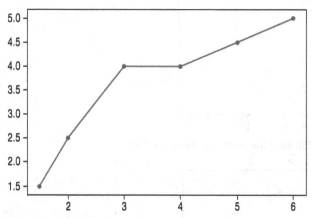

Figure 6.14: The line now fits the points perfectly

And guess what? You get an R-Squared value of 1! However, before you celebrate your success in finding the perfect algorithm in your prediction, you need to realize that while your algorithm may fit the training data perfectly, it is unlikely to perform well with new data. This is a known as *overfitting*, and the next section will discuss this topic in more detail.

Understanding Bias and Variance

The inability for a machine learning algorithm to capture the true relationship between the variables and the outcome is known as the *bias*. Figure 6.15 shows a straight line trying to fit all the points. Because it doesn't cut through all of the points, it has a high bias.

The curvy line in Figure 6.16, however, is able to fit all of the points and thus has a low bias.

While the straight line can't fit through all of the points and has high bias, when it comes to applying unseen observations, it gives a pretty good estimate. Figure 6.17 shows the testing points (in pink). The RSS (Residual Sum of Squares), which is the sum of the errors of prediction, is pretty low compared to that of the curvy line when using the same test points (see Figure 6.18).

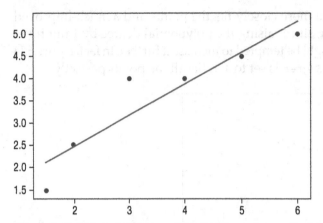

Figure 6.15: The straight line can't fit all of the points, so the bias is high

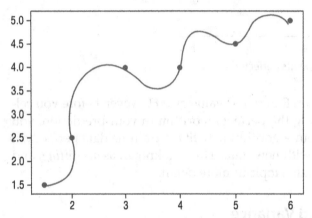

Figure 6.16: The curvy line fits all of the points, so the bias is low

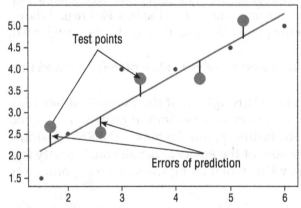

Figure 6.17: The straight line works well with unseen data, and its result does not vary much with different datasets. Hence, it has low variance.

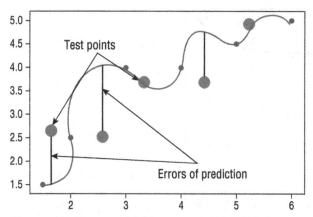

Figure 6.18: The curvy line does not work well with unseen data, and its result varies with different datasets. Hence, it has high variance.

In machine learning, the fit between the datasets is known as *variance*. In this example, the curvy line has *high variance* because it will result in vastly different RSS for different datasets. That is, you can't really predict how well it will perform with future datasets—sometimes it will do well with certain datasets and at other times it may fail badly. On the other hand, the straight line has a *low variance*, as the RSS is similar for different datasets.

> **TIP**   In machine learning, when we try to find a curve that tries to fit all of the points perfectly, it is known as *overfitting*. On the other hand, if we have a line that does not fit most points, it is known as *underfitting*.

Ideally, we should find a line that accurately expresses the relationships between the independent variables and that of the outcome. Expressed in terms of bias and variance, the ideal algorithm should have the following:

High bias, with the line hugging as many points as possible

Low variance, with the line resulting in consistent predictions using different datasets

Figure 6.19 shows such an ideal curve—high bias and low variance.

To strike a balance between finding a simple model and a complex model, you can use techniques such as *Regularization, Bagging,* and *Boosting*:

- *Regularization* is a technique that automatically penalizes the extra features you used in your modeling.

- *Bagging* (or *bootstrap aggregation*) is a specific type of machine learning process that uses *ensemble learning* to evolve machine learning models. Bagging uses a subset of the data and each sample trains a weaker learner. The weak learners can then be combined (through averaging or max vote) to create a strong learner that can make accurate predictions.

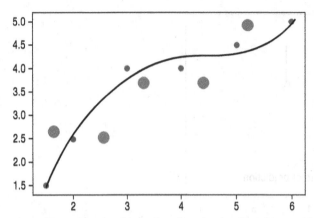

Figure 6.19: You should aim for a line that has high bias and low variance

- *Boosting* is also similar to Bagging, except that it uses all of the data to train each learner, but data points that were misclassified by previous learners are given more weight so that subsequent learners will give more focus to them during training.

> **TIP** *Ensemble learning* is a technique where you use several models working together on a single dataset and then combine its result.

Using Polynomial Multiple Regression on the Boston Dataset

Earlier in this chapter, you used multiple linear regression and trained a model based on the Boston dataset. After learning about the polynomial regression in the previous section, now let's try to apply it to the Boston dataset and see if we can improve the model.

As usual, let's load the data and split the dataset into training and testing sets:

```
import matplotlib.pyplot as plt
import pandas as pd
import numpy as np

from sklearn.preprocessing import PolynomialFeatures
from sklearn.linear_model import LinearRegression
from sklearn.datasets import load_boston

dataset = load_boston()

df = pd.DataFrame(dataset.data, columns=dataset.feature_names)
df['MEDV'] = dataset.target

x = pd.DataFrame(np.c_[df['LSTAT'], df['RM']], columns = ['LSTAT','RM'])
Y = df['MEDV']
```

```
from sklearn.model_selection import train_test_split
x_train, x_test, Y_train, Y_test = train_test_split(x, Y, test_size = 0.3,
                                                random_state=5)
```

You then use the polynomial function with degree 2:

```
#---use a polynomial function of degree 2---
degree = 2
polynomial_features= PolynomialFeatures(degree = degree)
x_train_poly = polynomial_features.fit_transform(x_train)
```

When using a polynomial function of degree 2 on two independent variables x_1 and x_2, the formula becomes:

$$Y = \beta_0 + \beta_1 x_1 + \beta_2 x_2 + \beta_3 x_1^2 + \beta_4 x_1 x_2 + \beta_5 x_2^2$$

where Y is the dependent variable, β_0 is the intercept, and β_1, β_2, β_3, and β_4 are the coefficients of the various combinations of the two features x_1 and x_2, respectively. You can verify this by printing out the feature names:

```
#---print out the formula---
print(polynomial_features.get_feature_names(['x','y']))
```

You should see the following, which coincides with the formula:

```
# ['1', 'x', 'y', 'x^2', 'x y', 'y^2']
```

TIP   Knowing the polynomial function formula is useful when plotting the 3D hyperplane, which you will do shortly.

You can then train your model using the `LinearRegression` class:

```
model = LinearRegression()
model.fit(x_train_poly, Y_train)
```

Now let's evaluate the model using the testing set:

```
x_test_poly = polynomial_features.fit_transform(x_test)
print('R-Squared: %.4f' % model.score(x_test_poly,
                                        Y_test))
```

You will see the result as follows:

```
R-Squared: 0.7340
```

You can also print the intercept and coefficients:

```
print(model.intercept_)
print(model.coef_)
```

You should see the following:

```
26.9334305238
[   0.00000000e+00    1.47424550e+00   -6.70204730e+00    7.93570743e-04
   -3.66578385e-01    1.17188007e+00]
```

With these values, the formula now becomes:

$$Y = \beta_0 + \beta_1 x_1 + \beta_2 x_2 + \beta_3 x_1^2 + \beta_4 x_1 x_2 + \beta_5 x_2^2$$

$$Y = 26.9334305238 + 1.47424550e + 00\, x_1 + (-6.70204730e + 00)\, x_2 + 7.93570743e$$
$$-04\, x_1^2 + (-3.66578385e - 01)\, x_1 x_2 + 1.17188007e + 00\, x_2^2$$

Plotting the 3D Hyperplane

Since you know the intercept and coefficients of the polynomial multiple regression function, you can plot out the 3D hyperplane of function easily. Save the following code snippet as a file named `boston2.py`:

```python
import matplotlib.pyplot as plt
import pandas as pd
import numpy as np

from mpl_toolkits.mplot3d import Axes3D
from sklearn.preprocessing import PolynomialFeatures
from sklearn.linear_model import LinearRegression
from sklearn.datasets import load_boston

dataset = load_boston()

df = pd.DataFrame(dataset.data, columns=dataset.feature_names)
df['MEDV'] = dataset.target

x = pd.DataFrame(np.c_[df['LSTAT'], df['RM']], columns = ['LSTAT','RM'])
Y = df['MEDV']

fig = plt.figure(figsize=(18,15))
ax = fig.add_subplot(111, projection='3d')

ax.scatter(x['LSTAT'],
           x['RM'],
           Y,
           c='b')
```

```
ax.set_xlabel("LSTAT")
ax.set_ylabel("RM")
ax.set_zlabel("MEDV")

#---create a meshgrid of all the values for LSTAT and RM---
x_surf = np.arange(0, 40, 1)    #---for LSTAT---
y_surf = np.arange(0, 10, 1)    #---for RM---
x_surf, y_surf = np.meshgrid(x_surf, y_surf)

#---use a polynomial function of degree 2---
degree = 2
polynomial_features= PolynomialFeatures(degree = degree)
x_poly = polynomial_features.fit_transform(x)
print(polynomial_features.get_feature_names(['x','y']))

#---apply linear regression---
model = LinearRegression()
model.fit(x_poly, Y)

#---calculate z (MEDC) based on the model---
z = lambda x,y: (model.intercept_ +
                (model.coef_[1] * x) +
                (model.coef_[2] * y) +
                (model.coef_[3] * x**2) +
                (model.coef_[4] * x*y) +
                (model.coef_[5] * y**2))

ax.plot_surface(x_surf, y_surf, z(x_surf,y_surf),
                rstride=1,
                cstride=1,
                color='None',
                alpha = 0.4)

plt.show()
```

To run the code, type the following in Terminal:

```
$ python boston2.py
```

You will see the 3D chart, as shown in Figure 6.20.

You can drag to rotate the chart. Figure 6.21 shows the different perspectives of the hyperplane.

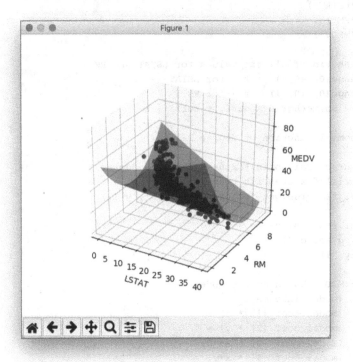

Figure 6.20: The hyperplane in the polynomial multiple regression

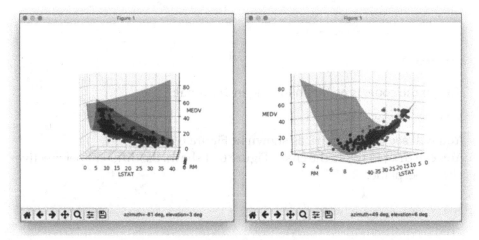

Figure 6.21: Rotate the chart to see the different perspectives of the hyperplane

Summary

In this chapter, you learned about the various types of linear regression. In particular, you learned about the following:

Multiple Regression   Linear relationships between two or more independent variables and one dependent variable.

Polynomial Regression   Modeling the relationship between one independent variable and one dependent variable using an nth degree polynomial function.

Polynomial Multiple Regression   Modeling the relationship between two or more independent variables and one dependent variable using an nth degree polynomial function.

You also learned how to plot the hyperplane showing the relationships between two independent variables and the label.

7

Supervised Learning— Classification Using Logistic Regression

What Is Logistic Regression?

In the previous chapter, you learned about linear regression and how you can use it to predict future values. In this chapter, you will learn another supervised machine learning algorithm—*logistic regression*. Unlike linear regression, logistic regression does not try to predict the value of a numeric variable given a set of inputs. Instead, the output of logistic regression is the probability of a given input point belonging to a specific class. The output of logistic regression always lies in [0,1].

To understand the use of logistic regression, consider the example shown in Figure 7.1. Suppose that you have a dataset containing information about voter income and voting preferences. For this dataset, you can see that low-income voters tend to vote for candidate B, while high-income voters tend to favor candidate A.

With this dataset, you would be very interested in trying to predict which candidate future voters will vote for based on their income level. At first glance, you might be tempted to apply what you have just learned to this problem; that is, using linear regression. Figure 7.2 shows what it looks like when you apply linear regression to this problem.

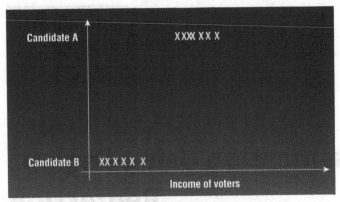

Figure 7.1: Some problems have binary outcomes

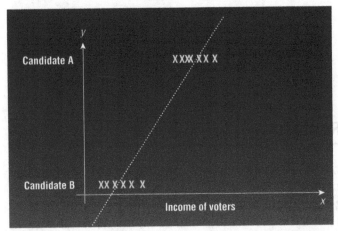

Figure 7.2: Using linear regression to solve the voting preferences problem leads to strange values

The main problem with linear regression is that the predicted value does not always fall within the expected range. Consider the case of a very low-income voter (near to 0), and you can see from the chart that the predicted result is a negative value. What you really want is a way to return the prediction as a value from 0 to 1, where this value represents the probability of an event happening.

Figure 7.3 shows how logistic regression solves this problem. Instead of drawing a straight line cutting through the points, you now use a curved line to try to fit all of the points on the chart.

Using logistic regression, the output will be a value from 0 to 1, where anything less than (or equal to) 0.5 (known as the *threshold*) will be considered as voting for candidate B, and anything greater than 0.5 will be considered as voting for candidate A.

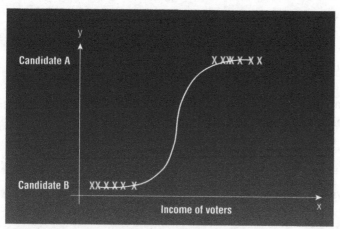

Figure 7.3: Logistic regression predicts the probability of an outcome, rather than a specific value

Understanding Odds

Before we discuss the details of the logistic regression algorithm, we first need to discuss one important term—*odds*. Odds are defined as the ratio of the probability of success to the probability of failure (see Figure 7.4).

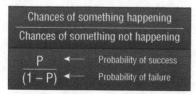

Figure 7.4: How to calculate the odds of an event happening

For example, the odds of landing a head when you flip a coin are 1. This is because you have a 0.5 probability of landing a head and a 0.5 probability of landing a tail. When you say that the odds of landing a head are 1, this means you have a 50 percent chance of landing a head.

But if the coin is rigged in such a way that the probability of landing a head is 0.8 and the probability of landing a tail is 0.2, then the odds of landing a head is 0.8/0.2 = 4. That is, you are 4 times more likely to land a head than a tail. Likewise, the odds of getting a tail are 0.2/0.8 = 0.25.

Logit Function

When you apply the natural logarithm function to the odds, you get the *logit function*. The logit function is the logarithm of the odds (see Figure 7.5).

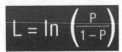

Figure 7.5: The formula for the logit function

The logit function transfers a variable on (0, 1) into a new variable on (−∞, ∞). To see this relationship, you can use the following code snippet:

```
%matplotlib inline
import pandas as pd
import numpy as np
import matplotlib.pyplot as plt

def logit(x):
    return np.log( x / (1 - x) )

x = np.arange(0.001,0.999, 0.0001)
y = [logit(n) for n in x]
plt.plot(x,y)
plt.xlabel("Probability")
plt.ylabel("Logit - L")
```

Figure 7.6 shows the logit curve plotted using the preceding code snippet.

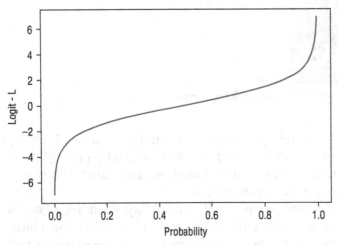

Figure 7.6: The logit curve

Sigmoid Curve

For the logit curve, observe that the x-axis is the probability and the y-axis is the real-number range. For logistic regression, what you really want is a function that maps numbers on the real-number system to the probabilities, which is exactly what you get when you flip the axes of the logit curve (see Figure 7.7).

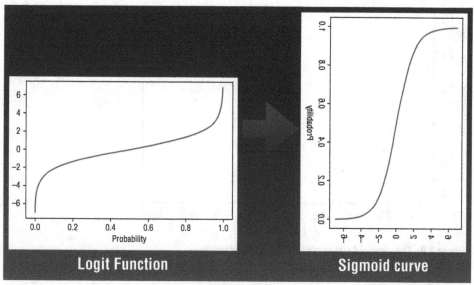

Figure 7.7: Flipping the logit curve into a Sigmoid curve

When you flip the axes, the curve that you get is called the *sigmoid curve*. The sigmoid curve is obtained using the *Sigmoid function*, which is the inverse of the logit function. The Sigmoid function is used to transform values on (−∞, ∞) into numbers on (0, 1). The Sigmoid function is shown in Figure 7.8.

$$P = \frac{1}{(1 + e^{-(L)})}$$

Figure 7.8: The formula for the Sigmoid function

The following code snippet shows how the sigmoid curve is obtained:

```
def sigmoid(x):
    return (1 / (1 + np.exp(-x)))

x = np.arange(-10, 10, 0.0001)
y = [sigmoid(n) for n in x]
plt.plot(x,y)
plt.xlabel("Logit - L")
plt.ylabel("Probability")
```

Figure 7.9 shows the sigmoid curve.

Just like you try to plot a straight line that fits through all of the points in linear regression (as explain in Chapter 5), in logistics regression, we would also like to plot a sigmoid curve that fits through all of the points. Mathematically, this can be expressed by the formula shown in Figure 7.10.

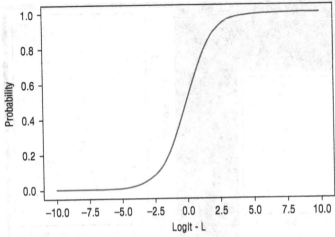

Figure 7.9: The sigmoid curve plotted using matplotlib

$$P = \frac{1}{\left(1 + e^{-(\beta_0 + x\beta)}\right)}$$

Figure 7.10: Expressing the sigmoid function using the intercept and coefficient

Notice that the key difference between the formula shown in Figure 7.8 and 7.10 is that now L has been replaced by β_0 and $x\beta$. The coefficients β_0 and β are unknown, and they must be estimated based on the available training data using a technique known as *Maximum Likelihood Estimation (MLE)*. In logistics regression, β_0 is known as the intercept and $x\beta$ is known as the coefficient.

Using the Breast Cancer Wisconsin (Diagnostic) Data Set

Scikit-learn ships with the Breast Cancer Wisconsin (Diagnostic) Data Set. It is a classic dataset that is often used to illustrate binary classifications. This dataset contains 30 features, and they are computed from a digitized image of a fine needle aspirate (FNA) of a breast mass. The label of the dataset is a binary classification—M for malignant or B for benign. Interested readers can check out more information at `https://archive.ics.uci.edu/ml/datasets/Breast+Cancer+Wisconsin+(Diagnostic)`.

Examining the Relationship Between Features

You can load the Breast Cancer dataset by first importing the `datasets` module from `sklearn`. Then use the `load_breast_cancer()` function as follows:

```
from sklearn.datasets import load_breast_cancer
cancer = load_breast_cancer()
```

Now that the Breast Cancer dataset has been loaded, it is useful to examine the relationships between some of its features.

Plotting the Features in 2D

For a start, let's plot the first two features of the dataset in 2D and examine their relationships. The following code snippet:

- Loads the Breast Cancer dataset
- Copies the first two features of the dataset into a two-dimensional list
- Plots a scatter plot showing the distribution of points for the two features
- Displays malignant growths in red and benign growths in blue

```
%matplotlib inline

import matplotlib.pyplot as plt
from sklearn.datasets import load_breast_cancer

cancer = load_breast_cancer()

#---copy from dataset into a 2-d list---
X = []
for target in range(2):
    X.append([[], []])
    for i in range(len(cancer.data)):            # target is 0 or 1
        if cancer.target[i] == target:
            X[target][0].append(cancer.data[i][0]) # first feature -
mean radius
            X[target][1].append(cancer.data[i][1]) # second feature -
mean texture

colours = ("r", "b")   # r: malignant, b: benign
fig = plt.figure(figsize=(10,8))
ax = fig.add_subplot(111)
for target in range(2):
    ax.scatter(X[target][0],
               X[target][1],
               c=colours[target])

ax.set_xlabel("mean radius")
ax.set_ylabel("mean texture")
plt.show()
```

Figure 7.11 shows the scatter plot of the points.

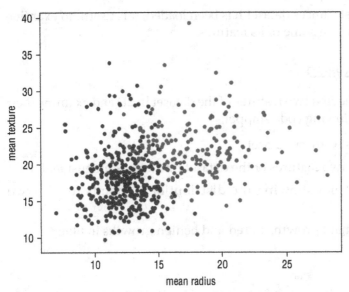

Figure 7.11: The scatter plot showing the relationships between the mean radius and mean texture of the tumor

From this scatter plot, you can gather that as the tumor grows in radius and increases in texture, the more likely that it would be diagnosed as malignant.

Plotting in 3D

In the previous section, you plotted the points based on two features using a scatter plot. It would be interesting to be able to visualize more than two features. In this case, let's try to visualize the relationships between three features. You can use matplotlib to plot a 3D plot. The following code snippet shows how this is done. It is very similar to the code snippet in the previous section, with the additional statements in bold:

```
%matplotlib inline

import matplotlib.pyplot as plt
from mpl_toolkits.mplot3d import Axes3D
from sklearn.datasets import load_breast_cancer

cancer = load_breast_cancer()

#---copy from dataset into a 2-d array---
X = []
for target in range(2):
    X.append([[], [], []])
    for i in range(len(cancer.data)):     # target is 0,1
        if cancer.target[i] == target:
```

```
                X[target][0].append(cancer.data[i][0])
                X[target][1].append(cancer.data[i][1])
                X[target][2].append(cancer.data[i][2])

colours = ("r", "b")    # r: malignant, b: benign
fig = plt.figure(figsize=(18,15))
ax = fig.add_subplot(111, projection='3d')
for target in range(2):
    ax.scatter(X[target][0],
               X[target][1],
               X[target][2],
               c=colours[target])

ax.set_xlabel("mean radius")
ax.set_ylabel("mean texture")
ax.set_zlabel("mean perimeter")
plt.show()
```

Instead of plotting using two features, you now have a third feature: mean perimeter. Figure 7.12 shows the 3D plot.

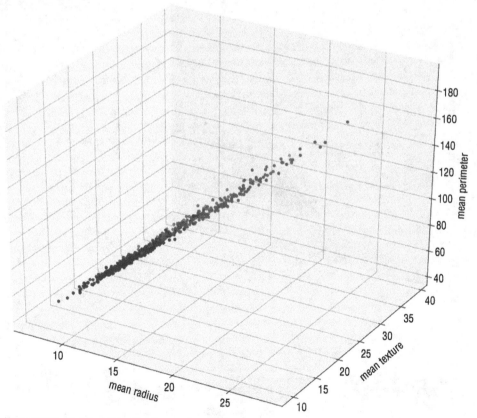

Figure 7.12: Plotting three features using a 3D map

Jupyter Notebook displays the 3D plot statically. As you can see from Figure 7.12, you can't really have a good look at the relationships between the three features. A much better way to display the 3D plot would be to run the preceding code snippet outside of Jupyter Notebook. To do so, save the code snippet (minus the first line containing the statement "`%matplotlib inline`") to a file named, say, `3dplot.py`. Then run the file in Terminal using the `python` command, as follows:

```
$ python 3dplot.py
```

Once you do that, matplotlib will open a separate window to display the 3D plot. Best of all, you will be able to interact with it. Use your mouse to drag the plot, and you are able to visualize the relationships better between the three features. Figure 7.13 gives you a better perspective: as the mean perimeter of the tumor growth increases, the chance of the growth being malignant also increases.

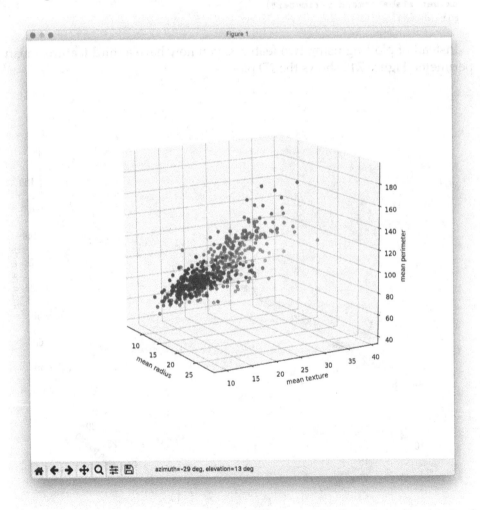

Figure 7.13: You can interact with the 3D plot when you run the application outside of Jupyter Notebook

Training Using One Feature

Let's now use logistic regression to try to predict if a tumor is cancerous. To get started, let's use only the first feature of the dataset: mean radius. The following code snippet plots a scatter plot showing if a tumor is malignant or benign based on the mean radius:

```
%matplotlib inline
import pandas as pd
import matplotlib.pyplot as plt
import matplotlib.patches as mpatches

from sklearn.datasets import load_breast_cancer

cancer = load_breast_cancer()    # Load dataset
x = cancer.data[:,0]             # mean radius
y = cancer.target               # 0: malignant, 1: benign
colors = {0:'red', 1:'blue'}    # 0: malignant, 1: benign

plt.scatter(x,y,
            facecolors='none',
            edgecolors=pd.DataFrame(cancer.target)[0].apply(lambda x:
colors[x]),
            cmap=colors)

plt.xlabel("mean radius")
plt.ylabel("Result")

red   = mpatches.Patch(color='red',  label='malignant')
blue  = mpatches.Patch(color='blue', label='benign')

plt.legend(handles=[red, blue], loc=1)
```

Figure 7.14 shows the scatter plot.

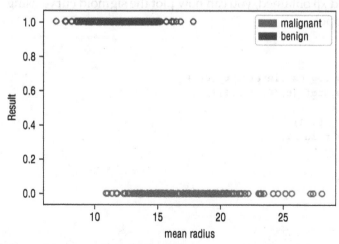

Figure 7.14: Plotting a scatter plot based on one feature

As you can see, this is a good opportunity to use logistic regression to predict if a tumor is cancerous. You could try to plot an "s" curve (albeit flipped horizontally).

Finding the Intercept and Coefficient

Scikit-learn comes with the `LogisticRegression` class that allows you to apply logistic regression to train a model. Thus, in this example, you are going to train a model using the first feature of the dataset:

```
from sklearn import linear_model
import numpy as np

log_regress = linear_model.LogisticRegression()

#---train the model---
log_regress.fit(X = np.array(x).reshape(len(x),1),
                y = y)

#---print trained model intercept---
print(log_regress.intercept_)       # [ 8.19393897]

#---print trained model coefficients---
print(log_regress.coef_)            # [[-0.54291739]]
```

Once the model is trained, what we are most interested in at this point is the intercept and coefficient. If you recall from the formula in Figure 7.10, the intercept is β_0 and the coefficient is $x\beta$. Knowing these two values allows us to plot the sigmoid curve that tries to fit the points on the chart.

Plotting the Sigmoid Curve

With the values of β_0 and $x\beta$ obtained, you can now plot the sigmoid curve using the following code snippet:

```
def sigmoid(x):
    return (1 / (1 +
        np.exp(-(log_regress.intercept_[0] +
        (log_regress.coef_[0][0] * x)))))

x1 = np.arange(0, 30, 0.01)
y1 = [sigmoid(n) for n in x1]

plt.scatter(x,y,
    facecolors='none',
```

```
    edgecolors=pd.DataFrame(cancer.target)[0].apply(lambda x:
colors[x]),
    cmap=colors)

plt.plot(x1,y1)
plt.xlabel("mean radius")
plt.ylabel("Probability")
```

Figure 7.15 shows the sigmoid curve.

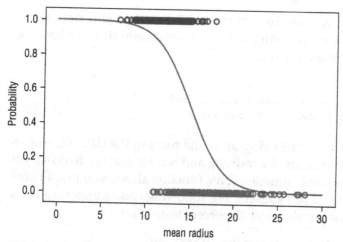

Figure 7.15: The sigmoid curve fitting to the two sets of points

Making Predictions

Using the trained model, let's try to make some predictions. Let's try to predict the result if the mean radius is 20:

```
print(log_regress.predict_proba(20))  # [[0.93489354 0.06510646]]
print(log_regress.predict(20)[0])      # 0
```

As you can see from the output, the `predict_proba()` function in the first statement returns a two-dimensional array. The result of 0.93489354 indicates the probability that the prediction is 0 (malignant) while the result of 0.06510646 indicates the probability that the prediction is 1. Based on the default *threshold* of 0.5, the prediction is that the tumor is malignant (value of 0), since its predicted probability (0.93489354) of 0 is more than 0.5.

The `predict()` function in the second statement returns the class that the result lies in (which in this case can be a 0 or 1). The result of 0 indicates that the prediction is that the tumor is malignant. Try another example with the mean radius of 8 this time:

```
print(log_regress.predict_proba(8))    # [[0.02082411 0.97917589]]
print(log_regress.predict(8)[0])        # 1
```

As you can see from the result, the prediction is that the tumor is benign.

Training the Model Using All Features

In the previous section, you specifically trained the model using one feature. Let's now try to train the model using all of the features and then see how well it can accurately perform the prediction.

First, load the dataset:

```
from sklearn.datasets import load_breast_cancer
cancer = load_breast_cancer()    # Load dataset
```

Instead of training the model using all of the rows in the dataset, you are going to split it into two sets, one for training and one for testing. To do so, you use the `train_test_split()` function. This function allows you to split your data into random train and test subsets. The following code snippet splits the dataset into a 75 percent training and 25 percent testing set:

```
from sklearn.model_selection import train_test_split
train_set, test_set, train_labels, test_labels = train_test_split(
                          cancer.data,              # features
                          cancer.target,            # labels
                          test_size = 0.25,         # split ratio
                          random_state = 1,         # set random
seed
                          stratify = cancer.target)  # randomize
based on labels
```

Figure 7.16 shows how the dataset is split. The `random_state` parameter of the `train_test_split()` function specifies the seed used by the random number generator. If this is not specified, every time you run this function you will get a different training and testing set. The `stratify` parameter allows you to specify which column (feature/label) to use so that the split is proportionate. For example, if the column specified is a categorical variable with 80 percent 0s and 20 percent 1s, then the training and test sets would each have 80 percent of 0s and 20 percent of 1s.

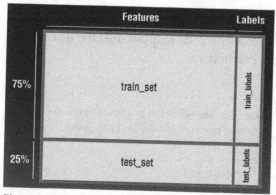

Figure 7.16: Splitting the dataset into training and test sets

Once the dataset is split, it is now time to train the model. The following code snippet trains the model using logistic regression:

```
from sklearn import linear_model
x = train_set[:,0:30]            # mean radius
y = train_labels                 # 0: malignant, 1: benign
log_regress = linear_model.LogisticRegression()
log_regress.fit(X = x,
                y = y)
```

In this example, we are training it with all of the 30 features in the dataset. When the training is done, let's print out the intercept and model coefficients:

```
print(log_regress.intercept_)     #
print(log_regress.coef_)          #
```

The following output shows the intercept and coefficients:

```
[0.34525124]
[[ 1.80079054e+00  2.55566824e-01 -3.75898452e-02 -5.88407941e-03
  -9.57624689e-02 -3.16671611e-01 -5.06608094e-01 -2.53148889e-01
  -2.26083101e-01 -1.03685977e-02  4.10103139e-03  9.75976632e-01
   2.02769521e-01 -1.22268760e-01 -8.25384020e-03 -1.41322029e-02
  -5.49980366e-02 -3.32935262e-02 -3.05606774e-02  1.09660157e-04
   1.62895414e+00 -4.34854352e-01 -1.50305237e-01 -2.32871932e-02
  -1.94311394e-01 -9.91201314e-01 -1.42852648e+00 -5.40594994e-01
  -6.28475690e-01 -9.04653541e-02]]
```

Because we have trained the model using 30 features, there are 30 coefficients.

Testing the Model

It's time to make a prediction. The following code snippet uses the test set and feeds it into the model to obtain the predictions:

```python
import pandas as pd

#---get the predicted probablities and convert into a dataframe---
preds_prob = pd.DataFrame(log_regress.predict_proba(X=test_set))

#---assign column names to prediction---
preds_prob.columns = ["Malignant", "Benign"]

#---get the predicted class labels---
preds = log_regress.predict(X=test_set)
preds_class = pd.DataFrame(preds)
preds_class.columns = ["Prediction"]

#---actual diagnosis---
original_result = pd.DataFrame(test_labels)
original_result.columns = ["Original Result"]

#---merge the three dataframes into one---
result = pd.concat([preds_prob, preds_class, original_result], axis=1)
print(result.head())
```

The results of the predictions are then printed out. The predictions and original diagnosis are displayed side-by-side for easy comparison:

	Malignant	Benign	Prediction	Original Result
0	0.999812	1.883317e-04	0	0
1	0.998356	1.643777e-03	0	0
2	0.057992	9.420079e-01	1	1
3	1.000000	9.695339e-08	0	0
4	0.207227	7.927725e-01	1	0

Getting the Confusion Matrix

While it is useful to print out the predictions together with the original diagnosis from the test set, it does not give you a clear picture of how good the model is in predicting if a tumor is cancerous. A more scientific way would be to use the *confusion matrix*. The confusion matrix shows the number of actual and predicted labels and how many of them are classified correctly. You can use Pandas's crosstab() function to print out the confusion matrix:

```python
#---generate table of predictions vs actual---
print("---Confusion Matrix---")
print(pd.crosstab(preds, test_labels))
```

The `crosstab()` function computes a simple cross-tabulation of two factors. The preceding code snippet prints out the following:

```
---Confusion Matrix---
col_0   0   1
row_0
0      48   3
1       5  87
```

The output is interpreted as shown in Figure 7.17.

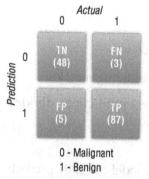

Figure 7.17: The confusion matrix for the prediction

The columns represent the actual diagnosis (0 for malignant and 1 for benign). The rows represent the prediction. Each individual box represents one of the following:

■ *True Positive (TP)*: The model correctly predicts the outcome as positive. In this example, the number of TP (87) indicates the number of correct predictions that a tumor is benign.

■ *True Negative (TN)*: The model correctly predicts the outcome as negative. In this example, tumors were correctly predicted to be malignant.

■ *False Positive (FP)*: The model incorrectly predicted the outcome as positive, but the actual result is negative. In this example, it means that the tumor is actually malignant, but the model predicted the tumor to be benign.

■ *False Negative (FN)*: The model incorrectly predicted the outcome as negative, but the actual result is positive. In this example, it means that the tumor is actually benign, but the model predicted the tumor to be malignant.

This set of numbers is known as the *confusion matrix*.

Besides using the `crosstab()` function, you can also use the `confusion_matrix()` function to print out the confusion matrix:

```
from sklearn import metrics
#---view the confusion matrix---
print(metrics.confusion_matrix(y_true = test_labels,   # True labels
                               y_pred = preds))         # Predicted labels
```

Note that the output is switched for the rows and columns.

```
[[48  5]
 [ 3 87]]
```

Computing Accuracy, Recall, Precision, and Other Metrics

Based on the confusion matrix, you can calculate the following metrics:

- *Accuracy*: This is defined as the sum of all correct predictions divided by the total number of predictions, or mathematically:

$$(TP / TN) / (TP + TN + FP + FN)$$

- This metric is easy to understand. After all, if the model correctly predicts 99 out of 100 samples, the accuracy is 0.99, which would be very impressive in the real world. But consider the following situation: Imagine that you're trying to predict the failure of equipment based on the sample data. Out of 1,000 samples, only three are defective. If you use a dumb algorithm that always returns negative (meaning no failure) for all results, then the accuracy is 997/1000, which is 0.997. This is very impressive, but does this mean it's a good algorithm? No. If there are 500 defective items in the dataset of 1,000 items, then the accuracy metric immediately indicates the flaw of the algorithm. In short, accuracy works best with evenly distributed data points, but it works really badly for a skewed dataset. Figure 7.18 summarizes the formula for accuracy.

- *Precision*: This metric is defined to be TP / (TP + FP). This metric is concerned with number of correct positive predictions. You can think of precision as "of those predicted to be positive, how many were actually predicted correctly?" Figure 7.19 summarizes the formula for precision.

- *Recall* (also known as *True Positive Rate (TPR)*): This metric is defined to be TP / (TP + FN). This metric is concerned with the number of correctly predicted positive events. You can think of recall as "of those positive events, how many were predicted correctly?" Figure 7.20 summarizes the formula for recall.

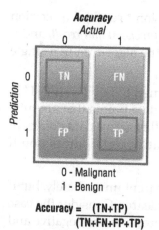

Figure 7.18: Formula for calculating accuracy

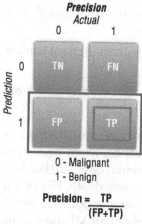

Figure 7.19: Formula for calculating precision

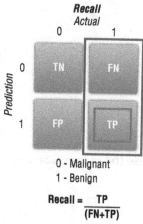

Figure 7.20: Formula for calculating recall

- *F1 Score:* This metric is defined to be 2 * (precision * recall) / (precision + recall). This is known as the *harmonic mean of precision and recall,* and it is a good way to summarize the evaluation of the algorithm in a single number.

- *False Positive Rate (FPR):* This metric is defined to be FP / (FP+TN). FPR corresponds to the proportion of negative data points that are mistakenly considered as positive, with respect to all negative data points. In other words, the higher FPR, the more negative data points you'll misclassify.

The concept of precision and recall may not be apparent immediately, but if you consider the following scenario, it will be much clearer. Consider the case of breast cancer diagnosis. If a malignant tumor is represented as negative and a benign tumor is represented as positive, then:

- If the precision or recall is high, it means that more patients with benign tumors are diagnosed correctly, which indicates that the algorithm is good.

- If the precision is low, it means that more patients with malignant tumors are diagnosed as benign.

- If the recall is low, it means that more patients with benign tumors are diagnosed as malignant.

For the last two points, having a low precision is more serious than a low recall (although wrongfully diagnosed as having breast cancer when you do not have it will likely result in unnecessary treatment and mental anguish) because it causes the patient to miss treatment and potentially causes death. Hence, for cases like diagnosing breast cancer, it's important to consider both the precision and recall metrics when evaluating the effectiveness of an ML algorithm.

To get the accuracy of the model, you can use the `score()` function of the model:

```
#---get the accuracy of the prediction---
print("---Accuracy---")
print(log_regress.score(X = test_set ,
                        y = test_labels))
```

You should see the following result:

```
---Accuracy---
0.9440559440559441
```

To get the precision, recall, and F1-score of the model, use the `classification_report()` function of the `metrics` module:

```
# View summary of common classification metrics
print("---Metrices---")
```

```
print(metrics.classification_report(
    y_true = test_labels,
    y_pred = preds))
```

You will see the following results:

```
---Metrices---
              precision    recall  f1-score   support

           0       0.94      0.91      0.92        53
           1       0.95      0.97      0.96        90

avg / total       0.94      0.94      0.94       143
```

Receiver Operating Characteristic (ROC) Curve

With so many metrics available, what is an easy way to examine the effectiveness of an algorithm? One way would be to plot a curve known as the *Receiver Operating Characteristic (ROC) curve*. The ROC curve is created by plotting the TPR against the FPR at various threshold settings.

So how does it work? Let's run through a simple example. Using the existing project that you have been working on, you have derived the confusion matrix based on the default threshold of 0.5 (meaning that all of those predicted probabilities less than or equal to 0.5 belong to one class, while those greater than 0.5 belong to another class). Using this confusion matrix, you then find the recall, precision, and subsequently FPR and TPR. Once the FPR and TPR are found, you can plot the point on the chart, as shown in Figure 7.21.

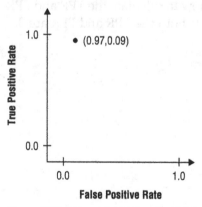

Figure 7.21: The point at threshold 0.5

Then you regenerate the confusion matrix for a threshold of 0, and recalculate the recall, precision, FPR, and TPR. Using the new FPR and TPR, you plot another point on the chart. You then repeat this process for thresholds of 0.1, 0.2, 0.3, and so on, all the way to 1.0.

At threshold 0, in order for a tumor to be classified as benign (1), the predicted probability must be greater than 0. Hence, all of the predictions would be classified as benign (1). Figure 7.22 shows how to calculate the TPR and FPR. For a threshold of 0, both the TPR and FPR are 1.

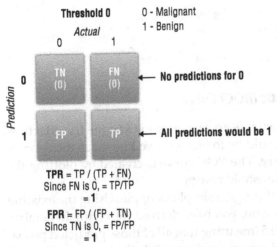

Figure 7.22: The value of TPR and FPR for threshold 0

At threshold 1.0, in order for a tumor to be classified as benign (1), the predicted probability must be equal to exactly 1. Hence, all of the predictions would be classified as malignant (0). Figure 7.23 shows how to calculate the TPR and FPR when the threshold is 1.0. For a threshold of 1.0, both the TPR and FPR are 0.

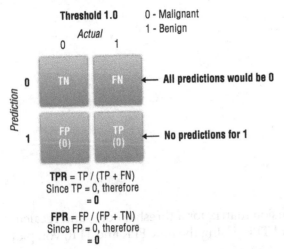

Figure 7.23: The value of TPR and FPR for threshold 1

We can now plot two more points on our chart (see Figure 7.24).

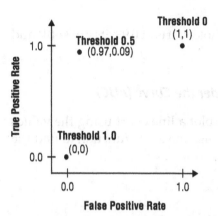

Figure 7.24: Plotting the points for threshold 0, 0.5, and 1.0.

You then calculate the metrics for the other threshold values. Calculating all of the metrics based on different threshold values is a very tedious process. Fortunately, Scikit-learn has the `roc_curve()` function, which will calculate the FPR and TPR automatically for you based on the supplied test labels and predicted probabilities:

```
from sklearn.metrics import roc_curve, auc

#---find the predicted probabilities using the test set
probs = log_regress.predict_proba(test_set)
preds = probs[:,1]

#---find the FPR, TPR, and threshold---
fpr, tpr, threshold = roc_curve(test_labels, preds)
```

The `roc_curve()` function returns a tuple containing the FPR, TPR, and threshold. You can print them out to see the values:

```
print(fpr)
print(tpr)
print(threshold)
```

You should see the following:

```
[ 0.          0.          0.01886792  0.01886792  0.03773585  0.03773585
  0.09433962  0.09433962  0.11320755  0.11320755  0.18867925  0.18867925
  1.          ]

[ 0.01111111  0.88888889  0.88888889  0.91111111  0.91111111  0.94444444
  0.94444444  0.96666667  0.96666667  0.98888889  0.98888889  1.
  1.          ]

[ 9.99991063e-01  9.36998422e-01  9.17998921e-01  9.03158173e-01
  8.58481867e-01  8.48217940e-01  5.43424515e-01  5.26248925e-01
```

```
3.72174142e-01    2.71134211e-01    1.21486104e-01    1.18614069e-01
1.31142589e-21]
```

As you can see from the output, the threshold starts at 0.99999 (9.99e-01) and goes down to 1.311e-21.

Plotting the ROC and Finding the Area Under the Curve (AUC)

To plot the ROC, you can use matplotlib to plot a line chart using the values stored in the *fpr* and *tpr* variables. You can use the auc() function to find the area under the ROC:

```
#---find the area under the curve---
roc_auc = auc(fpr, tpr)

import matplotlib.pyplot as plt
plt.plot(fpr, tpr, 'b', label = 'AUC = %0.2f' % roc_auc)
plt.plot([0, 1], [0, 1],'r--')
plt.xlim([0, 1])
plt.ylim([0, 1])
plt.ylabel('True Positive Rate (TPR)')
plt.xlabel('False Positive Rate (FPR)')
plt.title('Receiver Operating Characteristic (ROC)')
plt.legend(loc = 'lower right')
plt.show()
```

The area under an ROC curve is a measure of the usefulness of a test in general, where a greater area means a more useful test and the areas under ROC curves are used to compare the usefulness of tests. Generally, aim for the algorithm with the highest AUC.

Figure 7.25 shows the ROC curve as well as the AUC.

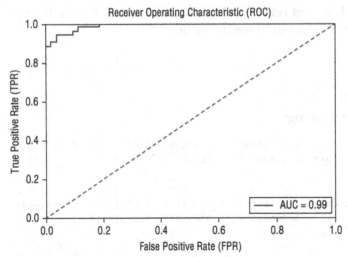

Figure 7.25: Plotting the ROC curve and calculating the AUC

Summary

In this chapter, you learned about another supervised machine learning algorithm—logistics regression. You first learned about the logit function and how to transform it into a sigmoid function. You then applied the logistic regression to the breast cancer dataset and used it to predict if a tumor is malignant or benign. More importantly, this chapter discussed some of the metrics that are useful in determining the effectiveness of a machine learning algorithm. In addition, you learned about what an ROC curve is, how to plot it, and how to calculate the area under the curve.

CHAPTER

8

Supervised Learning—
Classification Using Support
Vector Machines

What Is a Support Vector Machine?

In the previous chapter, you saw how to perform classification using logistics regression. In this chapter, you will learn another supervised machine learning algorithm that is also very popular among data scientists—*Support Vector Machines (SVM)*. Like logistics regression, SVM is also a classification algorithm.

The main idea behind SVM is to draw a line between two or more classes in the best possible manner (see Figure 8.1).

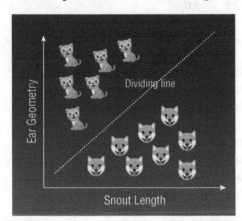

Figure 8.1: Using SVM to separate two classes of animals

Once the line is drawn to separate the classes, you can then use it to predict future data. For example, given the snout length and ear geometry of a new unknown animal, you can now use the dividing line as a classifier to predict if the animal is a dog or a cat.

In this chapter, you will learn how SVM works and the various techniques you can use to adapt SVM for solving nonlinearly-separable datasets.

Maximum Separability

How does SVM separate two or more classes? Consider the set of points in Figure 8.2. Before you look at the next figure, visually think of a straight line dividing the points into two groups.

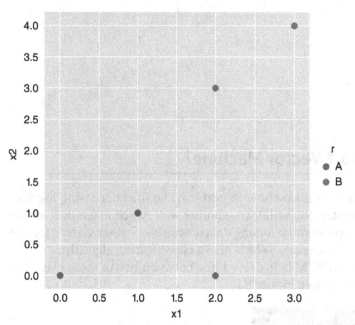

Figure 8.2: A set of points that can be separated using SVM

Now look at Figure 8.3, which shows two possible lines separating the two groups of points. Is this what you had in mind?

Though both lines separate the points into two distinct groups, which one is the right one? For SVM, the right line is the one that has the widest margins (with each margin touching at least a point in each class), as shown in Figure 8.4. In that figure, d1 and d2 are the width of the margins. The goal is to find the largest possible width for the margin that can separate the two groups. Hence, in this case d2 is the largest. Thus the line chosen is the one on the right.

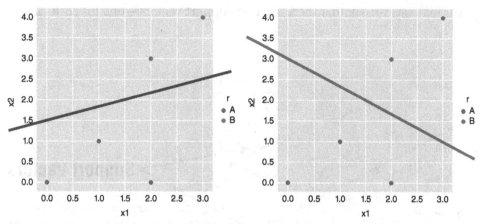

Figure 8.3: Two possible ways to split the points into two classes

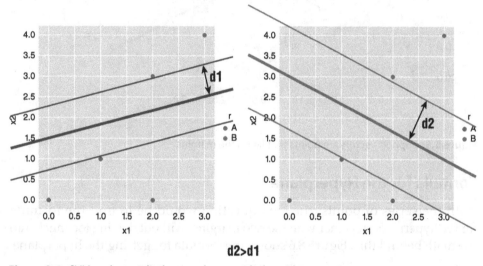

d2>d1

Figure 8.4: SVM seeks to split the two classes with the widest margin

Each of the two margins touches the closest point(s) to each group of points, and the center of the two margins is known as the *hyperplane*. The hyperplane is the line separating the two groups of points. We use the term "hyperplane" instead of "line" because in SVM we typically deal with more than two dimensions, and using the word "hyperplane" more accurately conveys the idea of a plane in a multidimensional space.

Support Vectors

A key term in SVM is *support vectors*. Support vectors are the points that lie on the two margins. Using the example from the previous section, Figure 8.5 shows the two support vectors lying on the two margins.

In this case, we say that there are two support vectors—one for each class.

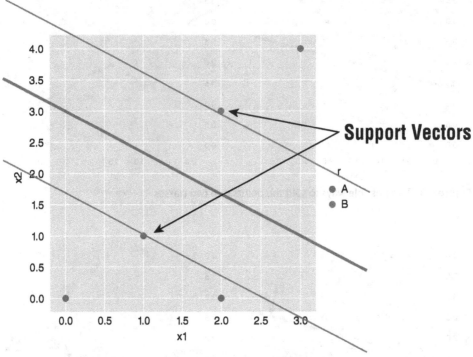

Figure 8.5: Support vectors are points that lie on the margins

Formula for the Hyperplane

With the series of points, the next question would be to find the formula for the hyperplane, together with the two margins. Without delving too much into the math behind this, Figure 8.6 shows the formula for getting the hyperplane.

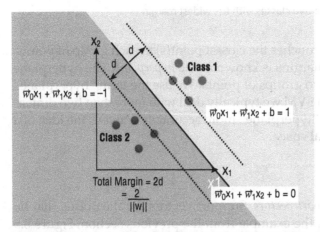

Figure 8.6: The formula for the hyperplane and its accompanying two margins

As you can see from Figure 8.6, the formula for hyperplane (g) is given as:

$$g(x) = \vec{W}_0 x_1 + \vec{W}_1 x_2 + b$$

where x_1 and x_2 are the inputs, $\vec{W}_0$ and $\vec{W}_1$ are the weight vectors, and b is the bias.

If the value of g is >= 1, then the point specified is in Class 1, and if the value of g is <= −1, then the point specified is in Class 2. As mentioned, the goal of SVM is to find the widest margins that divide the classes, and the total margin (2d) is defined by:

$$2 / \|w\|$$

where $\|w\|$ is the normalized weight vectors ($\vec{W}_0$ and $\vec{W}_1$). Using the training set, the goal is to minimize the value of $\|w\|$ so that you can get the maximum separability between the classes. Once this is done, you will be able to get the values of $\vec{W}_0$, $\vec{W}_1$, and b.

Finding the margin is a *Constrained Optimization* problem, which can be solved using the *Larange Multipliers* technique. It is beyond the scope of this book to discuss how to find the margin based on the dataset, but suffice it to say that we will make use of the Scikit-learn library to find them.

Using Scikit-learn for SVM

Now let's work on an example to see how SVM works and how to implement it using Scikit-learn. For this example, we have a file named svm.csv containing the following data:

```
x1,x2,r
0,0,A
1,1,A
2,3,B
2,0,A
3,4,B
```

The first thing that we will do is to plot the points using Seaborn:

```
%matplotlib inline
import pandas as pd
import numpy as np
import seaborn as sns; sns.set(font_scale=1.2)
import matplotlib.pyplot as plt

data = pd.read_csv('svm.csv')
sns.lmplot('x1', 'x2',
           data=data,
           hue='r',
           palette='Set1',
           fit_reg=False,
           scatter_kws={"s": 50});
```

Figure 8.7 shows the points plotted using Seaborn.

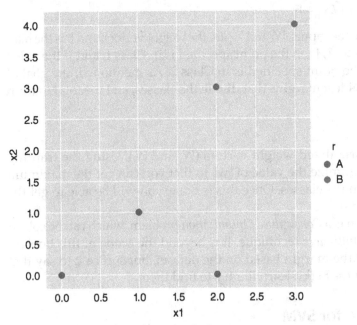

Figure 8.7: Plotting the points using Seaborn

Using the data points that we have previously loaded, now let's use Scikit-learn's svm module's svc class to help us derive the value for the various variables that we need to compute otherwise. The following code snippet uses the *linear kernel* to solve the problem. The linear kernel assumes that the dataset can be separated linearly.

```
from sklearn import svm
#---Converting the Columns as Matrices---
points = data[['x1','x2']].values
result = data['r']

clf = svm.SVC(kernel = 'linear')
clf.fit(points, result)

print('Vector of weights (w) = ',clf.coef_[0])
print('b = ',clf.intercept_[0])
print('Indices of support vectors = ', clf.support_)
print('Support vectors = ', clf.support_vectors_)
print('Number of support vectors for each class = ', clf.n_support_)
print('Coefficients of the support vector in the decision function = ',
      np.abs(clf.dual_coef_))
```

The svc stands for *Support Vector Classification.* The svm module contains a series of classes that implement SVM for different purposes:

svm.LinearSVC: Linear Support Vector Classification

svm.LinearSVR: Linear Support Vector Regression

svm.NuSVC: Nu-Support Vector Classification

svm.NuSVR: Nu-Support Vector Regression

svm.OneClassSVM: Unsupervised Outlier Detection

svm.SVC: C-Support Vector Classification

svm.SVR: Epsilon-Support Vector Regression

> **TIP** For this chapter, our focus is on using SVM for classification, even though SVM can also be used for regression.

The preceding code snippet yields the following output:

```
Vector of weights (w) =  [0.4 0.8]
b =  -2.2
Indices of support vectors =  [1 2]
Support vectors =  [[1. 1.]
 [2. 3.]]
Number of support vectors for each class =  [1 1]
Coefficients of the support vector in the decision function =  [[0.4 0.4]]
```

As you can see, the vector of weights has been found to be [0.4 0.8], meaning that $\vec{W}_0$ is now 0.4 and $\vec{W}_1$ is now 0.8. The value of b is –2.2, and there are two support vectors. The index of the support vectors is 1 and 2, meaning that the points are the ones in bold:

```
x1   x2   r
0    0    0   A
1    1    1   A
2    2    3   B
3    2    0   A
4    3    4   B
```

Figure 8.8 shows the relationship between the various variables in the formula and the variables in the code snippet.

$$g(x) = \vec{w}_0 x_1 + \vec{w}_1 x_2 + b$$

clf.coef_[0][0]

clf.coef_[0][1]

clf.intercept_[0]

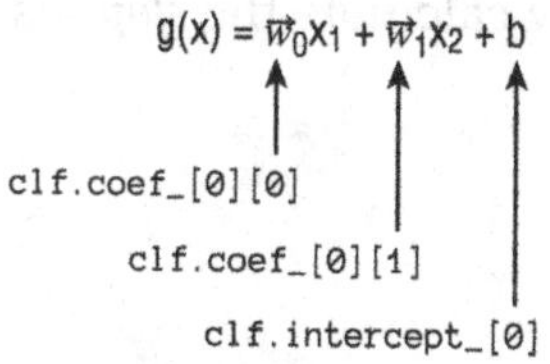

Figure 8.8: Relationships between the variables in the formula and the variables in the code snippet

Plotting the Hyperplane and the Margins

With the values of the variables all obtained, it is now time to plot the hyperplane and its two accompanying margins. Do you remember the formula for the hyperplane? It is as follows:

$$g(x) = \vec{W}_{0X_1} + \vec{W}_{1X_2} + b,$$

To plot the hyperplane, set $\vec{W}_{0X_1} + \vec{W}_{1X_2} + b$ to 0, like this:

$$\vec{W}_{0X_1} + \vec{W}_{1X_2} + b = 0$$

In order to plot the hyperplane (which is a straight line in this case), we need two points: one on the x-axis and one on the y-axis.

Using the preceding formula, when $x_1 = 0$, we can solve for x_2 as follows:

```
W₀(0)  +  W₁ₓ₂  +  b  =  0
W₁ₓ₂  =  -b
x₂=  -b/W₁
```

When $x_2 = 0$, we can solve for x_1 as follows:

```
W₀ₓ₁  +  W₁(0)  +  b  =  0
W₀ₓ₁  =  -b
x₁  =  -b/W₀
```

The point $(0, -b/\vec{W}_1)$ is the *y-intercept* of the straight line. Figure 8.9 shows the two points on the two axes.

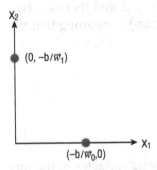

Figure 8.9: The two intercepts for the hyperplane

Once the points on each axis are found, you can now calculate the *slope* as follows:

```
Slope  =  (-b/W₁)  /  (b/W₀)
Slope  =  - (W₀/W₁)
```

With the slope and y-intercept of the line found, you can now go ahead and plot the hyperplane. The following code snippet does just that:

```
#---w is the vector of weights---
w = clf.coef_[0]

#---find the slope of the hyperplane---
slope = -w[0] / w[1]

b = clf.intercept_[0]

#---find the coordinates for the hyperplane---
xx = np.linspace(0, 4)
yy = slope * xx - (b / w[1])

#---plot the margins---
s = clf.support_vectors_[0]      #---first support vector---
yy_down = slope * xx + (s[1] - slope * s[0])

s = clf.support_vectors_[-1]     #---last support vector---
yy_up   = slope * xx + (s[1] - slope * s[0])

#---plot the points---
sns.lmplot('x1', 'x2', data=data, hue='r', palette='Set1',
fit_reg=False, scatter_kws={"s": 70})

#---plot the hyperplane---
plt.plot(xx, yy, linewidth=2, color='green');

#---plot the 2 margins---
plt.plot(xx, yy_down, 'k--')
plt.plot(xx, yy_up, 'k--')
```

Figure 8.10 shows the hyperplane and the two margins.

Making Predictions

Remember, the goal of SVM is to separate the points into two or more classes, so that you can use it to predict the classes of future points. Having trained your model using SVM, you can now perform some predictions using the model.

The following code snippet uses the model that you have trained to perform some predictions:

```
print(clf.predict([[3,3]])[0])   # 'B'
print(clf.predict([[4,0]])[0])   # 'A'
print(clf.predict([[2,2]])[0])   # 'B'
print(clf.predict([[1,2]])[0])   # 'A'
```

Check the points against the chart shown in Figure 8.10 and see if it makes sense to you.

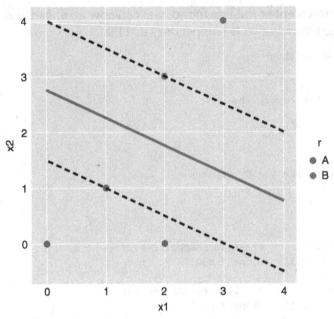

Figure 8.10: The hyperplane and the two margins

Kernel Trick

Sometimes, the points in a dataset are not always linearly separable. Consider the points shown in Figure 8.11.

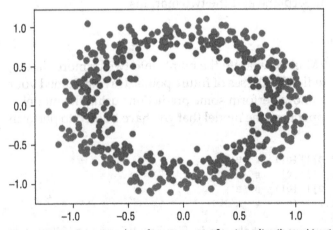

Figure 8.11: A scatter plot of two groups of points distributed in circular fashion

You can see that it is not possible to draw a straight line to separate the two sets of points. With some manipulation, however, you can make this set of points linearly separable. This technique is known as the *kernel trick*. The kernel trick is a technique in machine learning that transforms data into a higher dimension space so that, after the transformation, it has a clear dividing margin between classes of data.

Adding a Third Dimension

To do so, we can add a third dimension, say the z-axis, and define z to be:

$$z = x^2 + y^2$$

Once we plot the points using a 3D chart, the points are now linearly separable. It is difficult to visualize this unless you plot the points out. The following code snippet does just that:

```
%matplotlib inline

from mpl_toolkits.mplot3d import Axes3D
import matplotlib.pyplot as plt
import numpy as np
from sklearn.datasets import make_circles

#---X is features and c is the class labels---
X, c = make_circles(n_samples=500, noise=0.09)

rgb = np.array(['r', 'g'])
plt.scatter(X[:, 0], X[:, 1], color=rgb[c])
plt.show()

fig = plt.figure(figsize=(18,15))
ax = fig.add_subplot(111, projection='3d')
z = X[:,0]**2 + X[:,1]**2
ax.scatter(X[:, 0], X[:, 1], z, color=rgb[c])
plt.xlabel("x-axis")
plt.ylabel("y-axis")
plt.show()
```

We first create two sets of random points (a total of 500 points) distributed in circular fashion using the `make_circles()` function. We then plot them out on a 2D chart (as what was shown in Figure 8.11). We then add the third axis, the z-axis, and plot the chart in 3D (see Figure 8.12).

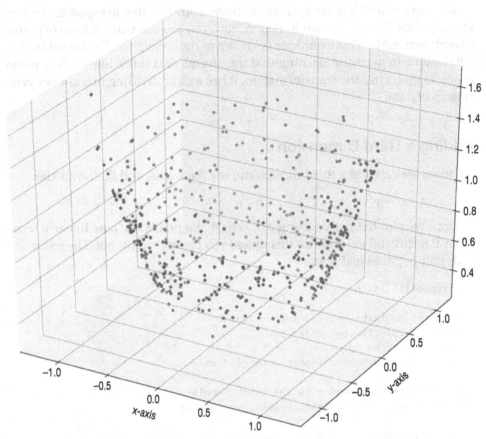

Figure 8.12: Plotting the points in the three dimensions

> **TIP** If you run the preceding code in Terminal (just remove the `%matplotlib inline` statement at the top of the code snippet) using the `python` command, you will be able to rotate and interact with the chart. Figure 8.13 shows the different perspectives of the 3D chart.

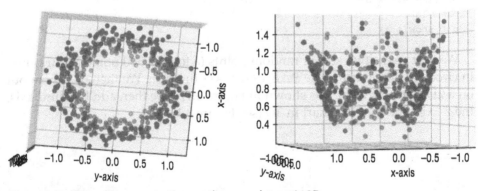

Figure 8.13: The various perspectives on the same dataset in 3D

Plotting the 3D Hyperplane

With the points plotted in a 3D chart, let's now train the model using the third dimension:

```
#---combine X (x-axis,y-axis) and z into single ndarray---
features = np.concatenate((X,z.reshape(-1,1)), axis=1)

#---use SVM for training---
from sklearn import svm

clf = svm.SVC(kernel = 'linear')
clf.fit(features, c)
```

First, we combined the three axes into a single `ndarray` using the `np.concat-enate()` function. We then trained the model as usual. For a linearly-separable set of points in two dimensions, the formula for the hyperplane is as follows:

$$g(x) = \vec{W}_{0x1} + \vec{W}_{1x2} + b$$

For the set of points now in three dimensions, the formula now becomes the following:

$$g(x) = \vec{W}_{0x1} + \vec{W}_{1x2} + \vec{W}_{2x3} + b$$

In particular, $\vec{W}_2$ is now represented by `clf.coef_[0][2]`, as shown in Figure 8.14.

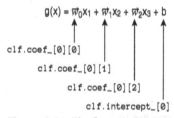

$$g(x) = \vec{w}_0 x_1 + \vec{w}_1 x_2 + \vec{w}_2 x_3 + b$$

```
clf.coef_[0][0]
      clf.coef_[0][1]
            clf.coef_[0][2]
                  clf.intercept_[0]
```

Figure 8.14: The formula for the hyperplane in 3D and its corresponding variables in the code snippet

The next step is to draw the hyperplane in 3D. In order to do that, you need to find the value of x3, which can be derived, as shown in Figure 8.15.

$$\vec{w}_0 x_1 + \vec{w}_1 x_2 + \vec{w}_2 x_3 + b = 0$$
$$\vec{w}_2 x_3 = -\vec{w}_0 x_1 - \vec{w}_1 x_2 - b$$
$$x_3 = \frac{-\vec{w}_0 x_1 - \vec{w}_1 x_2 - b}{\vec{w}_2}$$

Figure 8.15: Formula for finding the hyperplane in 3D

This can be expressed in code as follows:

```
x3 = lambda x,y: (-clf.intercept_[0] - clf.coef_[0][0] * x-clf.coef_[0][1] * y) /
                 clf.coef_[0][2]
```

To plot the hyperplane in 3D, use the `plot_surface()` function:

```
tmp = np.linspace(-1.5,1.5,100)
x,y = np.meshgrid(tmp,tmp)

ax.plot_surface(x, y, x3(x,y))
plt.show()
```

The entire code snippet is as follows:

```
from mpl_toolkits.mplot3d import Axes3D
import matplotlib.pyplot as plt
import numpy as np
from sklearn.datasets import make_circles

#---X is features and c is the class labels---
X, c = make_circles(n_samples=500, noise=0.09)
z = X[:,0]**2 + X[:,1]**2

rgb = np.array(['r', 'g'])

fig = plt.figure(figsize=(18,15))
ax = fig.add_subplot(111, projection='3d')
ax.scatter(X[:, 0], X[:, 1], z, color=rgb[c])
plt.xlabel("x-axis")
plt.ylabel("y-axis")
# plt.show()

#---combine X (x-axis,y-axis) and z into single ndarray---
features = np.concatenate((X,z.reshape(-1,1)), axis=1)

#---use SVM for training---
from sklearn import svm

clf = svm.SVC(kernel = 'linear')
clf.fit(features, c)
x3 = lambda x,y: (-clf.intercept_[0] - clf.coef_[0][0] * x-clf.coef_[0][1]
                 * y) / clf.coef_[0][2]
```

```
tmp = np.linspace(-1.5,1.5,100)
x,y = np.meshgrid(tmp,tmp)

ax.plot_surface(x, y, x3(x,y))
plt.show()
```

Figure 8.16 shows the hyperplane, as well as the points, plotted in 3D.

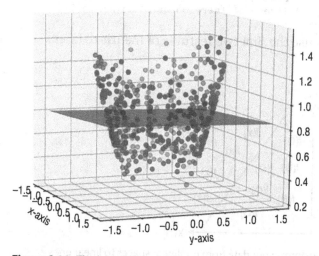

Figure 8.16: The hyperplane in 3D cutting through the two sets of points

Types of Kernels

Up to this point, we only discussed one type of SVM—linear SVM. As the name implies, linear SVM uses a straight line to separate the points. In the previous section, you also learned about the use of kernel tricks to separate two sets of data that are distributed in a circular fashion and then used linear SVM to separate them.

Sometimes, not all points can be separated linearly, nor can they be separated using the kernel tricks that you observed in the previous section. For this type of data, you need to "bend" the lines to separate them. In machine learning, *kernels* are functions that transform your data from nonlinear spaces to linear ones (see Figure 8.17).

To understand how kernels work, let's use the Iris dataset as an example. The following code snippet loads the Iris dataset and prints out the features, target, and target names:

```
%matplotlib inline
import pandas as pd
import numpy as np
```

```
from sklearn import svm, datasets
import matplotlib.pyplot as plt

iris = datasets.load_iris()
print(iris.data[0:5])        # print first 5 rows
print(iris.feature_names)    # ['sepal length (cm)', 'sepal width (cm)',
                             #  'petal length (cm)', 'petal width (cm)']
print(iris.target[0:5])      # print first 5 rows
print(iris.target_names)     # ['setosa' 'versicolor' 'virginica']
```

To illustrate, we will only use the first two features of the Iris dataset:

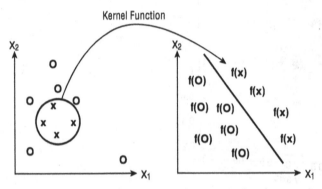

Figure 8.17: A kernel function transforms your data from nonlinear spaces to linear ones

```
X = iris.data[:, :2]        #  take the first two features
y = iris.target
```

We will plot the points using a scatter plot (see Figure 8.18):

```
#---plot the points---
colors = ['red', 'green', 'blue']
for color, i, target in zip(colors, [0, 1, 2], iris.target_names):
    plt.scatter(X[y==i, 0], X[y==i, 1], color=color, label=target)

plt.xlabel('Sepal length')
plt.ylabel('Sepal width')
plt.legend(loc='best', shadow=False, scatterpoints=1)

plt.title('Scatter plot of Sepal width against Sepal length')
plt.show()
```

Next, we will use the SVC class with the linear kernel:

```
C = 1  # SVM regularization parameter
clf = svm.SVC(kernel='linear', C=C).fit(X, y)
title = 'SVC with linear kernel'
```

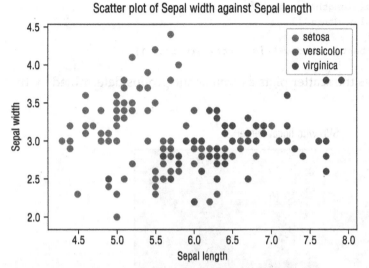

Figure 8.18: Scatter plot of the Iris dataset's first two features

TIP   Notice that this time around, we have a new parameter C. We will discuss this in a moment.

Instead of drawing lines to separate the three groups of Iris flowers, this time we will paint the groups in colors using the `contourf()` function:

```
#---min and max for the first feature---
x_min, x_max = X[:, 0].min() - 1, X[:, 0].max() + 1

#---min and max for the second feature---
y_min, y_max = X[:, 1].min() - 1, X[:, 1].max() + 1

#---step size in the mesh---
h = (x_max / x_min)/100

#---make predictions for each of the points in xx,yy---
xx, yy = np.meshgrid(np.arange(x_min, x_max, h),
                     np.arange(y_min, y_max, h))

Z = clf.predict(np.c_[xx.ravel(), yy.ravel()])

#---draw the result using a color plot---
Z = Z.reshape(xx.shape)
plt.contourf(xx, yy, Z, cmap=plt.cm.Accent, alpha=0.8)

#---plot the training points---
colors = ['red', 'green', 'blue']
for color, i, target in zip(colors, [0, 1, 2], iris.target_names):
    plt.scatter(X[y==i, 0], X[y==i, 1], color=color, label=target)
```

```
plt.xlabel('Sepal length')
plt.ylabel('Sepal width')
plt.title(title)
plt.legend(loc='best', shadow=False, scatterpoints=1)
```

Figure 8.19 shows the scatter plots as well as the groups determined by the SVM linear kernel.

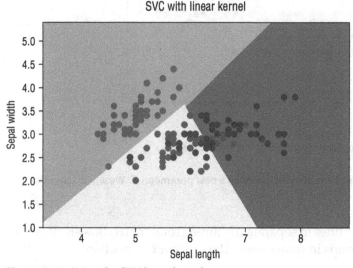

Figure 8.19: Using the SVM linear kernel

Once the training is done, we will perform some predictions:

```
predictions = clf.predict(X)
print(np.unique(predictions, return_counts=True))
```

The preceding code snippet returns the following:

```
(array([0, 1, 2]), array([50, 53, 47]))
```

This means that after the feeding the model with the Iris dataset, 50 are classified as "setosa," 53 are classified as "versicolor," and 47 are classified as "virginica."

C

In the previous section, you saw the use of the C parameter:

```
C = 1
clf = svm.SVC(kernel='linear', C=C).fit(X, y)
```

C is known as the *penalty parameter of the error term*. It controls the tradeoff between the smooth decision boundary and classifying the training points correctly. For example, if the value of C is high, then the SVM algorithm will seek to ensure that all points are classified correctly. The downside to this is that it may result in a narrower margin, as shown in Figure 8.20.

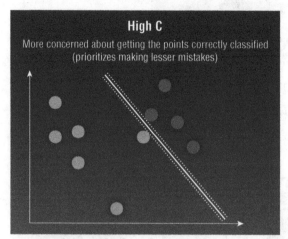

Figure 8.20: A high C focuses more on getting the points correctly classified

In contrast, a lower C will aim for the widest margin possible, but it will result in some points being classified incorrectly (see Figure 8.21).

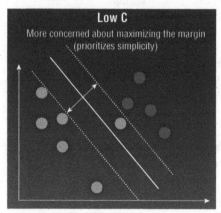

Figure 8.21: A low C aims for the widest margin, but may classify some points incorrectly

Figure 8.22 shows the effects of varying the value of C when applying the SVM linear kernel algorithm. The result of the classification appears at the bottom of each chart.

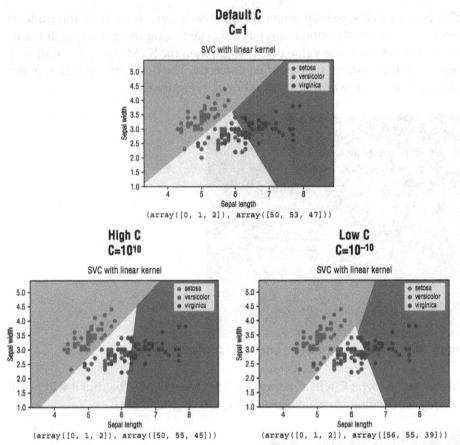

Figure 8.22: Using SVM with varying values of C

Note that when C is 1 or 10^{10}, there isn't too much difference among the classification results. However, when C is small (10^{-10}), you can see that a number of points (belonging to "versicolor" and "virginica") are now misclassified as "setosa."

TIP In short, a low C makes the decision surface smooth while trying to classify *most* points, while a high C tries to classify *all* of the points correctly.

Radial Basis Function (RBF) Kernel

Besides the linear kernel that we have seen so far, there are some commonly used nonlinear kernels:

- *Radial Basis function (RBF),* also known as *Gaussian Kernel*
- Polynomial

The first, RBF, gives value to each point based on its distance from the origin or a *fixed* center, commonly on a Euclidean space. Let's use the same example that we used in the previous section, but this time modify the kernel to use rbf:

```
C = 1
clf = svm.SVC(kernel='rbf', gamma='auto', C=C).fit(X, y)
title = 'SVC with RBF kernel'
```

Figure 8.23 shows the same sample trained using the RBF kernel.

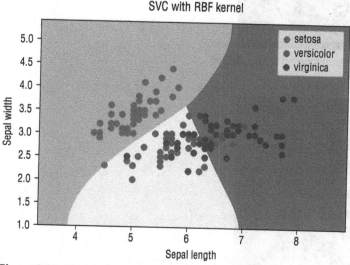

Figure 8.23: The Iris dataset trained using the RBF kernel

Gamma

If you look at the code snippet carefully, you will discover a new parameter—gamma. *Gamma* defines how far the influence of a single training example reaches. Consider the set of points shown in Figure 8.24. There are two classes of points—x's and o's.

A low Gamma value indicates that every point has a far reach (see Figure 8.25).

On the other hand, a high Gamma means that the points closest to the decision boundary have a close reach. The higher the value of Gamma, the more it will try to fit the training dataset exactly, resulting in overfitting (see Figure 8.26).

Figure 8.27 shows the classification of the points using RBF, with varying values of C and Gamma.

Note that if Gamma is high (10), overfitting occurs. You can also see from this figure that the value of C controls the smoothness of the curve.

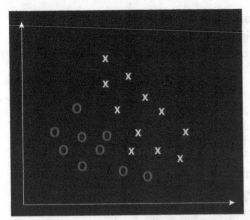

Figure 8.24: A set of points belonging to two classes

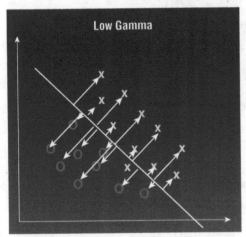

Figure 8.25: A low Gamma value allows every point to have equal reach

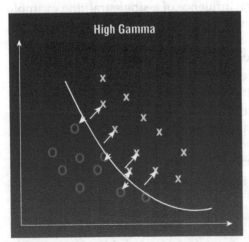

Figure 8.26: A high Gamma value focuses more on points close to the boundary

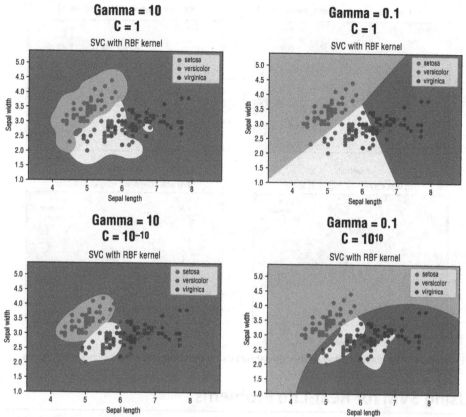

Figure 8.27: The effects of classifying the points using varying values of C and Gamma

> **TIP** To summarize, C controls the smoothness of the boundary and Gamma determines if the points are overfitted.

Polynomial Kernel

Another type of kernel is called the *polynomial kernel*. A polynomial kernel of degree 1 is similar to that of the linear kernel. Higher-degree polynomial kernels afford a more flexible decision boundary. The following code snippet shows the Iris dataset trained using the polynomial kernel with degree 4:

```
C = 1  # SVM regularization parameter
clf = svm.SVC(kernel='poly', degree=4, C=C, gamma='auto').fit(X, y)
title = 'SVC with polynomial (degree 4) kernel'
```

Figure 8.28 shows the dataset separated with polynomial kernels of degree 1 to 4.

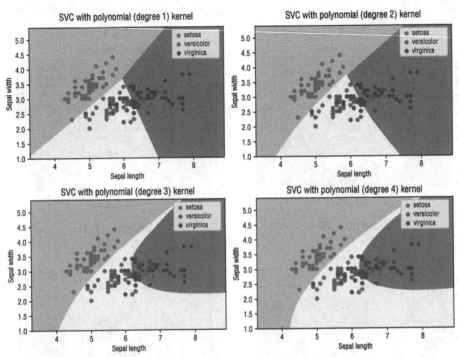

Figure 8.28: The classification of the Iris dataset using polynomial kernel of varying degrees

Using SVM for Real-Life Problems

We will end this chapter by applying SVM to a common problem in our daily lives. Consider the following dataset (saved in a file named `house_sizes_prices_svm` `.csv`) containing the size of houses and their asking prices (in thousands) for a particular area:

```
size,price,sold
550,50,y
1000,100,y
1200,123,y
1500,350,n
3000,200,y
2500,300,y
750, 45,y
1500,280,n
780,400,n
1200, 450,n
2750, 500,n
```

The third column indicates if the house was sold. Using this dataset, you want to know if a house with a specific asking price would be able to sell.

First, let's plot out the points:

```
%matplotlib inline

import pandas as pd
import numpy as np
from sklearn import svm
import matplotlib.pyplot as plt
import seaborn as sns; sns.set(font_scale=1.2)

data = pd.read_csv('house_sizes_prices_svm.csv')

sns.lmplot('size', 'price',
           data=data,
           hue='sold',
           palette='Set2',
           fit_reg=False,
           scatter_kws={"s": 50});
```

Figure 8.29 shows the points plotted as a scatter plot.

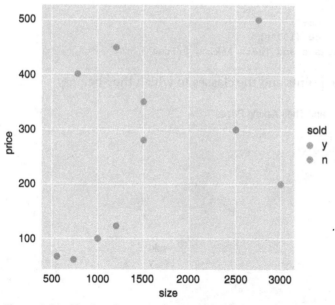

Figure 8.29: Plotting the points on a scatter plot

Visually, you can see that this is a problem that can be solved with SVM's linear kernel:

```
X = data[['size','price']].values
y = np.where(data['sold']=='y', 1, 0) #--1 for Y and 0 for N---
model = svm.SVC(kernel='linear').fit(X, y)
```

With the trained model, you can now perform predictions and paint the two classes:

```
#---min and max for the first feature---
x_min, x_max = X[:, 0].min() - 1, X[:, 0].max() + 1

#---min and max for the second feature---
y_min, y_max = X[:, 1].min() - 1, X[:, 1].max() + 1

#---step size in the mesh---
h = (x_max / x_min) / 20

#---make predictions for each of the points in xx,yy---
xx, yy = np.meshgrid(np.arange(x_min, x_max, h),
                     np.arange(y_min, y_max, h))

Z = model.predict(np.c_[xx.ravel(), yy.ravel()])

#---draw the result using a color plot---
Z = Z.reshape(xx.shape)
plt.contourf(xx, yy, Z, cmap=plt.cm.Blues, alpha=0.3)

plt.xlabel('Size of house')
plt.ylabel('Asking price (1000s)')
plt.title("Size of Houses and Their Asking Prices")
```

Figure 8.30 shows the points and the classes to which they belong.

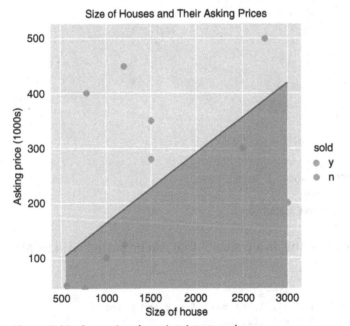

Figure 8.30: Separating the points into two classes

You can now try to predict if a house of a certain size with a specific selling price will be able to sell:

```
def will_it_sell(size, price):
    if(model.predict([[size, price]]))==0:
        print('Will not sell!')
    else:
        print('Will sell!')

#---do some prediction---
will_it_sell(2500, 400)  # Will not sell!
will_it_sell(2500, 200)  # Will sell!
```

Summary

In this chapter, you learned about how Support Vector Machines help in classification problems. You learned about the formula for finding the hyperplane, as well as the two accompanying margins. Fortunately, Scikit-learn provides the classes needed for training models using SVM, and with the parameters returned, you can plot the hyperplane and margins visually so that you can understand how SVM works. You also learned about the various kernels that you can apply to your SVM algorithms so that the dataset can be separated linearly.

CHAPTER

9

Supervised Learning— Classification Using K-Nearest Neighbors (KNN)

What Is K-Nearest Neighbors?

Up until this point, we have discussed three supervised learning algorithms: linear regression, logistics regression, and support vector machines. In this chapter, we will dive into another supervised machine learning algorithm known as *K-Nearest Neighbors (KNN)*.

KNN is a relatively simple algorithm compared to the other algorithms that we have discussed in previous chapters. It works by comparing the query instance's distance to the other training samples and selecting the K-nearest neighbors (hence its name). It then takes the majority of these K-neighbor classes to be the prediction of the query instance.

Figure 9.1 sums this up nicely. When k = 3, the closest three neighbors of the circle are the two squares and the one triangle. Based on the simple rule of majority, the circle is classified as a square. If k = 5, then the closest five neighbors are the two squares and the three triangles. Hence, the circle is classified as a triangle.

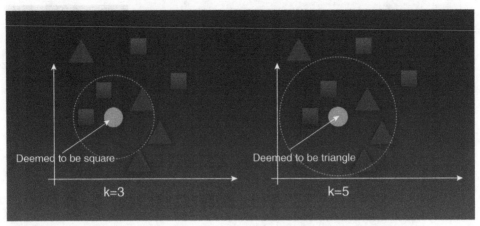

Figure 9.1: The classification of a point depends on the majority of its neighbors

> **TIP**   KNN is also sometimes used for regression in addition to classification.
> For example, it can be used to calculate the average of the numerical target of the
> K-nearest neighbors. For this chapter, however, we are focusing solely on its more
> common use as a classification algorithm.

Implementing KNN in Python

Now that you have seen how KNN works, let's try to implement KNN from
scratch using Python. As usual, first let's import the modules that we'll need:

```
import pandas as pd
import numpy as np
import operator
import seaborn as sns
import matplotlib.pyplot as plt
```

Plotting the Points

For this example, you will use a file named knn.csv containing the following data:

```
x,y,c
1,1,A
2,2,A
4,3,B
3,3,A
3,5,B
5,6,B
5,4,B
```

As we have done in the previous chapters, a good way is to plot the points using Seaborn:

```
data = pd.read_csv("knn.csv")
sns.lmplot('x', 'y', data=data,
           hue='c', palette='Set1',
           fit_reg=False, scatter_kws={"s": 70})
plt.show()
```

Figure 9.2 shows the distribution of the various points. Points that belong to class A are displayed in red while those belonging to class B are displayed in blue.

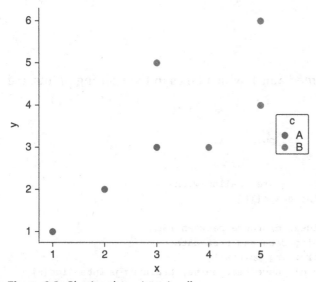

Figure 9.2: Plotting the points visually

Calculating the Distance Between the Points

In order to find the nearest neighbor of a given point, you need to calculate the Euclidean distance between two points.

> **TIP** In geometry, Euclidean space encompasses the two-dimensional Euclidean plane, the three-dimensional space of Euclidean geometry, and similar spaces of higher dimension.

Given two points, $p = (p_1, p_2, \ldots, p_n)$ and $q = (q_1 q_2, \ldots, q_n)$ the distance between p and q is given by the following formula:

$$\sqrt{\left((q_1 - p_1)^2 + (q_2 - p_2)^2 + \ldots + (q_n - p_n)^2\right)}$$

Based on this formula, you can now define a function named `euclidean_distance()` as follows:

```
#---to calculate the distance between two points---
def euclidean_distance(pt1, pt2, dimension):
    distance = 0
    for x in range(dimension):
        distance += np.square(pt1[x] - pt2[x])
    return np.sqrt(distance)
```

The `Euclidean_distance()` function can find the distance between two points in any dimension. For this example, the points that we are dealing with are in 2D.

Implementing KNN

Next, define a function named `knn()`, which takes in the training points, the test point, and the value of k:

```
#---our own KNN model---
def knn(training_points, test_point, k):
    distances = {}

    #---the number of axes we are dealing with---
    dimension = test_point.shape[1]

    #--calculating euclidean distance between each
    # point in the training data and test data
    for x in range(len(training_points)):
        dist = euclidean_distance(test_point, training_points.iloc[x],
                                  dimension)
        #---record the distance for each training points---
        distances[x] = dist[0]

    #---sort the distances---
    sorted_d = sorted(distances.items(), key=operator.itemgetter(1))

    #---to store the neighbors---
    neighbors = []

    #---extract the top k neighbors---
    for x in range(k):
        neighbors.append(sorted_d[x][0])

    #---for each neighbor found, find out its class---
    class_counter = {}
    for x in range(len(neighbors)):
        #---find out the class for that particular point---
        cls = training_points.iloc[neighbors[x]][-1]
```

```
        if cls in class_counter:
            class_counter[cls] += 1
        else:
            class_counter[cls] = 1

    #---sort the class_counter in descending order---
    sorted_counter = sorted(class_counter.items(),
                            key=operator.itemgetter(1),
                            reverse=True)

    #---return the class with the most count, as well as the
    #neighbors found---
    return(sorted_counter[0][0], neighbors)
```

The function returns the class to which the test point belongs, as well as the indices of all the nearest k neighbors.

Making Predictions

With the `knn()` function defined, you can now make some predictions:

```
#---test point---
test_set = [[3,3.9]]
test = pd.DataFrame(test_set)
cls,neighbors = knn(data, test, 5)
print("Predicted Class: " + cls)
```

The preceding code snippet will print out the following output:

```
Predicted Class: B
```

Visualizing Different Values of K

It is useful to be able to visualize the effect of applying various values of k. The following code snippet draws a series of concentric circles around the test point based on the values of k, which range from 7 to 1, with intervals of –2:

```
#---generate the color map for the scatter plot---
#---if column 'c' is A, then use Red, else use Blue---
colors = ['r' if i == 'A' else 'b'  for i in data['c']]
ax = data.plot(kind='scatter', x='x', y='y', c = colors)
plt.xlim(0,7)
plt.ylim(0,7)

#---plot the test point---
plt.plot(test_set[0][0],test_set[0][1], "yo", markersize='9')

for k in range(7,0,-2):
    cls,neighbors = knn(data, test, k)
```

```
        print("============")
        print("k = ", k)
        print("Class", cls)
        print("Neighbors")
        print(data.iloc[neighbors])

        furthest_point = data.iloc[neighbors].tail(1)

        #---draw a circle connecting the test point
        #and the furthest point---
        radius = euclidean_distance(test, furthest_point.iloc[0], 2)

        #---display the circle in red if classification is A,
        # else display circle in blue---
        c = 'r' if cls=='A' else 'b'
        circle = plt.Circle((test_set[0][0], test_set[0][1]),
                            radius, color=c, alpha=0.3)
        ax.add_patch(circle)

plt.gca().set_aspect('equal', adjustable='box')
plt.show()
```

The preceding code snippet prints out the following output:

```
============
k =  7
Class B
Neighbors
   x  y  c
3  3  3  A
4  3  5  B
2  4  3  B
6  5  4  B
1  2  2  A
5  5  6  B
0  1  1  A
============
k =  5
Class B
Neighbors
   x  y  c
3  3  3  A
4  3  5  B
2  4  3  B
6  5  4  B
1  2  2  A
============
k =  3
Class B
Neighbors
```

```
    x   y   c
3   3   3   A
4   3   5   B
2   4   3   B
============
k =  1
Class A
Neighbors
    x   y   c
3   3   3   A
```

Figure 9.3 shows the series of circles centered around the test point, with varying values of k. The innermost circle is for k = 1, with the next outer ring for k = 3, and so on. As you can see, if k = 1, the circle is red, meaning that the yellow point has been classified as class A. If the circle is blue, this means that the yellow point has been classified as class B. This is evident in the outer three circles.

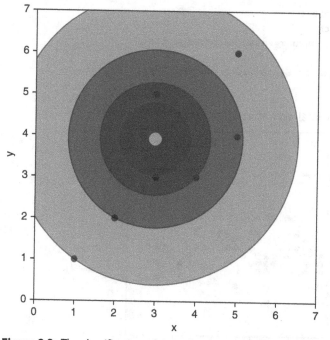

Figure 9.3: The classification of the yellow point based on the different values of k

Using Scikit-Learn's KNeighborsClassifier Class for KNN

Now that you have seen how KNN works and how it can be implemented manually in Python, let's use the implementation provided by Scikit-learn.

The following code snippet loads the Iris dataset and plots it out using a scatter plot:

```
%matplotlib inline
import pandas as pd
import numpy as np
import matplotlib.patches as mpatches
from sklearn import svm, datasets
import matplotlib.pyplot as plt

iris = datasets.load_iris()

X = iris.data[:, :2]        #  take the first two features
y = iris.target

#---plot the points---
colors = ['red', 'green', 'blue']
for color, i, target in zip(colors, [0, 1, 2], iris.target_names):
    plt.scatter(X[y==i, 0], X[y==i, 1], color=color, label=target)

plt.xlabel('Sepal length')
plt.ylabel('Sepal width')
plt.legend(loc='best', shadow=False, scatterpoints=1)

plt.title('Scatter plot of Sepal width against Sepal length')
plt.show()
```

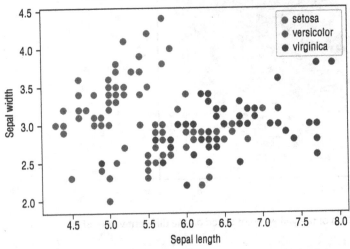

Figure 9.4: Plotting out the Sepal width against the Sepal length in a scatter plot

Figure 9.4 shows the scatter plot of the Sepal width against the Sepal length.

Exploring Different Values of K

We can now use Scikit-learn's `KNeighborsClassifier` class to help us train a model on the Iris dataset using KNN. For a start, let's use a k of 1:

```python
from sklearn.neighbors import KNeighborsClassifier

k = 1
#---instantiate learning model---
knn = KNeighborsClassifier(n_neighbors=k)

#---fitting the model---
knn.fit(X, y)

#---min and max for the first feature---
x_min, x_max = X[:, 0].min() - 1, X[:, 0].max() + 1

#---min and max for the second feature---
y_min, y_max = X[:, 1].min() - 1, X[:, 1].max() + 1

#---step size in the mesh---
h = (x_max / x_min)/100

#---make predictions for each of the points in xx,yy---
xx, yy = np.meshgrid(np.arange(x_min, x_max, h),
                     np.arange(y_min, y_max, h))

Z = knn.predict(np.c_[xx.ravel(), yy.ravel()])

#---draw the result using a color plot---
Z = Z.reshape(xx.shape)
plt.contourf(xx, yy, Z, cmap=plt.cm.Accent, alpha=0.8)

#---plot the training points---
colors = ['red', 'green', 'blue']
for color, i, target in zip(colors, [0, 1, 2], iris.target_names):
    plt.scatter(X[y==i, 0], X[y==i, 1], color=color, label=target)

plt.xlabel('Sepal length')
plt.ylabel('Sepal width')
plt.title(f'KNN (k={k})')
plt.legend(loc='best', shadow=False, scatterpoints=1)

predictions = knn.predict(X)

#--classifications based on predictions---
print(np.unique(predictions, return_counts=True))
```

The preceding code snippet creates a *meshgrid* (a rectangular grid of values) of points scattered across the x- and y-axes. Each point is then used for prediction, and the result is drawn using a color plot.

Figure 9.5 shows the classification boundary using a k of 1. Notice that for k = 1, you perform your prediction based solely on a single sample—your nearest neighbor. This makes your prediction very sensitive to all sorts of distortions, such as outliers, mislabeling, and so on. In general, setting k = 1 usually leads to *overfitting*, and as a result your prediction is usually not very accurate.

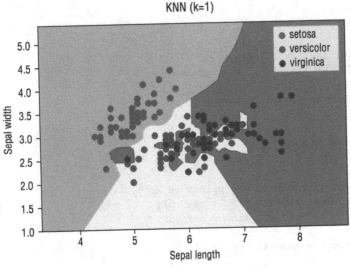

Figure 9.5: The classification boundary based on k = 1

> **TIP** *Overfitting* in machine learning means that the model you have trained fits the training data too well. This happens when all of the noises and fluctuations in your training data are picked up during the training process. In simple terms, this means that your model is trying very hard to fit all of your data perfectly. The key problem with an overfitted model is that it will not work well with new, unseen data.
>
> *Underfitting*, on the other hand, occurs when a machine learning model cannot accurately capture the underlying trend of the data. Specifically, the model does not fit the data well enough.
>
> Figure 9.6 shows an easy way to understand overfitting, underfitting, and a generally good fit.

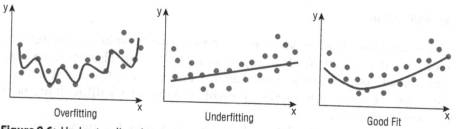

Figure 9.6: Understanding the concept of overfitting, underfitting, and a good fit

For KNN, setting k to a higher value tends to make your prediction more robust against noise in your data.

Using the same code snippet, let's vary the values of k. Figure 9.7 shows the classifications based on four different values of k.

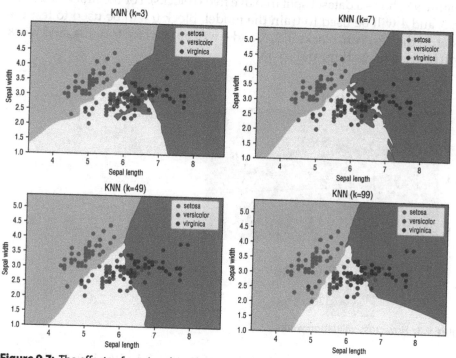

Figure 9.7: The effects of varying the values of k

Note that as k increases, the boundary becomes smoother. But it also means that more points will be classified incorrectly. When k increases to a large value, *underfitting* occurs.

The key issue with KNN is then how do you find out the ideal value of k to use?

Cross-Validation

In the previous few chapters, you have witnessed that we split our dataset into two individual sets—one for training and one for testing. However, the data in your dataset may not be distributed evenly, and as a result your test set may be too simple or too hard to predict, thereby making it very difficult to know if your model works well.

Instead of using part of the data for training and part for testing, you can split the data into *k-folds* and train the models *k* times, rotating the training and testing sets. By doing so, each data point is now being used for training and testing.

> **TIP** Do not confuse the *k* in k-folds with the *k* in KNN—they are not related.

Figure 9.8 shows a dataset split into five folds (blocks). For the first run, blocks 1, 2, 3, and 4 will be used to train the model. Block 0 will be used to test the model. In the next run, blocks 0, 2, 3, and 4 will be used for training, and block 1 will be used for testing, and so on.

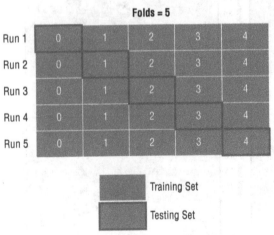

Figure 9.8: How cross-validation works

At the end of each run, the model is scored. At the end of the k-runs, the score is averaged. This averaged score will give you a good indication of how well your algorithm performs.

> **TIP** The purpose of *cross-validation* is not for training your model, but rather it is for model checking. Cross-validation is useful when you need to compare different machine learning algorithms to see how they perform with the given dataset. Once the algorithm is selected, you will use all of the data for training the model.

Parameter-Tuning K

Now that you understand cross-validation, let's use it on our Iris dataset. We will train the model using all of the four features, and at the same time we shall use cross-validation on the dataset using 10 folds. We will do this for each value of k:

```
from sklearn.model_selection import cross_val_score

#---holds the cv (cross-validates) scores---
cv_scores = []

#---use all features---
X = iris.data[:, :4]
y = iris.target

#---number of folds---
folds = 10

#---creating odd list of K for KNN---
ks = list(range(1,int(len(X) * ((folds - 1)/folds))))

#---remove all multiples of 3---
ks = [k for k in ks if k % 3 != 0]

#---perform k-fold cross validation---
for k in ks:
    knn = KNeighborsClassifier(n_neighbors=k)

    #---performs cross-validation and returns the average accuracy---
    scores = cross_val_score(knn, X, y, cv=folds, scoring='accuracy')
    mean = scores.mean()
    cv_scores.append(mean)
    print(k, mean)
```

The Scikit-learn library provides the `cross_val_score()` function that performs cross-validation for you automatically, and it returns the metrics that you want (for example, accuracy).

When using cross-validation, be aware that at any one time, there will be *((folds-1)/folds) * total_rows* available for training. This is because *(1/folds) * total_rows* will be used for testing.

For KNN, there are three rules to which you must adhere:

- The value of k cannot exceed the number of rows for training.

- The value of k should be an odd number (so that you can avoid situations where there is a tie between the classes) for a two-class problem.

- The value of k must not be a multiple of the number of classes (to avoid ties, similar to the previous point).

Hence, the `ks` list in the preceding code snippet will contain the following values:

```
[1, 2, 4, 5, 7, 8, 10, 11, 13, 14, 16, 17, 19, 20, 22, 23, 25, 26, 28,
29, 31, 32, 34, 35, 37, 38, 40, 41, 43, 44, 46, 47, 49, 50, 52, 53, 55,
56, 58, 59, 61, 62, 64, 65, 67, 68, 70, 71, 73, 74, 76, 77, 79, 80, 82,
83, 85, 86, 88, 89, 91, 92, 94, 95, 97, 98, 100, 101, 103, 104, 106,
107, 109, 110, 112, 113, 115, 116, 118, 119, 121, 122, 124, 125, 127,
128, 130, 131, 133, 134]
```

After the training, the `cv_scores` will contain a list of accuracies based on the different values of k:

```
1 0.96
2 0.9533333333333334
4 0.9666666666666666
5 0.9666666666666668
7 0.9666666666666668
8 0.9666666666666668
10 0.9666666666666668
11 0.9666666666666668
13 0.9800000000000001
14 0.9733333333333334
...
128 0.6199999999999999
130 0.6066666666666667
131 0.5933333333333332
133 0.5666666666666667
134 0.5533333333333333
```

Finding the Optimal K

To find the optimal k, you simply find the value of k that gives the highest accuracy. Or, in this case, you will want to find the lowest *misclassification error (MSE)*.

The following code snippet finds the MSE for each k, and then finds the k with the lowest MSE. It then plots a line chart of MSE against k (see Figure 9.9):

```
#---calculate misclassification error for each k---
MSE = [1 - x for x in cv_scores]

#---determining best k (min. MSE)---
optimal_k = ks[MSE.index(min(MSE))]
print(f"The optimal number of neighbors is {optimal_k}")

#---plot misclassification error vs k---
plt.plot(ks, MSE)
plt.xlabel('Number of Neighbors K')
plt.ylabel('Misclassification Error')
plt.show()
```

The preceding code snippet prints out the following:

```
The optimal number of neighbors is 13
```

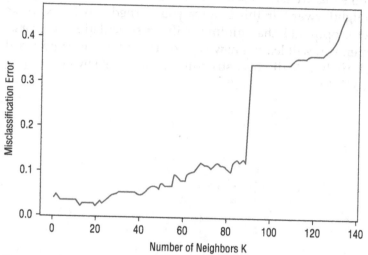

Figure 9.9: The chart of miscalculations for each k

Figure 9.10 shows the classification when k = 13.

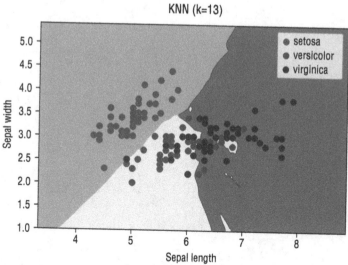

Figure 9.10: The optimal value of k at 13

Summary

Of the four algorithms that we have discussed in this book, KNN is considered one of the most straightforward. In this chapter, you learned how KNN works and how to derive the optimal k that minimizes the miscalculation of errors.

In the next chapter, you will learn a new type of algorithm—unsupervised learning. You will learn how to discover structures in your data by performing clustering using K-Means.

CHAPTER 10

Unsupervised Learning— Clustering Using K-Means

What Is Unsupervised Learning?

So far, all of the machine learning algorithms that you have seen are supervised learning. That is, the datasets have all been labeled, classified, or categorized. Datasets that have been labeled are known as *labeled data,* while datasets that have not been labeled are known as *unlabeled data.* Figure 10.1 shows an example of labeled data.

Features		*Label*
Size of House	Year Built	Price Sold

Figure 10.1: Labeled data

Based on the size of the house and the year in which it was built, you have the price at which the house was sold. The selling price of the house is the *label,* and your machine learning model can be trained to give the estimated worth of the house based on its size and the year in which it was built.

Unlabeled data, on the other hand, is data without label(s). For example, Figure 10.2 shows a dataset containing a group of people's waist circumference and corresponding leg length. Given this set of data, you can try to cluster them into groups based on the waist circumference and leg length, and from there you can figure out the average dimension in each group. This would be useful for clothing manufacturers to tailor different sizes of clothing to fit its customers.

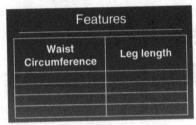

Figure 10.2: Unlabeled data

Unsupervised Learning Using K-Means

Since there is no label in unlabeled data, it is thus of interest to us that we are able to find patterns in that unlabeled data. This technique of finding patterns in unlabeled data is known as *clustering.* The main aim of clustering is to segregate groups with similar traits and assign them into groups (commonly known as *clusters*).

One of the common algorithms used for clustering is the K-Means algorithm. K-Means clustering is a type of unsupervised learning:

- Used when you have unlabeled data
- The goal is to find groups in data, with the number of groups represented by K

The goal of K-Means clustering is to achieve the following:

- K centroids representing the center of the clusters
- Labels for the training data

In the next section, you will learn how clustering using K-Means works.

How Clustering in K-Means Works

Let's walk through a simple example so that you can see how clustering using K-Means works. Suppose you have a series of unlabeled points, as shown in Figure 10.3.

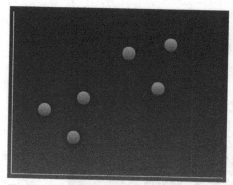

Figure 10.3: A set of unlabeled data points

Your job is to cluster all of these points into distinct groups so that you can discover a pattern among them. Suppose you want to separate them into two groups (that is, $K=2$). The end result would look like Figure 10.4.

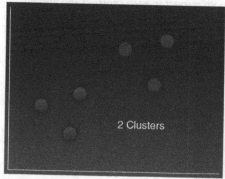

2 Clusters

Figure 10.4: Clustering the points into two distinct clusters

First, you will randomly put K number of centroids on the graph. In Figure 10.5, since K equals 2, we will randomly put two centroids on the graph: C_0 and C_1. For each point on the graph, measure the distance between itself and each of the centroids. As shown in the figure, the distance (represented by d_0) between a and c_0 is shorter than the distance (represented by d_1) between a and c_1. Hence, a is now classified as cluster 0. Likewise, for point b, the distance between itself and c_1 is shorter than the distance between itself and c_0. Hence, point b is classified as cluster 1. You repeat this process for all the points in the graph.

After the first round, the points would be clustered, as shown in Figure 10.6.

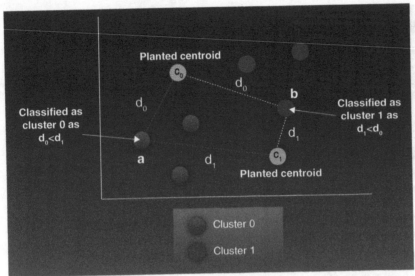

Figure 10.5: Measuring the distance of each point with respect to each centroid and finding the shortest distance

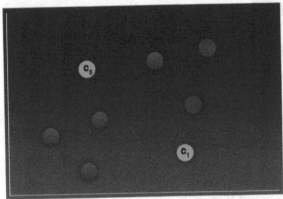

Figure 10.6: Groupings of the points after the first round of clustering

Now take the average of all of the points in each cluster and reposition the centroids using the newly calculated average. Figure 10.7 shows the new positions of the two centroids.

You now measure the distance between each of the old centroids and the new centroids (see Figure 10.8). If the distance is 0, that means that the centroid did not change position and hence the centroid is found. You repeat the entire process until all the centroids do not change position anymore.

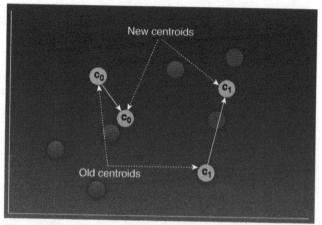

Figure 10.7: Repositioning the centroids by taking the average of all the points in each cluster

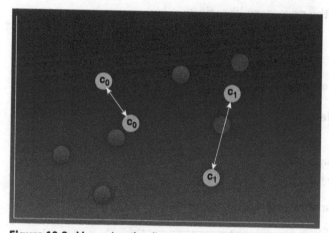

Figure 10.8: Measuring the distance between each centroid; if the distance is 0, the centroid is found

Implementing K-Means in Python

Now that you have a clear picture of how K-Means works, it is useful to implement this using Python. You will first implement K-Means using Python, and then see how you can use Scikit-learn's implementation of K-Means in the next section.

Suppose you have a file named `kmeans.csv` with the following content:

```
x,y
1,1
2,2
```

```
2,3
1,4
3,3
6,7
7,8
6,8
7,6
6,9
2,5
7,8
8,9
6,7
7,8
3,1
8,4
8,6
8,9
```

Let's first import all of the necessary libraries:

```
%matplotlib inline
import numpy as np
import pandas as pd
import matplotlib.pyplot as plt
```

Then load the CSV file into a Pandas dataframe, and plot a scatter plot showing the points:

```
df = pd.read_csv("kmeans.csv")
plt.scatter(df['x'],df['y'], c='r', s=18)
```

Figure 10.9 shows the scatter plot with the points.

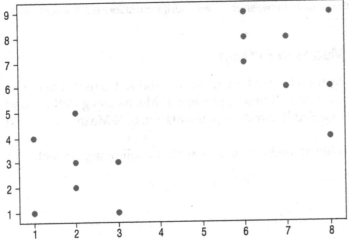

Figure 10.9: The scatter plot showing all the points

You can now generate some random centroids. You also need to decide on the value of K. Let's assume K to be 3 for now. You will learn how to determine the optimal K later in this chapter. The following code snippet generates three random centroids and marks them on the scatter plot:

```
#---let k assume a value---
k = 3

#---create a matrix containing all points---
X = np.array(list(zip(df['x'],df['y'])))

#---generate k random points (centroids)---
Cx = np.random.randint(np.min(X[:,0]), np.max(X[:,0]), size = k)
Cy = np.random.randint(np.min(X[:,1]), np.max(X[:,1]), size = k)

#---represent the k centroids as a matrix---
C = np.array(list(zip(Cx, Cy)), dtype=np.float64)
print(C)

#---plot the orginal points as well as the k centroids---
plt.scatter(df['x'], df['y'], c='r', s=8)
plt.scatter(Cx, Cy, marker='*', c='g', s=160)
plt.xlabel("x")
plt.ylabel("y")
```

Figure 10.10 shows the points, as well as the centroids on the scatter plot.

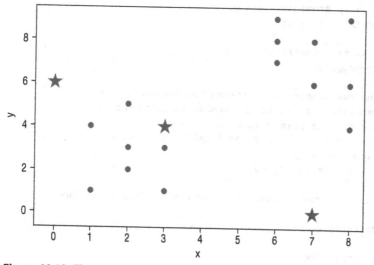

Figure 10.10: The scatter plot with the points and the three random centroids

Now comes the real meat of the program. The following code snippet implements the K-Means algorithm that we discussed earlier in the "How Clustering in K-Means Works" section:

```python
from copy import deepcopy

#---to calculate the distance between two points---
def euclidean_distance(a, b, ax=1):
    return np.linalg.norm(a - b, axis=ax)

#---create a matrix of 0 with same dimension as C (centroids)---
C_prev = np.zeros(C.shape)

#---to store the cluster each point belongs to---
clusters = np.zeros(len(X))

#---C is the random centroids and C_prev is all 0s---
#---measure the distance between the centroids and C_prev---
distance_differences = euclidean_distance(C, C_prev)

#---loop as long as there is still a difference in
# distance between the previous and current centroids---
while distance_differences.any() != 0:
    #---assign each value to its closest cluster---
    for i in range(len(X)):
        distances = euclidean_distance(X[i], C)

        #---returns the indices of the minimum values along an axis---
        cluster = np.argmin(distances)
        clusters[i] = cluster

    #---store the prev centroids---
    C_prev = deepcopy(C)

    #---find the new centroids by taking the average value---
    for i in range(k):  #---k is the number of clusters---
        #---take all the points in cluster i---
        points = [X[j] for j in range(len(X)) if clusters[j] == i]
        if len(points) != 0:
            C[i] = np.mean(points, axis=0)

    #---find the distances between the old centroids and the new
centroids---
    distance_differences = euclidean_distance(C, C_prev)

#---plot the scatter plot---
colors = ['b','r','y','g','c','m']
for i in range(k):
    points = np.array([X[j] for j in range(len(X)) if clusters[j] == i])
    if len(points) > 0:
```

```
        plt.scatter(points[:, 0], points[:, 1], s=10, c=colors[i])
    else:
        # this means that one of the clusters has no points
        print("Plesae regenerate your centroids again.")

    plt.scatter(points[:, 0], points[:, 1], s=10, c=colors[i])
    plt.scatter(C[:, 0], C[:, 1], marker='*', s=100, c='black')
```

With the preceding code snippet, the centroids would now be computed and displayed on the scatter plot, as shown in Figure 10.11.

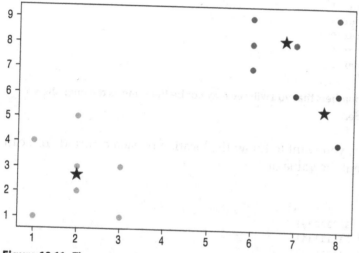

Figure 10.11: The scatter plot showing the clustering of the points as well as the new-found centroids

> **TIP** Due to the locations of the points, it is possible that the centroids you obtained may not be identical to the one shown in Figure 10.11.
>
> Also, there may be cases where after the clustering, there are no points belonging to a particular centroid. In this case, you have to regenerate the centroid and perform the clustering again.

You can now also print out the clusters to which each point belongs:

```
for i, cluster in enumerate(clusters):
    print("Point " + str(X[i]),
          "Cluster " + str(int(cluster)))
```

You should be able to see the following output:

```
Point [1 1] Cluster 2
Point [2 2] Cluster 2
Point [2 3] Cluster 2
```

```
Point [1 4] Cluster 2
Point [3 3] Cluster 2
Point [6 7] Cluster 1
Point [7 8] Cluster 1
Point [6 8] Cluster 1
Point [7 6] Cluster 0
Point [6 9] Cluster 1
Point [2 5] Cluster 2
Point [7 8] Cluster 1
Point [8 9] Cluster 1
Point [6 7] Cluster 1
Point [7 8] Cluster 1
Point [3 1] Cluster 2
Point [8 4] Cluster 0
Point [8 6] Cluster 0
Point [8 9] Cluster 1
```

TIP The cluster numbers that you will see may not be the same as the ones shown in the preceding code.

More importantly, you want to know the location of each centroid. You can do so via printing out the value of C:

```
print (C)
'''
[[ 7.66666667  5.33333333]
 [ 6.77777778  8.11111111]
 [ 2.         2.71428571]]
'''
```

Using K-Means in Scikit-learn

Rather than implementing your own K-Means algorithm, you can use the KMeans class in Scikit-learn to do clustering. Using the same dataset that you used in the previous section, the following code snippet creates an instance of the KMeans class with a cluster size of 3:

```
#---using sci-kit-learn---
from sklearn.cluster import KMeans
k=3
kmeans = KMeans(n_clusters=k)
```

You can now train the model using the fit() function:

```
kmeans = kmeans.fit(X)
```

To assign a label to all of the points, use the `predict()` function:

```
labels = kmeans.predict(X)
```

To get the centroids, use the `cluster_centers` property:

```
centroids = kmeans.cluster_centers_
```

Let's print the clusters label and centroids and see what you got:

```
print(labels)
print(centroids)
```

You should see the following:

```
[1 1 1 1 0 0 0 2 0 1 0 0 0 0 1 2 2 0]
[[ 6.77777778  8.11111111]
 [ 2.         2.71428571]
 [ 7.66666667  5.33333333]]
```

> **TIP**   Due to the locations of the points, it is possible that the centroids you
> obtained may not be identical to the one shown here in the text.

Let's now plot the points and centroids on a scatter plot:

```
#---map the labels to colors---
c = ['b','r','y','g','c','m']
colors = [c[i] for i in labels]

plt.scatter(df['x'],df['y'], c=colors, s=18)
plt.scatter(centroids[:, 0], centroids[:, 1], marker='*', s=100, c='black')
```

Figure 10.12 shows the result.

Using the model that you have just trained, you can use it to predict the cluster to which a point will belong using the `predict()` function:

```
#---making predictions---
cluster = kmeans.predict([[3,4]])[0]
print(c[cluster])  # r

cluster = kmeans.predict([[7,5]])[0]
print(c[cluster])  # y
```

The preceding statements print the cluster in which a point is located using its color: `r` for red and `y` for yellow.

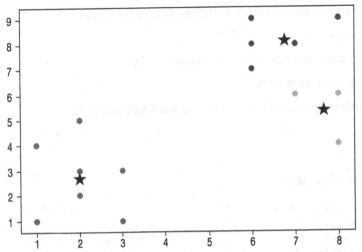

Figure 10.12: Using the KMeans class in Scikit-learn to do the clustering

TIP You may get different colors for the predicted points, which is perfectly fine.

Evaluating Cluster Size Using the Silhouette Coefficient

So far, we have been setting K to a fixed value of 3. How do you ensure that the value of K that you have set is the optimal number for the number of clusters? With a small dataset, it is easy to deduce the value of K by visual inspection; however, with a large dataset, it will be a more challenging task. Also, regardless of the dataset size, you will need a scientific way to prove that the value of K you have selected is the optimal one. To do that, you will use the Silhouette Coefficient.

The *Silhouette Coefficient* is a measure of the quality of clustering that you have achieved. It measures cluster cohesion, which is the space between clusters. The range of values for the Silhouette Coefficient is between –1 and 1.

The Silhouette Coefficient formula is given as:

$$1 - (a / b)$$

where:

- a is the average distance of a point to all other points in the same cluster; if a is small, cluster cohesion is good, as all of the points are close together
- b is the *lowest* average distance of a point to all other points in the closest cluster; if b is large, cluster separation is good, as the nearest cluster is far apart

If a is small and b is large, the Silhouette Coefficient is high. The value of k that yields the highest Silhouette Coefficient is known as the *optimal K*.

Calculating the Silhouette Coefficient

Let's walk through an example of how to calculate the Silhouette Coefficient of a point. Consider the seven points and the clusters (K=3) to which they belong, as shown in Figure 10.13.

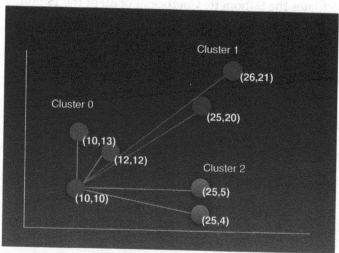

Figure 10.13: The set of points and their positions

Let's calculate the Silhouette Coefficient of a particular point and walk through the math. Consider the point (10,10) in cluster 0:

- Calculate its average distance to all other points in the same cluster:
  - $(10,10) - (12,12) = \sqrt{8} = 2.828$
  - $(10,10) - (10,13) = \sqrt{9} = 3$
  - Average: $(2.828 + 3.0) / 2 = 2.914$
- Calculate its average distance to all other points in cluster 1:
  - $(10,10) - (25,20) = \sqrt{325} = 18.028$
  - $(10,10) - (26,21) = \sqrt{377} = 19.416$
  - Average: $(18.028 + 19.416) / 2 = 18.722$
- Calculate its average distance to all other points in cluster 2:
  - $(10,10) - (25,5) = \sqrt{250} = 15.811$
  - $(10,10) - (25,4) = \sqrt{261} = 16.155$
  - Average: $(15.811 + 16.156) / 2 = 15.983$
- Minimum average distance from (10,10) to all the points in cluster 1 and 2 is min(18.722,15.983) = 15.983

Therefore, the Silhouette Coefficient of point (10,10) is $1 - (a/b) = 1 - (2.914/15.983)$ = 0.817681—and this is just for one point in the dataset. You need to calculate the Silhouette Coefficients of the other six points in the dataset. Fortunately, Scikit-learn contains the `metrics` module that automates this process.

Using the `kmean.csv` example that you used earlier in this chapter, the following code snippet calculates the Silhouette Coefficient of all of the 19 points in the dataset and prints out the average of the Silhouette Coefficient:

```
from sklearn import metrics

silhouette_samples = metrics.silhouette_samples(X, kmeans.labels_)
print(silhouette_samples)

print("Average of Silhouette Coefficients for k =", k)
print("==========================================")
print("Silhouette mean:", silhouette_samples.mean())
```

You should see the following results:

```
[ 0.67534567  0.73722797  0.73455072  0.66254937  0.6323039   0.33332111
  0.63792468  0.58821402  0.29141777  0.59137721  0.50802377  0.63792468
  0.52511161  0.33332111  0.63792468  0.60168807  0.51664787  0.42831295
  0.52511161]

Average of Silhouette Coefficients for k = 3
=============================================
Silhouette mean: 0.55780519852
```

In the preceding statements, you used the `metrics.silhouette_samples()` function to get an array of Silhouette Coefficients for the 19 points. You then called the `mean()` function on the array to get the average Silhouette Coefficient. If you are just interested in the average Silhouette coefficient and not the Silhouette Coefficient for the individual points, you can simply call the `metrics` `.silhouette_score()` function, like this:

```
print("Silhouette mean:", metrics.silhouette_score(X, kmeans.labels_))
# Silhouette mean: 0.55780519852
```

Finding the Optimal K

Now that you have seen how to calculate the mean Silhouette Coefficient for a dataset with K clusters, what you want to do next is to find the optimal K that gives you the highest average Silhouette Coefficient. You can start with a cluster size of 2, up to the cluster size of one less than the size of the dataset. The following code snippet does just that:

```
silhouette_avgs = []
min_k = 2

#---try k from 2 to maximum number of labels---
for k in range(min_k, len(X)):
    kmean = KMeans(n_clusters=k).fit(X)
    score = metrics.silhouette_score(X, kmean.labels_)
    print("Silhouette Coefficients for k =", k, "is", score)
    silhouette_avgs.append(score)

f, ax = plt.subplots(figsize=(7, 5))
ax.plot(range(min_k, len(X)), silhouette_avgs)

plt.xlabel("Number of clusters")
plt.ylabel("Silhouette Coefficients")

#---the optimal k is the one with the highest average silhouette---
Optimal_K = silhouette_avgs.index(max(silhouette_avgs)) + min_k
print("Optimal K is ", Optimal_K)
```

The code snippet will print out something similar to the following:

```
Silhouette Coefficients for k = 2 is 0.689711206994
Silhouette Coefficients for k = 3 is 0.55780519852
Silhouette Coefficients for k = 4 is 0.443038181464
Silhouette Coefficients for k = 5 is 0.442424857695
Silhouette Coefficients for k = 6 is 0.408647742839
Silhouette Coefficients for k = 7 is 0.393618055172
Silhouette Coefficients for k = 8 is 0.459039364508
Silhouette Coefficients for k = 9 is 0.447750636074
Silhouette Coefficients for k = 10 is 0.512411340842
Silhouette Coefficients for k = 11 is 0.469556467119
Silhouette Coefficients for k = 12 is 0.440983139813
Silhouette Coefficients for k = 13 is 0.425567707244
Silhouette Coefficients for k = 14 is 0.383836485201
Silhouette Coefficients for k = 15 is 0.368421052632
Silhouette Coefficients for k = 16 is 0.368421052632
Silhouette Coefficients for k = 17 is 0.368421052632
Silhouette Coefficients for k = 18 is 0.368421052632
Optimal K is  2
```

As you can see from the output, the optimal K is 2. Figure 10.14 shows the chart of the Silhouette Coefficients plotted against the number of clusters (k).

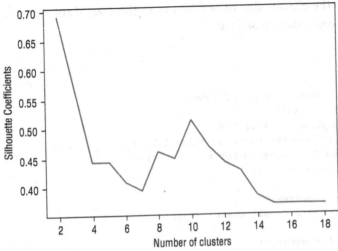

Figure 10.14: The chart showing the various values of K and their corresponding Silhouette Coefficients

Using K-Means to Solve Real-Life Problems

Suppose you are a clothing designer, and you have been tasked with designing a new series of Bermuda shorts. One of the design problems is that you need to come up with a series of sizes so that it can fit most people. Essentially, you need to have a series of sizes of people with different:

- Waist Circumference
- Upper Leg Length

So, how do you find the right combination of sizes? This is where the K-Means algorithm comes in handy. The first thing you need to do is to get ahold of a dataset containing the measurements of a group of people (of a certain age range). Using this dataset, you can apply the K-Means algorithm to group these people into clusters based on the specific measurement of their body parts. Once the clusters are found, you would now have a very clear picture of the sizes for which you need to design.

For the dataset, you can use the Body Measurement dataset from `https://data.world/rhoyt/body-measurements`. This dataset has 27 columns and 9338 rows. Among the 27 columns, two columns are what you need:

BMXWAIST: Waist Circumference (cm)

BMXLEG: Upper Leg Length (cm)

For this example, assume that the dataset has been saved locally with the filename `BMX_G.csv`.

Importing the Data

First, import the data into a Pandas dataframe:

```
%matplotlib inline
import numpy as np
import pandas as pd

df = pd.read_csv("BMX_G.csv")
```

Examine its shape, and you should see 9338 rows and 27 columns:

```
print(df.shape)
# (9338, 27)
```

Cleaning the Data

The dataset contains a number of missing values, so it is important to clean the data. To see how many empty fields each column contains, use the following statement:

```
df.isnull().sum()
```

You should see the following:

```
Unnamed: 0         0
seqn               0
bmdstats           0
bmxwt             95
bmiwt           8959
bmxrecum        8259
bmirecum        9307
bmxhead         9102
bmihead         9338
bmxht            723
bmiht           9070
bmxbmi           736
bmdbmic         5983
bmxleg          2383
bmileg          8984
bmxarml          512
bmiarml         8969
bmxarmc          512
bmiarmc         8965
bmxwaist        1134
bmiwaist        8882
bmxsad1         2543
bmxsad2         2543
bmxsad3         8940
```

```
bmxsad4       8940
bmdavsad      2543
bmdsadcm      8853
dtype: int64
```

Observe that the column `bmxleg` has 2383 missing values and `bmxwaist` has 1134 missing values, so you would need to remove them as follows:

```
df = df.dropna(subset=['bmxleg','bmxwaist'])  # remove rows with NaNs
print(df.shape)
# (6899, 27)
```

After removing the `bmxleg` and `bmxwaist` columns with missing values, there are now 6899 rows remaining.

Plotting the Scatter Plot

With the data cleaned, let's plot a scatter plot showing the distribution in upper leg length and waist circumference:

```
import matplotlib.pyplot as plt

plt.scatter(df['bmxleg'],df['bmxwaist'], c='r', s=2)
plt.xlabel("Upper leg Length (cm)")
plt.ylabel("Waist Circumference (cm)")
```

Figure 10.15 shows the scatter plot.

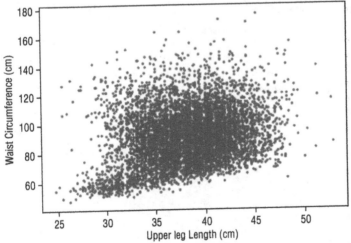

Figure 10.15: The scatter plot showing the distribution of waist circumference and upper leg length

Clustering Using K-Means

Assume that you want to create two sizes of Bermuda shorts. In this case, you would like to cluster the points into two clusters; that is, K=2. Again, we can use Scikit-learn's KMeans class for this purpose:

```
#---using sci-kit-learn---
from sklearn.cluster import KMeans

k = 2
X = np.array(list(zip(df['bmxleg'],df['bmxwaist'])))

kmeans = KMeans(n_clusters=k)
kmeans = kmeans.fit(X)
labels = kmeans.predict(X)
centroids = kmeans.cluster_centers_

#---map the labels to colors---
c = ['b','r','y','g','c','m']
colors = [c[i] for i in labels]

plt.scatter(df['bmxleg'],df['bmxwaist'], c=colors, s=2)
plt.scatter(centroids[:, 0], centroids[:, 1], marker='*', s=100, c='black')
```

Figure 10.16 shows the points separated into two clusters, red and blue, together with the two centroids.

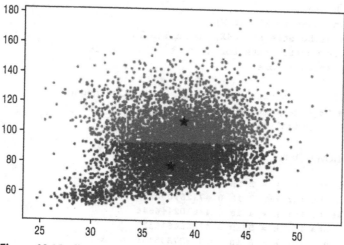

Figure 10.16: Clustering the points into two clusters

For you, the most important information is the value of the two centroids:

```
print(centroids)
```

You should get the following:

```
[[ 37.65663043   77.84326087]
 [ 38.81870146  107.9195713 ]]
```

This means that you can now design your Bermuda shorts with the follow-ing dimensions:

- Waist 77.8 cm, upper leg length 37.7 cm
- Waist 107.9 cm, upper leg length 38.8 cm

Finding the Optimal Size Classes

Before deciding on the actual different sizes to make, you wanted to see if the K=2 is the optimal one, hence you try out different values of K from 2 to 10 and look for the optimal K:

```
from sklearn import metrics

silhouette_avgs = []
min_k = 2

#---try k from 2 to maximum number of labels---
for k in range(min_k, 10):
    kmean = KMeans(n_clusters=k).fit(X)
    score = metrics.silhouette_score(X, kmean.labels_)
    print("Silhouette Coefficients for k =", k, "is", score)
    silhouette_avgs.append(score)

#---the optimal k is the one with the highest average silhouette---
Optimal_K = silhouette_avgs.index(max(silhouette_avgs)) + min_k
print("Optimal K is", Optimal_K)
```

The results are as shown here:

```
Silhouette Coefficients for k = 2 is 0.516551581494
Silhouette Coefficients for k = 3 is 0.472269050688
Silhouette Coefficients for k = 4 is 0.436102446644
Silhouette Coefficients for k = 5 is 0.418064636123
Silhouette Coefficients for k = 6 is 0.392927895139
Silhouette Coefficients for k = 7 is 0.378340717032
Silhouette Coefficients for k = 8 is 0.360716292593
Silhouette Coefficients for k = 9 is 0.341592231958
Optimal K is 2
```

The result confirms that the optimal K is 2. That is, you should have two different sizes for the Bermuda shorts that you are designing.

However, the company wanted you to have more sizes so that it can accommodate a wider range of customers. In particular, the company feels that four sizes would be a better decision. To do so, you just need to run the KMeans code snippet that you saw in the "Clustering Using K-Means" section and set k =4.

You should now see the clusters as shown in Figure 10.17.

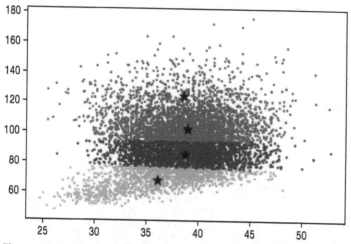

Figure 10.17: Clustering the points into four clusters

The centroids locations are as follows:

```
[[  38.73004292    85.05450644]
 [  38.8849217    102.17011186]
 [  36.04064872    67.30131125]
 [  38.60124294   124.07853107]]
```

This means that you can now design your Bermuda shorts with the following dimensions:

- Waist 67.3 cm, upper leg length 36.0 cm
- Waist 85.1 cm, upper leg length 38.7 cm
- Waist 102.2 cm, upper leg length 38.9 cm
- Waist 124.1 cm, upper leg length 38.6 cm

Summary

In this chapter, you learned about unsupervised learning. Unsupervised learning is a type of machine learning technique that allows you to find patterns in data. In unsupervised learning, the data that is used by the algorithm (for example, K-Means, as discussed in this chapter) is not labeled, and your role is to discover its hidden structures and assign labels to them.

Using Azure Machine Learning Studio

What Is Microsoft Azure Machine Learning Studio?

Microsoft Azure Machine Learning Studio (henceforth referred to as *MAML*) is an online collaborative, drag-and-drop tool for building machine learning models. Instead of implementing machine learning algorithms in languages like Python or R, MAML encapsulates the most-commonly used machine learning algorithms as modules, and it lets you build learning models visually using your dataset. This shields the beginning data science practitioners from the details of the algorithms, while at the same time offering the ability to fine-tune the hyperparameters of the algorithm for advanced users. Once the learning model is tested and evaluated, you can publish your learning models as web services so that your custom apps or BI tools, such as Excel, can consume it. What's more, MAML supports embedding your Python or R scripts within your learning models, giving advanced users the opportunity to write custom machine learning algorithms.

In this chapter, you will take a break from all of the coding that you have been doing in the previous few chapters. Instead of implementing machine learning using Python and Scikit-learn, you will take a look at how to use the MAML to perform machine learning visually using drag-and-drop.

An Example Using the Titanic Experiment

Now that you have a good sense of what machine learning is and what it can do, let's get started with an experiment using MAML. For this experiment, you will be using a classic example in machine learning—predicting the survival of a passenger on the Titanic.

In case you are not familiar with the Titanic, on April 15, 1912, during her maiden voyage, the Titanic sank after colliding with an iceberg, killing 1,502 out of 2,224 passengers and crew. While the main reason for the deaths was due to insufficient lifeboats, of those who survived, most of them were women, children, and the upper-class. As such, this presents a very interesting experiment in machine learning. If we are given a set of data points, containing the various profiles of passengers (such as gender, cabin class, age, and so forth) and whether they survived the sinking, it would be interesting for us to use machine learning to predict the survivability of a passenger based on his/her profile.

Interestingly, you can get the Titanic data from Kaggle (`https://www.kaggle.com/c/titanic/data`). Two sets of data are provided (see Figure 11.1):

- Training set
- Testing set

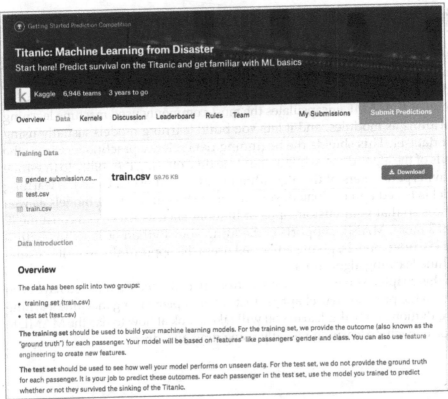

Figure 11.1: You can download the training and testing datasets from Kaggle

You use the training set to train your learning model so that you can use it to make predictions. Once your learning model is trained, you will make use of the testing set to predict the survivability of passengers.

Because the testing test does not contain a label specifying if a passenger survived, we will not use it for this experiment. Instead, we will only use the training set for training and testing our model.

Once the training set is downloaded, examine its contents (see Figure 11.2).

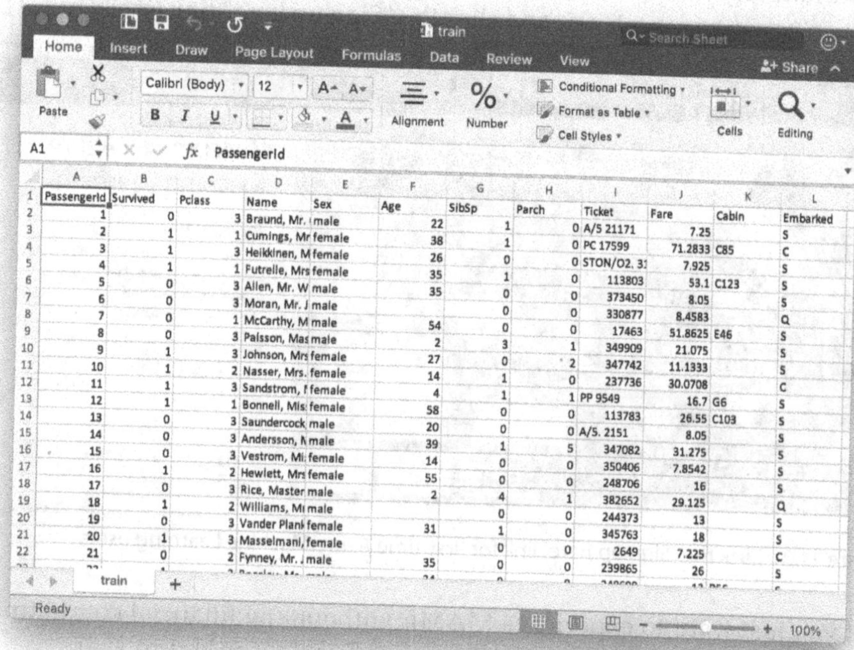

Figure 11.2: Examining the data in Excel

The training set should have the following fields:

PassengerId: A running number indicating the row of records.

Survived: If the particular passenger survived the sinking. This is the label of the dataset for our experiment.

Pclass: Ticket class that the passenger is holding.

Name: Name of the passenger.

Sex: Gender of the passenger.

Age: Age of the passenger.

SibSp: Number of siblings/spouses aboard the Titanic.

Parch: Number of parents/children aboard the Titanic.

Ticket: Ticket number.

Fare: Fare paid by the passenger.

Cabin: Cabin number of the passenger.

Embarked: Place of embarkation. Note that C = Cherbourg, Q = Queenstown, and S = Southampton.

Using Microsoft Azure Machine Learning Studio

We are now ready to load the data into MAML. Using your web browser, navigate to http://studio.azureml.net, and click the "Sign up here" link (see Figure 11.3).

Figure 11.3: Click the "Sign up here" link for first-time Azure Machine Learning users

If you just want to experience MAML without any financial commitment, choose the Free Workspace option and click Sign In (see Figure 11.4).

Figure 11.4: You can choose from the various options available to use MAML

Once you are signed in, you should see a list of items on the left side of the page (see Figure 11.5). I will highlight some of the items on this panel as we move along.

Figure 11.5: The left panel of MAML

Uploading Your Dataset

To create learning models, you need datasets. For this example, we will use the dataset that you have just downloaded.

Click the **+ NEW** item located at the bottom-left of the page. Select DATASET on the left (see Figure 11.6), and then click the item on the right labeled FROM LOCAL FILE.

Figure 11.6: Uploading a dataset to the MAML

Click the Choose File button (see Figure 11.7) and locate the training set downloaded earlier. When finished, click the tick button to upload the dataset to the MAML.

Upload a new dataset

SELECT THE DATA TO UPLOAD:

Choose File   train.csv

☐ This is the new version of an existing dataset
ENTER A NAME FOR THE NEW DATASET:

train.csv

SELECT A TYPE FOR THE NEW DATASET:

Generic CSV File with a header (.csv) ▲▼

PROVIDE AN OPTIONAL DESCRIPTION:

✓

Figure 11.7: Choose a file to upload as a dataset

Creating an Experiment

You are now ready to create an experiment in MAML. Click the **+ NEW** button at the bottom-left of the page and select Blank Experiment (see Figure 11.8).

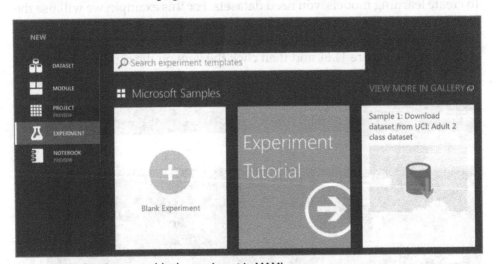

Figure 11.8: Creating a new blank experiment in MAML

You should now see the canvas, as shown in Figure 11.9.

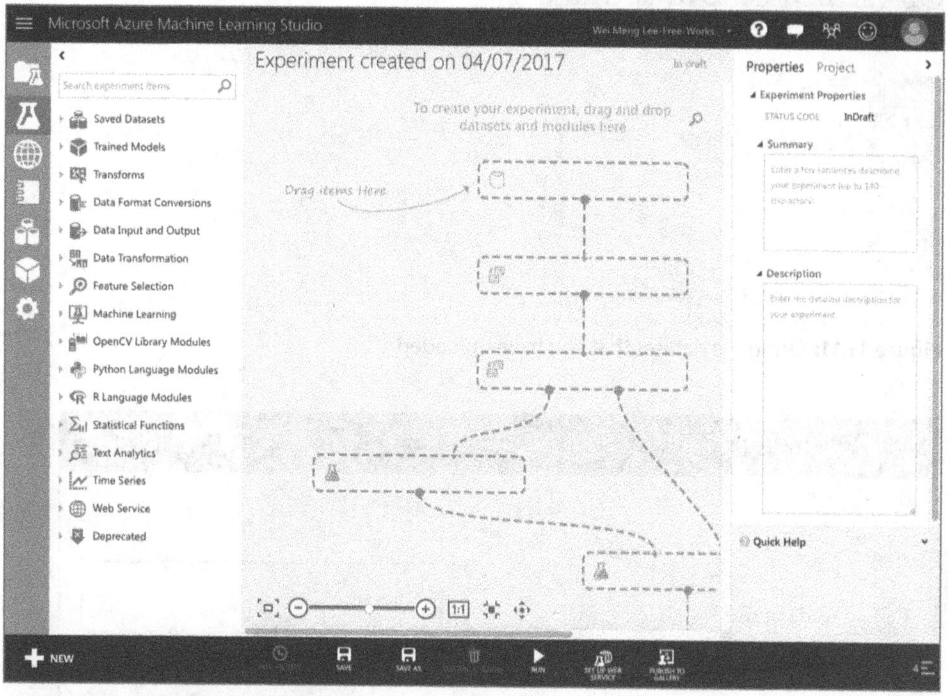

Figure 11.9: The canvas representing your experiment

You can give a name to your experiment by typing it over the default experiment name at the top (see Figure 11.10).

Figure 11.10: Naming your experiment

Once that is done, let's add our training dataset to the canvas. You can do so by typing the name of the training set in the search box on the left, and the matching dataset will now appear (see Figure 11.11).

Drag and drop the `train.csv` dataset onto the canvas (see Figure 11.12).

The `train.csv` dataset has an output port (represented by a circle with a 1 inside). Clicking it will reveal a context menu (see Figure 11.13).

Click Visualize to view the content of the dataset. The dataset is now displayed, as shown in Figure 11.14.

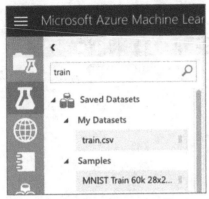

Figure 11.11: Using the dataset that you have uploaded

Figure 11.12: Dragging and dropping the dataset onto the canvas

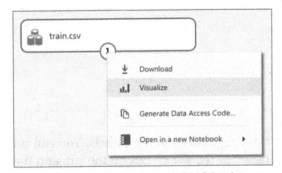

Figure 11.13: Visualizing the content of the dataset

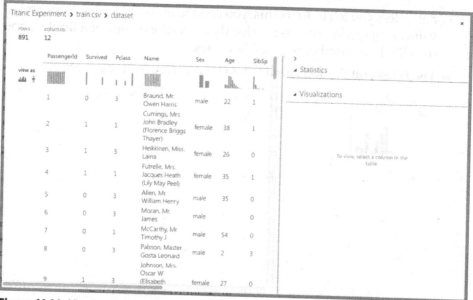

Figure 11.14: Viewing the dataset

Take a minute to scroll through the data. Observe the following:

- The **PassengerID** field is simply a running number, and it does not provide any information with regard to the passenger. This field should be discarded when training your model.

- The **Ticket** field contains the ticket number of the passengers. In this case, however, a lot of these numbers seem to be randomly generated. Thus, it is not very useful in helping us to predict the survivability of a passenger and hence should be discarded.

- The **Cabin** field contains a lot of missing data. Fields that have a lot of missing data do not provide insights to our learning model and hence should be discarded.

- If you select the **Survived** field, you will see the chart displayed on the bottom right of the window (see Figure 11.15). Because a passenger can either survive (represented by a 1) or die (represented by a 0), it does not make sense to have any values in between. However, since this value is represented as a numeric value, MAML would not be able to figure this out unless you tell it. To fix this, you need to make this value a categorical value. A *categorical value* is a value that can take on one of a limited, and usually fixed, number of possible values.

■ The **Pclass**, **SibSp**, and **Parch** fields should all be made categorical as well.

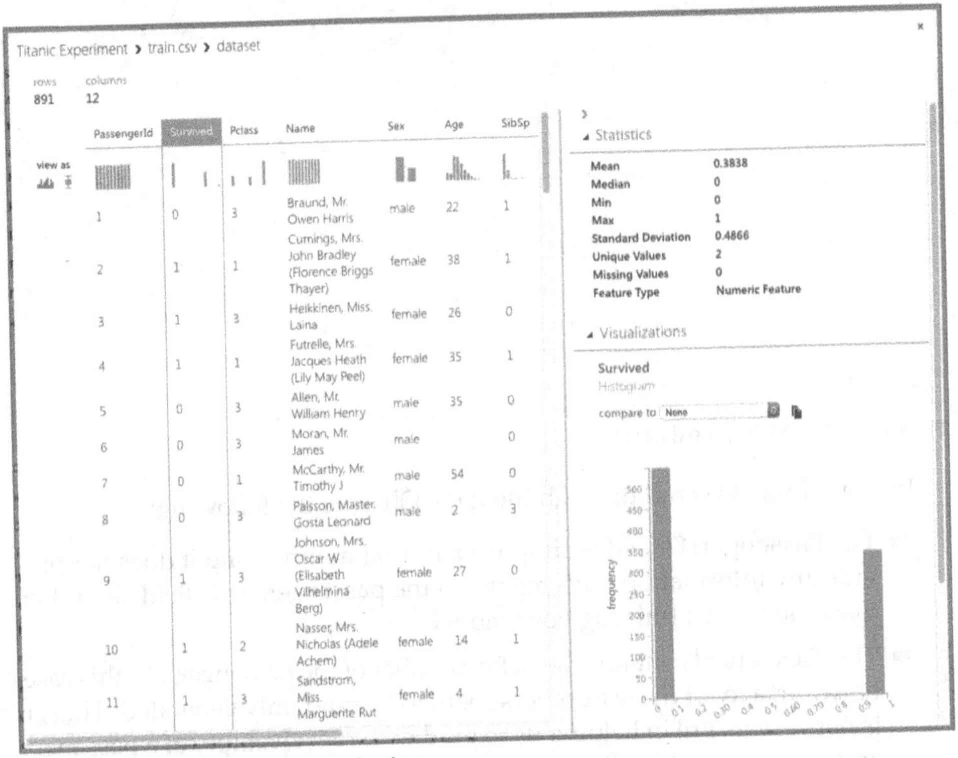

Figure 11.15: Viewing the Survived column

All of the fields that are not discarded are useful in helping us to create a learning model. These fields are known as *features*.

Filtering the Data and Making Fields Categorical

Now that we have identified the features we want, let's add the Select Columns in Dataset module to the canvas (see Figure 11.16).

In the Properties pane, click the Launch column selector and select the columns, as shown in Figure 11.17.

The Select Columns in Dataset module will reduce the dataset to the columns that you have specified. Next, we want to make some of the columns categorical. To do that, add the Edit Metadata module, as shown in Figure 11.18, and connect it as shown. Click the Launch column selector button, and select the **Survived**, **Pclass**, **SibSp**, and **Parch** fields. In the Categorical section of the properties pane, select "Make categorical."

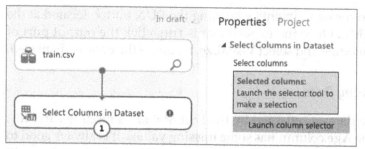

Figure 11.16: Use the Select Columns in Dataset module to filter columns

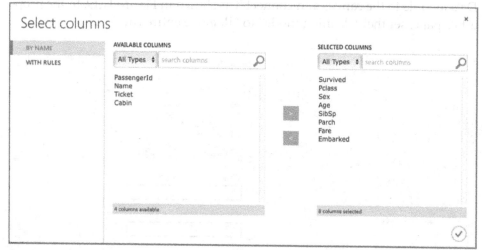

Figure 11.17: Selecting the fields that you want to use as features

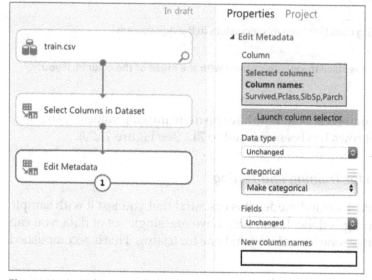

Figure 11.18: Making specific fields categorical

You can now run the experiment by clicking the RUN button located at the bottom of the MAML. Once the experiment is run, click the output port of the Edit Metadata module and select Visualize. Examine the dataset displayed.

Removing the Missing Data

If you examine the dataset returned by the Edit Metadata module carefully, you will see that the **Age** column has some missing values. It is always good to remove all those rows that have missing values so that those missing values will not affect the efficiency of the learning model. To do that, add a *Clean Missing Data* module to the canvas and connect it as shown in Figure 11.19. In the properties pane, set the "Cleaning mode" to "Remove entire row."

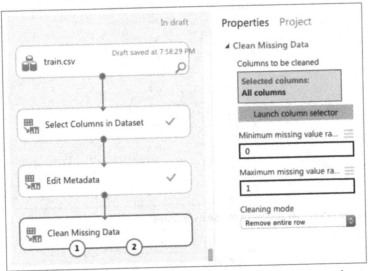

Figure 11.19: Removing rows that have missing values in the Age column

TIP   You can also replace the missing values with the mean of the column, if you prefer.

Click RUN. The dataset should now have no more missing values. Also notice that the number of rows has been reduced to 712 (see Figure 11.20).

Splitting the Data for Training and Testing

When building your learning model, it is essential that you test it with sample data after the training is done. If you only have one single set of data, you can split it into two parts—one for training and one for testing. This is accomplished by the Split Data module (see Figure 11.21). For this example, I am splitting 80 percent of the dataset for training and the remaining 20 percent for testing.

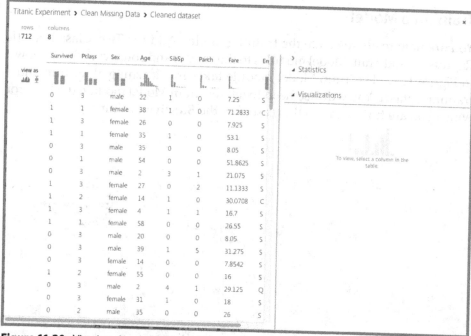

Figure 11.20: Viewing the cleaned and filtered dataset

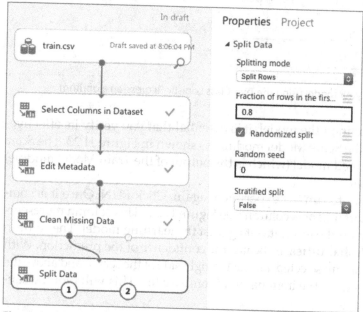

Figure 11.21: Splitting the data into training and testing datasets

The left output port of the Split Data module will return 80 percent of the dataset while the right output port will return the remaining 20 percent.

Training a Model

You are now ready to create the training model. Add the Two-Class Logistic Regression and Train Model modules to the canvas and connect them as shown in Figure 11.22. The Train Model module takes in a learning algorithm and a training dataset. You will also need to tell the Train Model module the label for which you are training it. In this case, it is the **Survived** column.

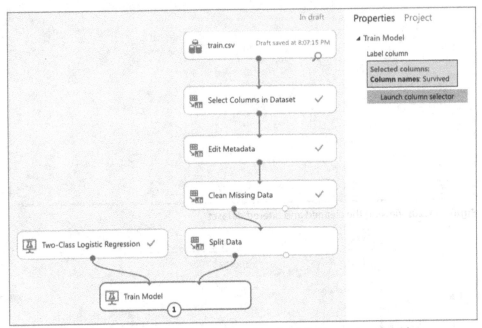

Figure 11.22: Training your model using the Two-Class Logistic Regression algorithm

Once you have trained the model, it is essential that you verify its effectiveness. To do so, use the Score Model module, as shown in Figure 11.23. The *Score Model* takes in a trained model (which is the output of the Train Model module) and a testing dataset.

You are now ready to run the experiment again. Click RUN. Once it is completed, select the **Scored Labels** column (see Figure 11.24). This column represents the results of applying the test dataset against the learning model. The column next to it, **Scored Probabilities**, indicates the confidence of the prediction. With the **Scored Labels** column selected, look at the right side of the screen and above the chart, select Survived for the item named "compare to." This will plot the confusion matrix.

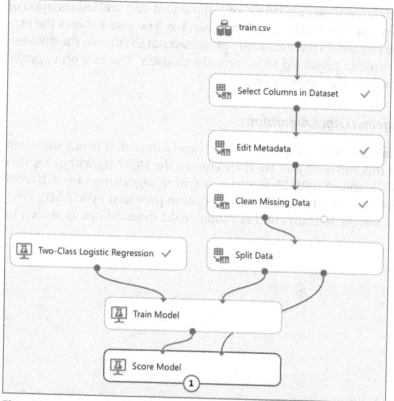

Figure 11.23: Scoring your model using the testing dataset and the trained model

	Survived	Pclass	Sex	Age	SibSp	Parch	Fare	Embarked	Scored Labels	Scored Probabilities
	0	1	male	61	0	0	32.3208	S	0	0.311036
	0	2	male	46	0	0	26	S	0	0.165802
	0	3	female	18	2	0	18	S	1	0.548405
	1	2	male	1	0	2	37.0042	C	0	0.371913
	1	3	male	25	0	0	0	S	0	0.115827
	1	2	male	0.67	1	1	14.5	S	0	0.398321
	1	1	male	48	1	0	76.7292	C	0	0.451904
	0	3	male	29	0	0	8.05	S	0	0.107689
	0	3	male	28	0	0	9.5	S	0	0.109675
	1	1	female	38	1	0	71.2833	C	1	0.920679
	0	2	male	21	0	0	73.5	S	0	0.249162
	0	3	male	24	0	0	9.225	S	0	0.120094
	0	3	male	19	0	0	7.8958	S	0	0.129034
	0	3	female	20	1	0	9.825	S	1	0.626984
	1	3	male	20	1	0	7.925	S	0	0.127833
	1	2	female	17	0	0	10.5	S	1	0.805102

Titanic Experiment ▸ Score Model ▸ Scored dataset

rows 142   columns 10

Statistics

Unique Values   2
Missing Values   0
Feature Type   Categorical Score

Visualizations

Scored Labels
Crosstab

compare to   Survived

Figure 11.24: Viewing the confusion matrix for the learning model

The y-axis of the confusion matrix shows the actual survival information of passengers: 1 for survived and 0 for did not survive. The x-axis shows the prediction. As you can see, 75 were correctly predicted not to survive the disaster, and 35 were correctly predicted to survive the disaster. The two other boxes show the predictions that were incorrect.

Comparing Against Other Algorithms

While the numbers for the predictions look pretty decent, it is not sufficient to conclude at this moment that we have chosen the right algorithm for this problem. MAML comes with 25 machine learning algorithms for different types of problems. Now let's use another algorithm provided by MAML, Two-Class Decision Jungle, to train another model. Add the modules as shown in Figure 11.25.

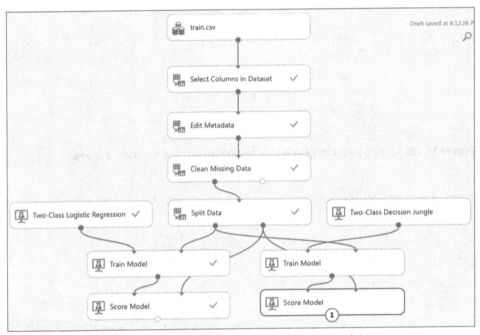

Figure 11.25: Using another algorithm for training the alternative model

> **TIP**   The Two-Class Decision Jungle algorithm is another machine learning algorithm that is based on decision trees. For this experiment, you can also use other algorithms provided by MAML, such as the Two-Class Logistic Regression and Two-Class Support Vector Machine.

Click Run. You can click the output port of the second Score Model module to view the result of the model, just like the previous learning model. However, it would be more useful to be able to compare them directly. You can accomplish this using the Evaluate Model module (see Figure 11.26).

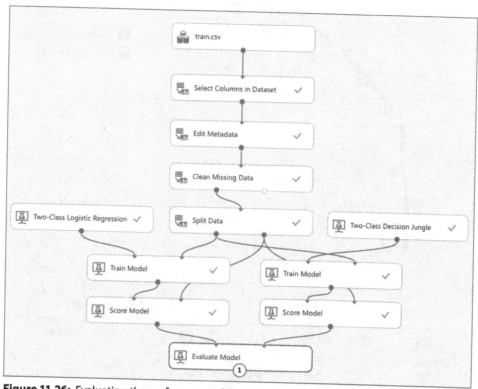

Figure 11.26: Evaluating the performance of the two models

Click RUN to run the experiment. When done, click the output port of the Evaluate Model module and you should see something like Figure 11.27.

The blue line represents the algorithm on the left input port of the Evaluate Model module (Two-Class Logistic Regression), while the red line represents the algorithm on the right (Two-Class Decision Jungle). When you click either the blue or red box, you will see the various metrics for each algorithm displayed below the chart.

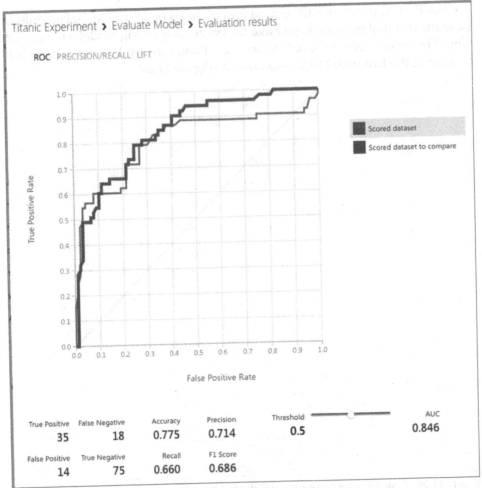

Titanic Experiment **>** Evaluate Model **>** Evaluation results

ROC PRECISION/RECALL LIFT

True Positive	False Negative	Accuracy	Precision	Threshold	AUC
35	18	0.775	0.714	0.5	0.846

False Positive	True Negative	Recall	F1 Score
14	75	0.660	0.686

Figure 11.27: Viewing the metrics for the two learning algorithms

Evaluating Machine Learning Algorithms

Now that you have seen an experiment performed using two specific machine learning algorithms—Two-Class Logistic Regression and Two-Class Decision Jungle—let's step back a little and examine the various metrics that were generated by the *Evaluate Model* module. Specifically, let's define the meaning of the following terms:

True Positive (TP) The model correctly predicts the outcome as positive. In this case, the number of TP indicates the number of correct predictions that a passenger survived (positive) the disaster.

True Negative (TN)   The model correctly predicts the outcome as negative (did not survive); that is, passengers were correctly predicted not to survive the disaster.

False Positive (FP)   The model incorrectly predicted the outcome as positive, but the actual result is negative. In the Titanic example, it means that the passenger did not survive the disaster, but the model predicted the passenger to have survived.

False Negative (FN)   The model incorrectly predicted the outcome as negative, but the actual result is positive. In this case, this means the model predicted that the passenger did not survive the disaster, but actually the passenger did.

This set of numbers is known as the *confusion matrix*. The confusion matrix is discussed in detail in Chapter 7, "Supervised Learning—Classification Using Logistic Regression." So if you are not familiar with it, be sure to read up on Chapter 7.

Publishing the Learning Model as a Web Service

Once the most effective machine learning algorithm has been determined, you can publish the learning model as a web service. Doing so will allow you to build custom apps to consume the service. Imagine that you are building a learning model to help doctors diagnose breast cancer. Publishing as a web service would allow you to build apps to pass the various features to the learning model to make the prediction. Best of all, by using MAML, there is no need to handle the details of publishing the web service—MAML will host it for you on the Azure cloud.

Publishing the Experiment

To publish our experiment as a web service:

- Select the left Train Model module (since it has a better performance compared to the other).

- At the bottom of the page, hover your mouse over the item named SET UP WEB SERVICE, and click Predictive Web Service (Recommended).

TIP   For this experiment, the best algorithm is the one that gives the highest AUC (Area Under the Curve) score.

This will create a new Predictive experiment, as shown in Figure 11.28.

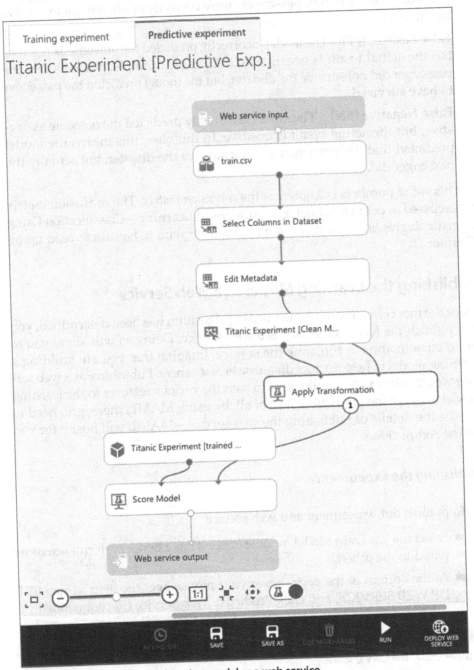

Figure 11.28: Publishing the learning model as a web service

Click RUN, and then DEPLOY WEB SERVICE. The page seen in Figure 11.29 will now be shown.

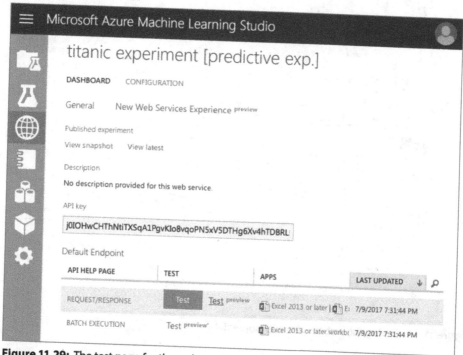

Figure 11.29: The test page for the web service

Testing the Web Service

Click the Test hyperlink. The test page shown in Figure 11.30 is displayed. You can click the Enable button to fill the various fields from your training set. This will save you the chore of filling in the various fields.

The fields should now be filled with values from the training data. At the bottom of the page, click Test Request/Response and the prediction will be shown on the right.

Programmatically Accessing the Web Service

At the top of the Test page, you should see a Consume link as shown in Figure 11.31. Click it.

You will see the credentials that you need to use in order to access your web service, as well as the URLs for the web service. At the bottom of the page, you will see the sample code generated for you that you could use to access the web service programmatically (see Figure 11.32). The sample code is available in C#, Python 2, Python 3, and R.

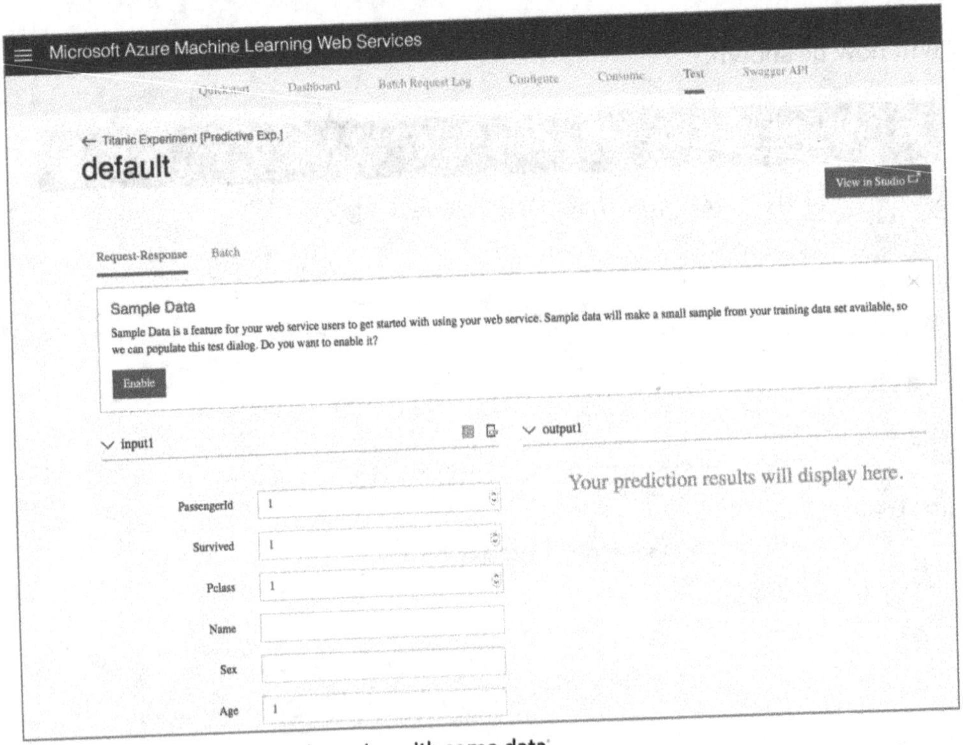

Figure 11.30: Testing the web service with some data

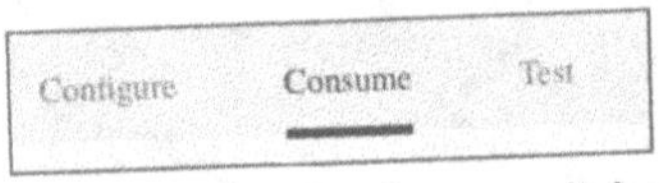

Figure 11.31: The Consume link at the top of the web service page

Click the Python 3+ tab, and copy the code generated. Click the View in Studio link at the top-right of the page to return to MAML. Back in MAML, click the + NEW button at the bottom of the screen. Click NOTEBOOK on the left, and you should be able to see the various notebooks, as shown in Figure 11.33.

TIP   The notebooks hosted by the MAML are the same as the Jupyter Notebook that you have installed on your local computer.

Click Python 3, give a name to your notebook, and paste in the Python code that you copied earlier (see Figure 11.34).

```
Request-Response        Batch
────────────────

C#      Python      Python 3+     R


// This code requires the Nuget package Microsoft.AspNet.WebApi.Client to be installed.
// Instructions for doing this in Visual Studio:
// Tools -> Nuget Package Manager -> Package Manager Console
// Install-Package Microsoft.AspNet.WebApi.Client

using System;
using System.Collections.Generic;
using System.IO;
using System.Net.Http;
using System.Net.Http.Formatting;
using System.Net.Http.Headers;
using System.Text;
using System.Threading.Tasks;

namespace CallRequestResponseService
{
    class Program
    {
        static void Main(string[] args)
        {
            InvokeRequestResponseService().Wait();
        }

        static async Task InvokeRequestResponseService()
        {
            using (var client = new HttpClient())
            {
```

Figure 11.32: The sample code for accessing the web service written in the three programming languages

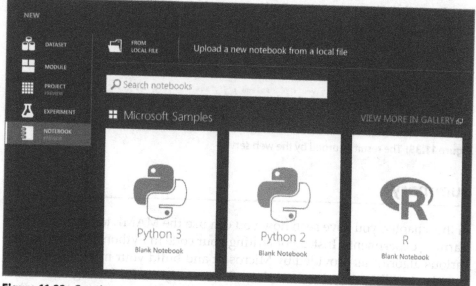

Figure 11.33: Creating a new notebook in MAML

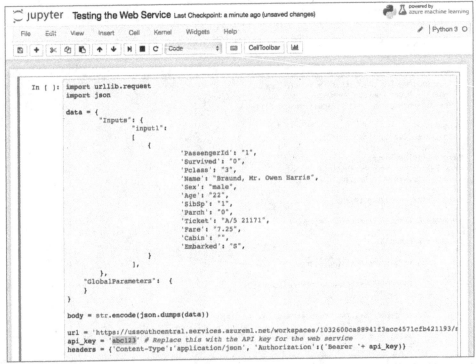

Figure 11.34: Testing the code in the Python notebook

Be sure to replace the value of the api _ key variable with that of your primary key. Press Ctrl+Enter to run the Python code. If the web service is deployed correctly, you should see the result at the bottom of the screen (see Figure 11.35).

```
b'{"Results":{"output1":[{"Survived":"0","Pclass":"3","Sex":"male","Age":"22","SibSp":"1","Pa
rch":"0","Fare":"7.25","Embarked":"S","Scored Labels":"0","Scored Probabilities":"0.123330034
315586"}]}}'
```

Figure 11.35: The result returned by the web service

Summary

In this chapter, you have seen how you can use the MAML to create machine learning experiments. Instead of writing your code in Python, you can use the various algorithms provided by Microsoft and build your machine learning models visually using drag and drop. This is very useful for beginners who want to get started with machine learning without diving into the details. Best of all, MAML helps you to deploy your machine learning as a web service automatically—and it even provides the code for you to consume it.

In the next chapter, you will learn how to deploy your machine learning models created in Python and Scikit-learn manually using Python and the Flask micro-framework.

Deploying Machine Learning Models

Deploying ML

The main goal of machine learning is to create a model that you can use for making predictions. Over the past few chapters in this book, you learned about the various algorithms used to build an ideal machine learning model. At the end of the entire process, what you really want is to make your model accessible to users so that they can utilize it to do useful tasks, like making predictions (such as helping doctors with their diagnosis, and so forth).

A good way to deploy your machine learning model is to build a *REST (REpresentational State Transfer) API*, so that the model is accessible by others who may not be familiar with how machine learning works. Using REST, you can build multi-platform front-end applications (such as iOS, Android, Windows, and so forth) and pass the data to the model for processing. The result can then be returned back to the application. Figure 12.1 summarizes the architecture that we will use for deploying our machine learning model.

In this chapter, we will go through a case study, build a machine learning model, and then deploy it as a REST service. Finally, we will build a console front-end application using Python to allow users to make some predictions.

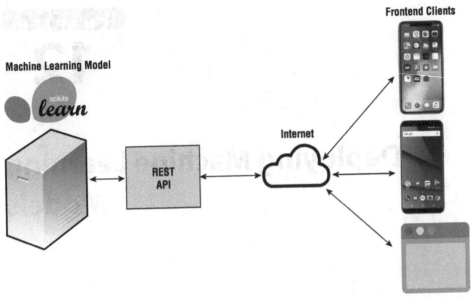

Figure 12.1: Deploying your machine learning model as a REST API allows front-end applications to use it for predictions

Case Study

For this case study, we are going to help predict the likelihood of a person being diagnosed with diabetes based on several diagnostic measurements of that person.

The dataset that you will be using in this chapter is from this database: https://www.kaggle.com/uciml/pima-indians-diabetes-database. This dataset contains several medical independent predictors and one target. Its features consist of the following:

- *Pregnancies*: Number of times pregnant
- *Glucose*: Plasma glucose concentration after 2 hours in an oral glucose tolerance test
- *BloodPressure*: Diastolic blood pressure (mm Hg)
- *SkinThickness*: Triceps skin fold thickness (mm)
- *Insulin*: 2-Hour serum insulin (mu U/ml)
- *BMI*: Body mass index (weight in kg/(height in m)^2)
- *DiabetesPedigreeFunction*: Diabetes pedigree function
- *Age*: Age (years)
- *Outcome*: 0 (non-diabetic) or 1 (diabetic)

The dataset has 768 records, and all patients are females at least 21 years of age and of Pima Indian descent.

Loading the Data

For this example, the dataset has been downloaded locally and named `diabetes.csv`.

The following code snippet loads the dataset and prints out information about the DataFrame using the `info()` function:

```
import numpy as np
import pandas as pd

df = pd.read_csv('diabetes.csv')
df.info()
```

You should see the following output:

```
<class 'pandas.core.frame.DataFrame'>
RangeIndex: 768 entries, 0 to 767
Data columns (total 9 columns):
Pregnancies                 768 non-null int64
Glucose                     768 non-null int64
BloodPressure               768 non-null int64
SkinThickness               768 non-null int64
Insulin                     768 non-null int64
BMI                         768 non-null float64
DiabetesPedigreeFunction    768 non-null float64
Age                         768 non-null int64
Outcome                     768 non-null int64
dtypes: float64(2), int64(7)
memory usage: 54.1 KB
```

Cleaning the Data

As with all datasets, your first job is to clean the data so that there are no missing or erroneous values. Let's first check for nulls in the dataset:

```
#---check for null values---
print("Nulls")
print("=====")
print(df.isnull().sum())
```

The result is as follows:

```
Nulls
=====
Pregnancies          0
Glucose              0
```

```
BloodPressure              0
SkinThickness              0
Insulin                    0
BMI                        0
DiabetesPedigreeFunction   0
Age                        0
Outcome                    0
dtype: int64
```

There are no nulls. Next, let's check for 0s:

```
#---check for 0s---
print("0s")
print("==")
print(df.eq(0).sum())
```

For features like Pregnancies and Outcome, having values of 0 is normal. For the other features, however, a value of 0 indicates that the values are not captured in the dataset.

```
0s
==
Pregnancies              111
Glucose                    5
BloodPressure             35
SkinThickness            227
Insulin                  374
BMI                       11
DiabetesPedigreeFunction   0
Age                        0
Outcome                  500
dtype: int64
```

There are many ways to deal with this case of 0 for features, but for simplicity, let's just replace the 0 values with NaN:

```
df[['Glucose','BloodPressure','SkinThickness',
    'Insulin','BMI','DiabetesPedigreeFunction','Age']] = \
    df[['Glucose','BloodPressure','SkinThickness',
        'Insulin','BMI','DiabetesPedigreeFunction','Age']].replace
(0,np.NaN)
```

Once the NaN values have replaced the 0s in the DataFrame, you can now replace them with the mean of each column as follows:

```
df.fillna(df.mean(), inplace = True)    # replace NaN with the mean
```

You can now check the DataFrame to verify that there are now no more 0s in the DataFrame:

```
print(df.eq(0).sum())
```

You should see this output:

```
Pregnancies                     111
Glucose                           0
BloodPressure                     0
SkinThickness                     0
Insulin                           0
BMI                               0
DiabetesPedigreeFunction          0
Age                               0
Outcome                         500
dtype: int64
```

Examining the Correlation Between the Features

The next step is to examine how the various independent features affect the outcome (whether a patient is diabetic or not). To do that, you can call the `corr()` function on the DataFrame:

```
corr = df.corr()
print(corr)
```

The `corr()` function computes the pairwise correlation of columns. For example, the following output shows that the glucose level of a patient after a 2-hour oral glucose tolerance test has little relationship to the number of pregnancies of a patient (0.127911), but it has a significant relationship to the outcome (0.492928):

```
                  Pregnancies    Glucose  BloodPressure  SkinThickness  \
Pregnancies          1.000000   0.127911       0.208522       0.082989
Glucose              0.127911   1.000000       0.218367       0.192991
BloodPressure        0.208522   0.218367       1.000000       0.192816
SkinThickness        0.082989   0.192991       0.192816       1.000000
Insulin              0.056027   0.420157       0.072517       0.158139
BMI                  0.021565   0.230941       0.281268       0.542398
DiabetesPedigree
Function            -0.033523   0.137060      -0.002763       0.100966
Age                  0.544341   0.266534       0.324595       0.127872
Outcome              0.221898   0.492928       0.166074       0.215299

                   Insulin       BMI  DiabetesPedigreeFunction  \
Pregnancies       0.056027  0.021565                 -0.033523
Glucose           0.420157  0.230941                  0.137060
BloodPressure     0.072517  0.281268                 -0.002763
SkinThickness     0.158139  0.542398                  0.100966
Insulin           1.000000  0.166586                  0.098634
BMI               0.166586  1.000000                  0.153400
DiabetesPedigree
Function          0.098634  0.153400                  1.000000
```

Age	0.136734	0.025519	0.033561
Outcome	0.214411	0.311924	0.173844

	Age	Outcome
Pregnancies	0.544341	0.221898
Glucose	**0.266534**	**0.492928**
BloodPressure	0.324595	0.166074
SkinThickness	0.127872	0.215299
Insulin	0.136734	0.214411
BMI	0.025519	0.311924
DiabetesPedigree		
Function	0.033561	0.173844
Age	1.000000	0.238356
Outcome	0.238356	1.000000

Our goal here is to find out which features significantly affect the outcome.

Plotting the Correlation Between Features

Rather than look at the various numbers representing the various correlations between the columns, it is useful to be able to picture it visually. The following code snippet uses the matshow() function to plot the results returned by the corr() function as a matrix. At the same time, the various correlation factors are also shown in the matrix:

```
%matplotlib inline
import matplotlib.pyplot as plt

fig, ax = plt.subplots(figsize=(10, 10))
cax     = ax.matshow(corr,cmap='coolwarm', vmin=-1, vmax=1)

fig.colorbar(cax)
ticks = np.arange(0,len(df.columns),1)
ax.set_xticks(ticks)

ax.set_xticklabels(df.columns)
plt.xticks(rotation = 90)

ax.set_yticklabels(df.columns)
ax.set_yticks(ticks)

#---print the correlation factor---
for i in range(df.shape[1]):
    for j in range(9):
        text = ax.text(j, i, round(corr.iloc[i][j],2),
                       ha="center", va="center", color="w")
plt.show()
```

Figure 12.2 shows the matrix. The cubes that have colors closest to red represent the highest correlation factors, while those closest to blue represent the lowest correlation factors.

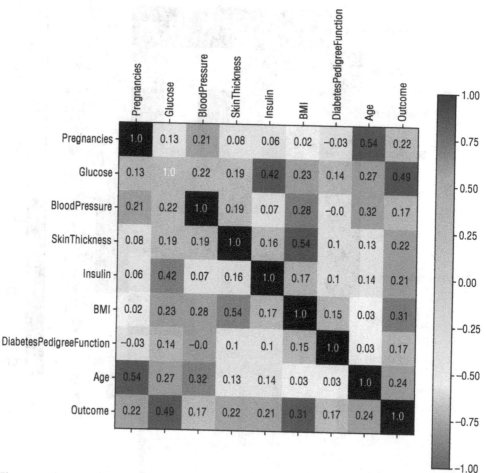

Figure 12.2: Matrix showing the various correlation factors

Another way to plot the correlation matrix is to use Seaborn's `heatmap()` function as follows:

```
import seaborn as sns

sns.heatmap(df.corr(),annot=True)

#---get a reference to the current figure and set its size---
fig = plt.gcf()
fig.set_size_inches(8,8)
```

Figure 12.3 shows the heatmap produced by Seaborn.

Now let's print out the top four features that have the highest correlation with the *Outcome*:

```
#---get the top four features that has the highest correlation---
print(df.corr().nlargest(4, 'Outcome').index)
```

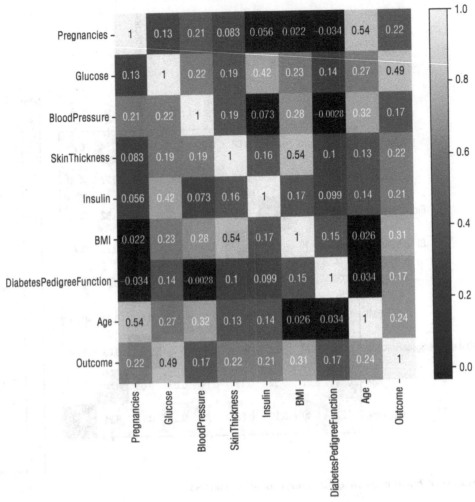

Figure 12.3: Heatmap produced by Seaborn showing the correlation factors

```
#---print the top 4 correlation values---
print(df.corr().nlargest(4, 'Outcome').values[:,8])
```

You should see the following output:

```
Index(['Outcome', 'Glucose', 'BMI', 'Age'], dtype='object')
[1.        0.49292767 0.31192439 0.23835598]
```

You can now see that apart from the Outcome feature, the three most influential features are Glucose, BMI, and Age. We can use these three features to train our model.

Evaluating the Algorithms

Before we train our model, it is always good to evaluate a few algorithms to find the one that gives the best performance. Accordingly, we will try the following algorithms:

- Logistic Regression
- K-Nearest Neighbors (KNN)
- Support Vector Machines (SVM)—Linear and RBF Kernels

Logistic Regression

For the first algorithm, we will use logistic regression. Instead of splitting the dataset into training and testing sets, we will use 10-fold cross-validation to obtain the average score of the algorithm used:

```
from sklearn import linear_model
from sklearn.model_selection import cross_val_score

#---features---
X = df[['Glucose','BMI','Age']]

#---label---
y = df.iloc[:,8]

log_regress = linear_model.LogisticRegression()
log_regress_score = cross_val_score(log_regress, X, y, cv=10,
scoring='accuracy').mean()

print(log_regress_score)
```

The result of training the model should use an average of 0.7617737525632263. We will also save this result to a list so that we can use it to compare with the scores of other algorithms:

```
result = []
result.append(log_regress_score)
```

K-Nearest Neighbors

The next algorithm that we will use is the K-Nearest Neighbors (KNN). In addition to using the 10-fold cross-validation to obtain the average score of the algorithm, we also need to try out the various values of k to obtain the optimal k so that we can get the best accuracy:

```
from sklearn.neighbors import KNeighborsClassifier

#---empty list that will hold cv (cross-validates) scores---
cv_scores = []
```

```
#---number of folds---
folds = 10

#---creating odd list of K for KNN---
ks = list(range(1,int(len(X) * ((folds - 1)/folds)), 2))

#---perform k-fold cross validation---
for k in ks:
    knn = KNeighborsClassifier(n_neighbors=k)
    score = cross_val_score(knn, X, y, cv=folds, scoring='accuracy').mean()
    cv_scores.append(score)

#---get the maximum score---
knn_score = max(cv_scores)

#---find the optimal k that gives the highest score---
optimal_k = ks[cv_scores.index(knn_score)]

print(f"The optimal number of neighbors is {optimal_k}")
print(knn_score)
result.append(knn_score)
```

You should get the following output:

```
The optimal number of neighbors is 19
0.7721462747778537
```

Support Vector Machines

The next algorithm we will use is Support Vector Machine (SVM). We will use two types of kernels for SVM: linear and RBF. The following code snippet uses the linear kernel:

```
from sklearn import svm

linear_svm = svm.SVC(kernel='linear')
linear_svm_score = cross_val_score(linear_svm, X, y,
                                    cv=10, scoring='accuracy').mean()

print(linear_svm_score)
result.append(linear_svm_score)
```

You should get an accuracy of:

```
0.7656527682843473
```

The next code snippet uses the RBF kernel:

```
rbf = svm.SVC(kernel='rbf')
rbf_score = cross_val_score(rbf, X, y, cv=10, scoring='accuracy').mean()
print(rbf_score)
result.append(rbf_score)
```

You should get an accuracy of:

```
0.6353725222146275
```

Selecting the Best Performing Algorithm

Now that we have evaluated the four different algorithms, we can choose the best performing one:

```
algorithms = ["Logistic Regression", "K Nearest Neighbors", "SVM Linear
Kernel", "SVM RBF Kernel"]
cv_mean = pd.DataFrame(result,index = algorithms)
cv_mean.columns=["Accuracy"]
cv_mean.sort_values(by="Accuracy",ascending=False)
```

	Accuracy
K Nearest Neighbors	0.772146
SVM Linear Kernel	0.765653
Logistic Regression	0.761774
SVM RBF Kernel	0.635373

Figure 12.4: Ranking the performance of the various algorithms

Figure 12.4 shows the output of the preceding code snippet.

Training and Saving the Model

Since the best performing algorithm for our dataset is KNN with k = 19, we can now go ahead and train our model using the entire dataset:

```
knn = KNeighborsClassifier(n_neighbors=19)
knn.fit(X, y)
```

Once the model is trained, you need to save it to disk so that the model can be retrieved later for prediction purposes:

```
import pickle

#---save the model to disk---
filename = 'diabetes.sav'

#---write to the file using write and binary mode---
pickle.dump(knn, open(filename, 'wb'))
```

The trained model is now saved to a file named `diabetes.sav`. Let's load it to ensure that it was saved properly:

```
#---load the model from disk---
loaded_model = pickle.load(open(filename, 'rb'))
```

Once the model is loaded, let's do some predictions:

```
Glucose = 65
BMI = 70
Age = 50

prediction = loaded_model.predict([[Glucose, BMI, Age]])
print(prediction)
if (prediction[0]==0):
    print("Non-diabetic")
else:
    print("Diabetic")
```

The output prints the word "Non-Diabetic" if the return value of the prediction is a 0; else it prints the word "Diabetic". You should see the following output:

```
[0]
Non-diabetic
```

We are also interested to know the probabilities of the prediction, and so you get the probabilities and convert them into percentages:

```
proba = loaded_model.predict_proba([[Glucose, BMI, Age]])
print(proba)
print("Confidence: " + str(round(np.amax(proba[0]) * 100 ,2)) + "%")
```

You should see the following:

```
[[0.94736842 0.05263158]]
Confidence: 94.74%
```

The probabilities printed show the probability of the result being 0, and the probability of the result being 1. The prediction is based on the one with the highest probability, and we use that probability and convert it into the confidence percentage.

Deploying the Model

It is now time to deploy our machine learning model as a REST API. First, however, you need to install the *Flask* micro-framework.

TIP *Flask* is a micro-framework for Python that allows you to build web-based applications. Micro-frameworks in Python have little to no dependencies to external libraries and are thus very lightweight. Flask is particularly useful for developing REST APIs. For more information on Flask, check out its documentation at `http://flask.pocoo.org/docs/1.0/`.

Type the following in Terminal or Command Prompt to install Flask:

```
$ pip install flask
```

Once Flask is installed, create a text file named REST _ API.py, and enter the following code snippet:

```python
import pickle
from flask import Flask, request, json, jsonify
import numpy as np


app = Flask(__name__)

#---the filename of the saved model---
filename = 'diabetes.sav'

#---load the saved model---
loaded_model = pickle.load(open(filename, 'rb'))

@app.route('/diabetes/v1/predict', methods=['POST'])
def predict():
    #---get the features to predict---
    features = request.json

    #---create the features list for prediction---
    features_list = [features["Glucose"],
                     features["BMI"],
                     features["Age"]]

    #---get the prediction class---
    prediction = loaded_model.predict([features_list])

    #---get the prediction probabilities---
    confidence = loaded_model.predict_proba([features_list])

    #---formulate the response to return to client---
    response = {}
    response['prediction'] = int(prediction[0])
    response['confidence'] = str(round(np.amax(confidence[0]) * 100 ,2))

    return  jsonify(response)

if __name__ == '__main__':
    app.run(host='0.0.0.0', port=5000)
```

The preceding code snippet accomplishes the following:

- Creates a route /diabetes/v1/predict using the route decorator.
- The route is accessible through the POST verb.

- To make a prediction, users make a call to this route and pass in the various features using a JSON string.

- The result of the prediction is returned as a JSON string.

> **NOTE**   A *decorator* in Python is a function that wraps and replaces another function.

Testing the Model

To test the REST API, run it in Terminal by entering the following command:

```
$ python REST_API.py
```

You should see the following output:

```
* Serving Flask app "REST_API" (lazy loading)
 * Environment: production
   WARNING: Do not use the development server in a production environment.
   Use a production WSGI server instead.
 * Debug mode: off
 * Running on http://0.0.0.0:5000/ (Press CTRL+C to quit)
```

This indicates that the service is up and listening at port 5000.

The easiest way to test the API is to use the cURL command (installed by default on macOS) from a separate Terminal or Command Prompt window:

```
$ curl -H "Content-type: application/json" -X POST
http://127.0.0.1:5000/diabetes/v1/predict
-d '{"BMI":30, "Age":29,"Glucose":100 }'
```

The preceding command sets the JSON header, and it uses the POST verb to connect to the REST API listening at port 5000. The features and their values to use for the prediction are sent as a JSON string.

> **TIP**   For Windows users, single quotes are not recognized by the cURL command. You have to use double quotes and turn off the special meaning of double quotes in the JSON string: "{\"BMI\":30, \"Age\":29,\"Glucose\":100 }".

When the REST API has received the data sent to it, it will use it to perform the prediction. You will see the prediction result returned as follows:

```
{"confidence":"78.95","prediction":0}
```

The result indicates that based on the data sent to it, it is not likely that the person has diabetes (78.95% confidence).

Go ahead and try some other values, like this:

```
$ curl -H "Content-type: application/json" -X POST
http://127.0.0.1:5000/diabetes/v1/predict
-d '{"BMI":65, "Age":29,"Glucose":150 }'
```

This time around, the prediction indicates that the person is likely to be diabetic with 68.42% confidence:

```
{"confidence":"68.42","prediction":1}
```

Creating the Client Application to Use the Model

Once the REST API is up and running, and it has been tested to be working correctly, you can build the client side of things. Since this book revolves around Python, it is fitting to build the client using Python. Obviously, in real life, you would most likely build your clients for the iOS, Android, macOS, and Windows platforms.

Our Python client is pretty straightforward—formulate the JSON string to send to the service, get the result back in JSON, and then retrieve the details of the result:

```
import json
import requests

def predict_diabetes(BMI, Age, Glucose):
    url = 'http://127.0.0.1:5000/diabetes/v1/predict'
    data = {"BMI":BMI, "Age":Age, "Glucose":Glucose}
    data_json = json.dumps(data)
    headers = {'Content-type':'application/json'}
    response = requests.post(url, data=data_json, headers=headers)
    result = json.loads(response.text)
    return result

if __name__ == "__main__":
    predictions = predict_diabetes(30,40,100)
    print("Diabetic" if predictions["prediction"] == 1 else "Not
Diabetic")
    print("Confidence: " + predictions["confidence"] + "%")
```

Running this in Jupyter Notebook yields the following result:

```
Not Diabetic
Confidence: 68.42%
```

Let's save the preceding code snippet into a file and add the code to allow users to enter the various values for BMI, Age, and Glucose. Save the following code snippet in a file named Predict_Diabetes.py:

```
import json
import requests

def predict_diabetes(BMI, Age, Glucose):
    url = 'http://127.0.0.1:5000/diabetes/v1/predict'
```

```
        data = {"BMI":BMI, "Age":Age, "Glucose":Glucose}
        data_json = json.dumps(data)
        headers = {'Content-type':'application/json'}
        response = requests.post(url, data=data_json, headers=headers)
        result = json.loads(response.text)
        return result

if __name__ == "__main__":
    BMI = input('BMI?')
    Age = input('Age?')
    Glucose = input('Glucose?')
    predictions = predict_diabetes(BMI,Age,Glucose)
    print("Diabetic" if predictions["prediction"] == 1 else "Not
Diabetic")
    print("Confidence: " + predictions["confidence"] + "%")
```

You can now run the application in Terminal:

```
$ python Predict_Diabetes.py
```

You can now enter the values:

```
BMI?55
Age?29
Glucose?120
```

The result will now be shown:

```
Not Diabetic
Confidence: 52.63%
```

Summary

In this final chapter, you saw how to deploy your machine learning model using the Flask micro-framework. You also saw how you can view the correlations between the various features and then only use those most useful features for training your model. It is always useful to evaluate several machine learning algorithms and choose the best performing one so that you can choose the correct algorithm for your specific dataset.

I hope that this book has given you a good overview of machine learning, and that it has jumpstarted and inspired you to continue learning. As I have mentioned, this book is a gentle introduction to machine learning, and there are some details that were purposely omitted to make it easy to follow along. Nevertheless, if you have tried all of the exercises in each chapter, you should now have a pretty good understanding of the fundamentals of machine learning!

Index

A

accuracy, computing of, 168–171

algorithms
  categories of in ML, 5
  comparing ML algorithms, 258–260
  evaluating ML algorithms, 260–261, 277–279
  supervised learning algorithms, 5
  Two-Class Decision Jungle algorithm, 258, 259, 260
  Two-Class Logistic Regression algorithm, 258, 259, 260
  Two-Class Support Vector Machine algorithm, 258
  unsupervised learning algorithms, 5, 7

Anaconda, 8–18

apply() function, 57, 58, 59

area under the curve (AUC), 174

argsort() function, 33

arrange() function, 20

array assignment, 34–38

array indexing, 22–26

array math, 27–34

arrays
  copying by reference, 34–35
  copying by value (deep copy), 37
  copying by view (shallow copy), 36–37
  creating NumPy arrays, 20–21
  reshaping of, 26–27
  slicing of, 23–25

asmatrix() function, 30

auc() function, 174

Auto MPG Data Set, 98

Azure Machine Learning Studio (MAML)
  comparing against other algorithms, 258–260
  creating experiment, 248–252
  evaluating machine learning algorithms, 260–261
  example using Titanic experiment, 244–246
  filtering data and making fields categorical, 252–254
  introduction, 243
  programmatically accessing web service, 263–266
  publishing experiment, 261–263
  publishing learning model as web service, 261–262

removing missing data, 254
splitting data for training and
        testing, 254–256
testing web service, 263
training a model, 256–258
uploading dataset, 247–248
use of, 246–266

B

Bagging, 143
bar chart
  defined, 73
  plotting of, 73–77
bar() function, 73
bias, 141–144
Boolean indexing, 22–23
Boosting, 143, 144
bootstrap aggregation, 143
Boston dataset, 120–124, 144–146
Breast Cancer Wisconsin (Diagnostic)
        Data Set, 156–174

C

C parameter, 194–196
case study in machine learning (ML)
  cleaning data, 271–273
  evaluating algorithms, 277–279
  examining correlation between
          features, 273–274
  introduction, 270–271
  loading data, 271
  plotting correlation between
          features, 274–276
  selecting best performing algorithm,
          279
  training and saving the model,
          279–282
catplot() function, 87
Census Income Data Set, 98
charts
  bar chart, 73–77
  line chart, 68–73
  pie chart, 77–82

classes
  DataFrame() class, 45
  KMeans class, 230, 232, 239
  KNeighborsClassifier class, 213
  LinearRegression class, 101–102,
          131, 139, 145
  LogisticRegression class, 162
  MinMaxScaler class, 112
  PolynomialFeatures class, 138
  Series class, 41
  SVC class, 182, 192
classification problems, described, 4
classification_report() function,
        170
clustering
  defined/described, 4, 5, 222
  using K-Means. See K-Means,
          clustering using
clusters, defined, 222
coefficient of determination, 105
coefficient of multiple determinations
        for multiple regressions, 105
conda, 8
confusion matrix, 166–168, 261
confusion_matrix() function, 168
Constrained Optimization, 181
contourf() function, 193
copy() function, 37
corr() function, 126, 273, 274
correlation
  examining correlation between
          features in ML case study,
          273–274
  negative correlation, 127
  plotting correlation between features
          in ML case study, 274–276
  positive correlation, 127
cross_val_score() function, 217
crosstab, 63–64
crosstab() function, 64, 166, 167
cross-validation, 216
cumsum() function, 31
cumulative sum, 31–32

D

data
cleaning data in clustering using
K-Means, 237–238
cleaning data in ML case study,
271–273
data cleansing in linear regression,
125–126
data cleansing in Scikit-learn,
106–117
filtering data and making fields
categorical in MAML, 252–254
importing data in clustering using
K-Means, 237
labeled data, 221
loading data in ML case study, 271
manipulation of tabular data using
Pandas, 39–65
removing missing data in MAML,
254
sorting of in Pandas DataFrame,
55–57
splitting data for training and testing
in MAML, 254–256
unlabeled data, 221, 222
data cleansing, 107–117, 125
data visualization, using matplotlib,
67–91
DataFrame, Pandas. *See* Pandas
DataFrame
DataFrame() class, 45
datasets
Boston dataset, 120–124, 144–146
getting datasets in Scikit-learn,
94–100
Iris dataset. *See* Iris dataset
Kaggle dataset, 97, 244, 270
labeled dataset, 5
uploading of in MAML, 247–248
date _ range() function, 42, 43
decorator, defined, 282
dependent variable, 119
describe() function, 48

dot() function, 29
dot product, 29–30
drop() function, 61, 62
drop _ duplicates() function, 111
dropna() function, 109
dump() function, 107
duplicated() function, 110, 111

E

ensemble learning, 143, 144
euclidean _ distance() function, 208
Evaluate Model, 260
explanatory variable, 120
explode parameter, 78–79
eye() function, 21

F

F1 Score, 170
False Negative (FN), 167, 261
False Positive (FP), 167, 261
False Positive Rate (FPR), 170, 171–172,
173
features
in case study, 273–276
independent variables as, 119
in linear regression, 126–128
in logistic regression, 156–174
in Titanic experiment with MAML,
252
Fisher, Ronald (biologist), 94
fit() function, 102, 230
Flask micro-framework, 280
flatten() function, 27
full() function, 21
functions
apply() function, 57, 58, 59
applying of to DataFrame, 57–60
argsort() function, 33
arrange() function, 20
asmatrix() function, 30
auc() function, 174
bar() function, 73
catplot() function, 87

classification _ report()
function, 170

confusion _ matrix() function, 168

contourf() function, 193

copy() function, 37

corr() function, 126, 273, 274

cross _ val _ score() function, 217

crosstab() function, 64, 166, 167

cumsum() function, 31

date _ range() function, 42, 43

describe() function, 48

dot() function, 29

drop() function, 61, 62

drop _ duplicates() function, 111

dropna() function, 109

dump() function, 107

duplicated() function, 110, 111

euclidean _ distance() function, 208

eye() function, 21

fit() function, 102, 230

flatten() function, 27

full() function, 21

get _ feature _ names() function, 139

head() function, 49

heatmap() function, 275

info() function, 125, 271

isnull() function, 108, 125

kernel function, 192

knn() function, 208, 209

legend() function, 72, 81

lmplot() function, 89

load() function, 107

load _ boston() function, 121

load _ breast _ cancer() function, 156

load _ dataset() function, 88

logit function, 153–154

make _ blobs() function, 98

make _ circles() function, 100, 187

make _ regression() function, 98

matshow() function, 274

mean() function, 48, 234

metrics.silhouette _ samples()
function, 234

metrics.silhouette _ score()
function, 234

np.add() function, 28

np.concatenate() function, 189

np.dot() function, 31

np.where() function, 114

outliers _ iqr() function, 114, 115

outliers _ z _ score() function, 116

pie() function, 81, 82

plot() function, 68, 71, 85

plot _ surface() function, 134, 190

polynomial function, 120, 138, 139, 145, 149

predict() function, 102, 163, 231

predict _ proba() function, 163

Radial Basis function (RBF), 196–197, 277, 278–279

randn() function, 45

random() function, 21

ravel() function, 27, 106

read _ csv() function, 46

reset _ index() function, 109

reshape() function, 26–27, 35

roc _ curve() function, 173

savefig() function, 82

scatter() function, 85

score() function, 106, 170

Sigmoid function, 155, 156

sns.get _ dataset _ names()
function, 88

sort() function, 33

sort _ index() function, 55, 56, 61

sort _ values() function, 55, 56

sq() function, 57, 58

sq _ root() function, 57, 58, 59

subplot() function, 85

sum() function, 59

tail() function, 49

title() function, 69

train _ test _ split() function, 131, 164

transpose() function, 54

view() function, 36
xlabel() function, 69
xticks() function, 76–77
ylabel() function, 69
zeros() function, 20

G
Gamma, 197–199
Gaussian Kernel, 196–197
get _ feature _ names() function, 139
The Grammar of Graphics: Statistics and Computing (Wilkinson), 70

H
harmonic mean of precision and recall, 170
head() function, 49
heatmap() function, 275
high bias, 143
high variance, 143
hyperplane
  defined, 179
  formula for in SVM, 180–181
  plotting of, 184–185, 189–191
  3D hyperplane, 133–135, 136, 146–147, 189–191

I
independent variable, 119
info() function, 125, 271
Interquartile Range (IQR), 113
Iris dataset, 89, 94, 96, 119, 191–194, 197, 199, 200, 212, 213, 217
isnull() function, 108, 125

J
Jupyter Notebook (formerly known as *iPython Notebook*), 8, 9–18, 67, 68, 69, 134, 160, 264, 283

K
k
  exploring different values of, 212–215
  finding optimal k, 218–219, 234–236

visualizing different values of, 209–211
Kaggle dataset, 97, 244, 270
kernel function, 192
kernel trick, 186–191
kernels
  defined, 191
  Gaussian Kernel, 196–197
  linear kernel, 182, 192, 194, 195, 196, 199, 201, 278, 279
  polynomial kernel, 199–200
  types of, 191–200
k-folds, 216
K-Means
  calculating Silhouette Coefficient, 233–234
  cleaning data, 237–238
  clustering using, 239–240
  evaluating cluster size using Silhouette Coefficient, 232–236
  finding optimal k, 234–236
  finding optimal size classes, 240–241
  how it works, 222–225
  implementing of in Python, 225–230
  importing data, 237
  plotting scatter plot, 238
  unsupervised learning using, 222
  using of in Scikit-learn, 230–232
  using of to solve real-life problems, 236–241
  what is unsupervised learning? 221–226
KMeans class, 230, 232, 239
K-Nearest Neighbors (KNN)
  calculating distance between points, 207–208
  cross-validation, 216
  described, 205–219
  evaluation of in ML case study, 277–278
  exploring different values of k, 212–215
  finding optimal k, 218–219
  implementing of in Python, 206–211

making predictions, 209
parameter-tuning k, 217–218
using Scikit-learn's
    KNeighborsClassifier class for,
    211–219
visualizing different values of k,
    209–211
KNeighborsClassifier class, 213
knn() function, 208, 209

L

label (dependent variable), 119
labeled data, 221
labeled dataset, 5
Larange Multipliers, 181
legend() function, 72, 81
line chart, plotting of, 68–73
linear kernel, 182, 192, 194, 195, 196,
    199, 201, 278, 279
linear regression
  data cleansing, 125–126
  defined, 100, 120
  feature selection, 126–128
  formula for polynomial regression,
    138
  getting gradient and intercept of
    linear regression line, 103–104
  getting intercept and coefficients, 133
  multiple regression, 128–130
  plotting 3D hyperplane, 133–135,
    146–147
  plotting linear regression line,
    102–103
  polynomial regression, 135–147
  training the model, 131–132
  types of, 119–120
  understanding bias and variance,
    141–144
  using polynomial multiple
    regression on Boston dataset,
    144–146
LinearRegression class, 101–102, 131,
    139, 145
list data type, 19–20
lmplot, 88–89

lmplot() function, 89
load() function, 107
load _ boston() function, 121
load _ breast _ cancer() function,
    156
load _ dataset() function, 88
logistic regression
  computing accuracy, recall,
    precision, and other metrics,
    168–171
  defined, 151–153
  evaluation of in ML case study, 277
  examining relationship between
    features, 156–161
  finding intercept and coefficient, 162
  getting the confusion matrix,
    166–168
  logit function, 153–154
  making predictions, 163–164
  plotting features in 2D, 157–158
  plotting in 3D, 158–160
  plotting ROC and finding area under
    the curve (AUC), 174
  plotting sigmoid curve, 162–163
  Receiver Operating Characteristic
    (ROC) curve, 171–174
  sigmoid curve, 154–156
  testing the model, 166
  training the model using all features,
    164–174
  training using one feature, 161–164
  Two-Class Logistic Regression
    algorithm, 258, 259, 260
  understanding odds, 153
  using Breast Cancer Wisconsin
    (Diagnostic) Data Set, 156–174
LogisticRegression class, 162
logit function, 153–154
low variance, 143

M

machine learning (ML)
  case study
    cleaning data, 271–273
    evaluating algorithms, 277–279

examining correlation between features, 273–274

introduction, 270–271

loading data, 271

plotting correlation between features, 274–276

selecting best performing algorithm, 279

training and saving the model, 279–280

categories of algorithms in, 5

creating client application to use the model, 283–284

defined, 1, 3

deployment of, 269–270

deployment of model of
introduction, 280–282
testing model, 282–283

described, 3

disciplines of, 3

main goal of, 269

make_blobs() function, 98

make_circles() function, 100, 187

make_regression() function, 98

mathematics, as discipline of machine learning, 3

matplotlib
defined, 67
plotting bar charts
adding another bar to chart, 74–75
changing tick marks, 75–77
introduction, 73–74
plotting line charts
adding legend, 72–73
adding title and labels, 69
introduction, 68–69
plotting multiple lines in same chart, 71–72
styling, 69–71
plotting pie charts
displaying custom colors, 79–80
displaying legend, 81
exploding slices, 78–79
introduction, 77–78

location strings and corresponding location codes, 82
rotating pie charts, 80
saving chart, 82
plotting scatter plots
combining plots, 83–84
introduction, 83
subplots, 84–85
plotting using Seaborn
displaying categorical plots, 86–88
displaying lmplots, 88–89
displaying swarmplots, 90–91
introduction, 85–86

matrix class, 30–31

matrix multiplication, 30

matshow() function, 274

mean() function, 48, 234

meshgrid, 214

metrics.silhouette_samples() function, 234

metrics.silhouette_score() function, 234

Microsoft Azure Machine Learning Studio (MAML)
comparing against other algorithms, 258–260
creating experiment, 248–252
evaluating machine learning algorithms, 260–261
example using Titanic experiment, 244–246
filtering data and making fields categorical, 252–254
introduction, 243
programmatically accessing web service, 263–266
publishing experiment, 261–263
publishing learning model as web service, 261–262
removing missing data, 254
splitting data for training and testing, 254–256
testing web service, 263
training a model, 256–258

uploading dataset, 247–248
use of, 246–266
`MinMaxScaler` class, 112
misclassification error (MSE), 218
model, a.k.a. program, 3
multi-class classification problem, 4
multiple linear regression, 120
multiple regression, 120, 128–130

N
`ndarray` (n-dimensional array), 20, 31
negative correlation, 127
normalization, 112–113
`np.add()` function, 28
`np.concatenate()` function, 189
`np.dot()` function, 31
`np.where()` function, 114
NumPy
  array assignment, 34–38
  array indexing, 22–26
  array math, 27–34
  creating NumPy arrays, 20–21
  described, 19–20
  NumPy slice as reference, 25
  reshaping arrays, 26–267
  slicing arrays, 23–25
  sorting in, 32–34

O
odds, understanding of, 153
optimal k, 218–219, 232, 234–236
outliers, 113–117
`outliers_iqr()` function, 114, 115
`outliers_z_score()` function, 116
overfitting, 143, 214–215

P
Pandas, described, 39–40
Pandas DataFrame
  adding/removing rows/columns in, 60–63
  applying functions to, 57–60
  checking to see if result is DataFrame or Series, 55
  common DataFrame operations, 65

  creation of, 45–46
  defined, 45
  examples of, 124
  extracting from, 49–54
  generating crosstab, 63–64
  selecting based on cell value, 54
  selecting single cell in, 54
  sorting data in, 55–57
  specifying index in, 46–47
  transformation of, 54–55
Pandas Series
  accessing elements in, 41–42
  creation of using specified index, 41
  date ranges, 43–44
  defined, 40
  generating descriptive statistics on, 47–48
  specifying datetime range as index of, 42–43
penalty parameter of the error term, 195
pie chart
  defined, 77
  plotting of, 77–82
`pie()` function, 81, 82
`plot()` function, 68, 71, 85
`plot_surface()` function, 134, 190
plotting
  of bar charts, 73–77
  of correlation between features in ML case study, 274–276
  of hyperplane, 184–185, 189–191
  of line charts, 68–73
  of linear regression line, 102–103
  of pie charts, 77–82
  plotting features in 2D (logistic regression), 157–158
  of ROC and finding area under the curve (AUC) (logistic regression), 174
  of scatter plots, 83–85, 238
  of sigmoid curve (logistic regression), 162–163
  of 3D hyperplane (linear regression), 133–135, 146–147

in 3D (logistic regression), 158–160
using Seaborn, 85–91, 182
polynomial function, 120, 138, 139, 145, 149
polynomial kernel, 199–200
polynomial multiple regression, 120, 144–146
polynomial regression, 120, 135–147
PolynomialFeatures class, 138
positive correlation, 127
precision, computing of, 168–171
predict() function, 102, 163, 231
predict_proba() function, 163
predictions
  making of in KNN, 209
  making of in logistic regression, 163–164
  making of in Scikit-learn, 102
  making of in SVM, 185–186

Q
quadratic regression, 138

R
Radial Basis function (RBF), 196–197, 277, 278–279
randn() function, 45
random() function, 21
ravel() function, 27, 106
read_csv() function, 46
recall, computing of, 168–171
Receiver Operating Characteristic (ROC) curve, 171–174
regression
  linear regression. See linear regression
  logistic regression. See logistic regression
  multiple linear regression, 120
  multiple regression, 120, 128–130
  polynomial multiple regression, 120, 144–146
  polynomial regression, 120, 135–147
  problems with, 4
  quadratic regression, 138

Two-Class Logistic Regression algorithm, 258, 259, 260
Regularization, 143
reset_index() function, 109
reshape() function, 26–27, 35
Residual Sum of Squares (RSS), 104–105, 141, 143
REST (REpresentational State Transfer) API, 269–270, 280, 283
ROC (Receiver Operating Characteristic) curve, 171–174
roc_curve() function, 173
R-squared method, 105, 132

S
savefig() function, 82
scatter() function, 85
scatter plot
  defined, 83
  examples of, 99, 129, 130, 132, 136, 158, 186, 193, 194, 201, 212, 226, 227, 229, 238
  plotting of, 83–85, 238
scientific computing, as discipline of machine learning, 3
Scikit-learn
  data cleansing
    cleaning rows with NaNs, 108
    introduction, 106–107
    normalizing columns, 112–113
    removing duplicate rows, 110–112
    removing outliers, 113–117
    removing rows, 109
    replacing NaN with mean of column, 109
  getting datasets
    clustered dataset, 98–99
    clustered dataset distributed in circular fashion, 100
    generating your own, 98
    introduction, 94
    linearly distributed dataset, 98
    using Kaggle dataset, 97
    using Scikit-learn dataset, 94–97

using UCI (University of California, Irvine) Machine Learning Repository, 97–98

getting started with

evaluating model using test dataset, 105–106

examining performance of model by calculating Residual Sum of Squares (RSS), 104–105

getting gradient and intercept of linear regression line, 103–104

introduction, 100–101

making predictions, 102

persisting the model, 106–107

plotting linear regression line, 102–103

using `LinearRegression` class for fitting model, 101–102

introduction to, 93–100

polynomial regression in, 138–141

use of for SVM, 181–183

use of `KNeighborsClassified` class for KNN, 211–219

using K-Means in, 230–232

`score()` function, 106, 170

Score Model, 256

Seaborn

defined, 85

plotting points using, 182

plotting using, 85–91

Series, Pandas. *See* Pandas Series

`Series` class, 41

shallow copy, 36

sigmoid curve, 154–156, 162–163

Sigmoid function, 155, 156

Silhouette Coefficient, 232–236

slope, 184

`sns.get_dataset_names()` function, 88

`sort()` function, 33

`sort_index()` function, 55, 56, 61

`sort_values()` function, 55, 56

`sq()` function, 57, 58

`sq_root()` function, 57, 58, 59

statistics, as discipline of machine learning, 3

StatLib library, 120

Student Performance Data Set, 98

`subplot()` function, 85

`sum()` function, 59

supervised learning

classification using K-Nearest Neighbors (KNN)

calculating distance between points, 207–208

cross-validation, 216

described, 205–219

exploring different values of k, 212–215

finding optimal k, 218–219

implementation of, 208–209

implementing KNN in Python, 206–211

making predictions, 209

parameter-tuning k, 217–218

using Scikit-learn's `KNeighborsClassifier` class for, 211–219

visualizing different values of k, 209–211

classification using Support Vector Machines (SVM)

adding third dimension, 187–188

C parameter, 194–196

formula for hyperplane, 180–181

Gamma, 197–199

introduction, 177–186

kernel trick, 186–191

making predictions, 185–186

maximum separability, 178–179

plotting 3D hyperplane, 189–191

plotting hyperplane and margins, 184–185

polynomial kernel, 199–200

Radial Basis function (RBF), 196–197

support vectors, 179–180

types of kernels, 191–200

using Scikit-learn for, 181–183
using SVM for real-life problems, 200–203
linear regression
data cleansing, 125–126
defined, 120
feature selection, 126–128
formula for polynomial regression, 138
getting intercept and coefficients, 133
multiple regression, 128–130
plotting 3D hyperplane, 133–135, 146–147
polynomial regression, 135–147
polynomial regression in Scikit-learn, 138–141
training the model, 131–132
types of, 119–120
understanding bias and variance, 141–144
using Boston dataset, 120–124
using polynomial multiple regression on Boston dataset, 144–146
logistic regression
defined, 151–153
examining relationship between features, 156–161
finding intercept and coefficient, 162
getting the confusion matrix, 166–168
logit function, 153–154
making predictions, 163–164
plotting features in 2D, 157–158
plotting in 3D, 158–160
plotting ROC and finding area under the curve (AUC), 174
plotting sigmoid curve, 162–163
Receiver Operating Characteristic (ROC) curve, 171–174
sigmoid curve, 154–156
testing the model, 166

training the model using all features, 164–174
training using one feature, 161–164
understanding odds, 153
using Breast Cancer Wisconsin (Diagnostic) Data Set, 156–174
supervised learning algorithms, 5–6
Support Vector Classification (SVC), 183
Support Vector Machines (SVM)
adding third dimension, 187–188
C parameter, 194–196
formula for hyperplane, 180–181
Gamma, 197–199
introduction, 177–186
kernel trick, 186–191
making predictions, 185–186
maximum separability, 178–179
plotting 3D hyperplane, 189–191
plotting hyperplane and margins, 184–185
polynomial kernel, 199–200
Radial Basis function (RBF), 196–197, 277, 278–279
support vectors, 179–180
types of kernels, 191–200
use of for real-life problems, 200–203
using Scikit-learn for, 181–183
support vectors, 179–180
svc class, 182, 192
swarmplots, 90–91

T
tabular data, manipulation of using Pandas, 39–65
tail() function, 49
targets, 120
3D hyperplane, 133–135, 136, 146–147, 189–191
threshold, 152, 163
Titanic, use of as experiment, 244–246
title() function, 69
traditional programming, described, 2

`train_test_split()` function, 131, 164

`transpose()` function, 54

True Negative (TN), 167, 261

True Positive Rate (TPR), 168, 171–172, 173

True Positive (TP), 167, 260

Tukey Fences, 113–115

two-class classification problem, 4

Two-Class Decision Jungle algorithm, 258, 259, 260

Two-Class Logistic Regression algorithm, 258, 259, 260

Two-Class Support Vector Machine algorithm, 258

U

UCI Machine Learning Repository, 97–98

underfitting, 143, 214–215

unlabeled data, 221, 222

unsupervised learning
  clustering using K-Means
    calculating Silhouette Coefficient, 233–234
    cleaning data, 237–238
    clustering using K-Means, 239–240
    evaluating cluster size using Silhouette Coefficient, 232–236
    finding optimal k, 234–236
    finding optimal size classes, 240–241
    how it works, 222–225
    implementing K-Means in Python, 225–230
    importing data, 237

plotting scatter plot, 238
  unsupervised learning using K-Means, 222
  using K-Means in Scikit-learn, 230–232
  using K-Means to solve real-life problems, 236–241
  what is unsupervised learning? 221–226
unsupervised learning algorithms, 5, 7

V

variables
  dependent variable, 119
  explanatory variable, 120
  independent variable, 119
variance, 141–144
`view()` function, 36

W

Wilkinson, Leland (author)
  The Grammar of Graphics: Statistics and Computing, 70

X

`xlabel()` function, 69
`xticks()` function, 76–77

Y

y-intercept, 184
`ylabel()` function, 69

Z

`zeros()` function, 20
Z-score, 116–117